Federalism and Rights

FEDERALISM AND RIGHTS

edited by
ELLIS KATZ and G. ALAN TARR

ROWMAN & LITTLEFIELD PUBLISHERS, INC.

ROWMAN & LITTLEFIELD PUBLISHERS, INC.

Published in the United States of America
by Rowman & Littlefield Publishers, Inc.
4720 Boston Way, Lanham, Maryland 20706

3 Henrietta Street
London WC2E 8LU, England

Chapter 6 originally appeared as "Federalism and the Protection of Individual Rights:
The American State Constitutional Perspective" in volume 11 of the *George State
University Law Review* (1995). Reprinted by permission.

British Cataloging in Publication Information Available

Library of Congress Cataloging-in-Publication Data

Federalism and rights / edited by Ellis Katz and G. Alan Tarr.
p. cm.
1. Federal government. 2. Civil rights. 3. Federal government—United States—
History. 4. Civil rights—United States—History. I. Katz, Ellis. II. Tarr, G. Alan
(George Alan)
JC355.F372 1995 321.02—dc20   95-8954   CIP

ISBN 0-8476-8089-4 (cloth : alk. paper)
ISBN 0-8476-8090-8 (pbk. : alk. paper)

Printed in the United States of America

♾™ The paper used in this publication meets the minimum requirements of
American National Standard for Information Sciences—Permanence of
Paper for Printed Library Materials, ANSI Z39.48–1984.

CONTENTS

FEDERALISM AND RIGHTS
IN COMPARATIVE PERSPECTIVE

ACKNOWLEDGMENTS

The essays that comprise this volume were initially presented at an international conference on "Federalism and Rights" held in Philadelphia in November 1992. For the success of that conference, we owe a debt of gratitude to the Center for the Study of Federalism at Temple University. The Center sponsored the conference and has supported the development of this volume for publication. More generally, it has for decades promoted serious scholarship on the subject of federalism, without which volumes like this one would be impossible.

We are also grateful to the National Endowment for the Humanities, which provided generous financial support for the conference, and to the United States Information Agency, which underwrote the expenses of foreign scholars and officials who attended and participated in the conference. Rutgers University (Camden), the U. S. Advisory Commission on Intergovernmental Relations, and the Philadelphia Bar Association all cosponsored the conference proceedings.

On behalf of the contributors to this volume, we would like to thank the distinguished scholars who served as paper commentators at the conference: Clement Keto, John Kincaid, Donald Kommers, Michael Libonati, Robert Licht, Rafael Porrata-Doria, Jr., John Pittenger, and Robert Williams. The essays in this volume owe much to their comments and to the provocative discussions that characterized the conference.

Ms. Deirdre Mullervy of Rowman & Littlefield eased each step of the process of transforming diverse essays into a book. At the Center for the Study of Federalism, Kimberly Robinson cheerfully and efficiently managed the preparation of the manuscript. Eric Katz was a wizard in solving myriad computer problems faced by the editors. Bobby Katz and Susan Tarr patiently endured the entire endeavor, from the planning of the conference to the completion of the book.

INTRODUCTION

G. Alan Tarr and Ellis Katz

Does federalism promote or undermine rights? The importance of this question can scarcely be overstated. Emerging democracies in Europe and elsewhere are currently attempting to design constitutions that combine effective government, recognition of the diversity within their populations, and protection for rights. Federalism and federal arrangements are among the options from which they must choose in seeking to achieve these objectives. In addition, in the decades since World War II, many nations have adopted federal systems, experimented with federal arrangements, or decided to band together in confederal arrangements. For those nations participating in - or contemplating joining - what one scholar has called "the federalist revolution," the effect of federalism on rights is crucial.[1] Finally, for mature federal democracies, in North America and elsewhere, the relationship between federalism and rights remains important because their compatibility remains controversial. Various commentators have either denied that federalism promotes the security of rights or contended that it in fact undermines rights, and these arguments must be confronted by all who espouse federalism.[2]

I

By diffusing governmental power, federalism permits the constituent units of a federal system to determine to a significant extent the ends that they will pursue and the means by which they will accomplish those ends. Implicit in federal arrangements is the expectation that the retention of these choices by the constituent governments will produce diversity; that given the opportunity, these governments will order their affairs in diverse ways. Thus, federalism can claim to serve the ends of both pluralism and self-government. In doing so, however, federalism necessarily sacrifices complete uniformity of treatment for those ruled by the various constituent governments. Put simply, in a federal system many of the laws one must obey, the benefits one receives, and the rights one enjoys depend on the political jurisdiction in which one resides.

It is this connection between residence and rights - and more particularly the notion that one's rights change when one moves from one part of a nation to another part - that raises important questions about the relationship between federalism and rights. For to speak in terms of rights is, typically, to speak the language of universality: rights belong to human beings *qua* human beings. Thus, the American Declaration of Independence recognizes that "all men are created equal and endowed by their Creator with certain inalienable rights," and the United Nations Declaration of Rights elaborates a detailed list of rights belonging to all human beings. Both the United States Congress and the President have at various times recognized rights as universal, arguing that American foreign policy should be guided by a concern for "human rights." In principle, these inalienable rights, these human rights, know no borders. Indeed, it can be argued, if a right deserves protection, then it should be equally protected for all people, regardless of where they happen to live.

If this argument is correct, then federalism and rights are necessarily at odds, for federalism countenances particularism and encourages diversity, while the protection of rights seems to require universal standards and uniform treatment. Yet, without reaching a final determination on the issue, it should be noted that the argument for the universality of rights ignores certain complexities in political theory and political practice. First of all, inherent in the concept of a right is the notion both of a realm of non-interference and of an authority that is obliged to respect and/or secure that realm. Thus, it is not inconceivable that one might have different rights as to different authorities. In addition, not all rights rise to the stature of natural or human - and hence universal - rights. The United States Constitution reflects this in distinguishing between the "privileges" and the "immunities" of citizens. This distinction, as explained in Blackstone's *Commentaries*, reflects the transformation of rights that accompanies the movement from a state of nature to civil society.[3] When one enters civil society, one gives up various rights possessed in the state of nature and receives in return certain "privileges" (*i.e.*, legal means to secure one's valid interests). These privileges quite properly vary from one civil society to another, reflecting the different circumstances that these societies confront and differences in their political judgment about how to achieve the ends for which they were created. Of course, when one enters civil society, one also retains certain "immunities"; that is, rights which are not surrendered in leaving the state of nature because they involve aspects of human life that need not be regulated to achieve valid societal ends.

Moreover, in practice rights in a democratic society are largely defined and enforced by political majorities. In a federal system, this entails dual majority rule - a national majority establishing rights *vis-a-vis* the federal government and sub-national majorities establishing rights *vis-a-vis* constituent governments. This dual majority rule affords more opportunity to secure rights. When the federal government is receptive to rights claims, there may be opportunities to nationalize the protection of various rights on a uniform basis. But when the federal government is indifferent to rights or holds a restrictive view of them, then there may be opportunities to expand the protection of some rights in those constituent units that are receptive, as well as the possibility for citizens to make their choice of residence among those units based on their rights policies. This dual protection for rights also accommodates sharp public disagreements over particular rights. In the United States, for example, thirty-seven states permit capital punishment, while thirteen view it as inconsistent with human dignity and ban it.

Furthermore, although discussions of human rights or natural rights characteristically focus on individual rights, our contemporary understanding of rights is not so limited. During the Middle Ages, one's rights depended on one's status or position. While the hierarchical aspect of this notion has disappeared, the idea that rights belong to groups or collectivities, as well as to individuals, continues to find wide acceptance. Indeed, recent decades have witnessed a reemergence of the sense that primordial ties are basic to one's individual identity, and with it a multiplication of claims based on notions of collective entitlement. Group rights have been tied to ethnicity (as in American affirmative action programs and in the concept of "federal character" in Nigeria), to language (as in Canada), and to a host of other factors. Federal systems, with their traditions of shared-rule and self-rule, have generally found it easier to respond to claims for group rights than have unitary systems. In fact, groups seeking recognition of their claims have frequently called for a devolution of political power or, in short, for some sort of federalism.

Finally, in considering the relation between federalism and rights, it bears mention that the world's great federal democracies (*e.g.*, Australia, Canada, Germany, Switzerland, and the United States) by and large have good records of protecting rights. One might dismiss the correlation between federalism and security of rights as spurious, the product of other factors. One might even seek to deny it; certainly, some nonfederal and quasi-federal nations - *e.g.*, France and Great Britain - have impressive records of protecting rights, while some federal systems - *e.g.*, India and Brazil - have had mixed records. Nonetheless, if, as it appears, federal systems have a better overall record of protecting rights than unitary systems have, then this fact deserves consideration in any assessment of the compatibility of federalism and rights.

II

In the United States the relationship between federalism and rights has been particularly controversial. For much of the twentieth century, the received wisdom was that federalism was the enemy of rights and that appeals to federalism were, as Michael Zuckert has noted, merely "thinly veiled attempts to maintain segregation and other morally suspect social practices."[4] This notion, based largely on Southern intransigence in opposing civil rights, contrasts sharply with the expectation voiced by James Madison in *Federalist No. 51*. Madison argued that American federalism would provide a "double security" for rights, because both federal and state governments could act to safeguard them. In practice, the relationship over time between federalism and rights in the United States has been both more complex - and more interesting - than is suggested by either of these positions. The division of responsibility between nation and state for protecting rights has varied throughout American history, and so too has the willingness of nation and state to live up to that responsibility.

Immediately after independence, the responsibility for protecting rights fell to the states, which in designing their constitutions typically prefaced these documents with declarations of rights. These guarantees, however, did not ensure adequate protection for rights, and state violations of rights were among the factors that prompted the Constitutional Convention of 1787. Nevertheless, the new Constitution did not dramatically alter the division of responsibility for rights protection. While the Constitution augmented national power and placed some restrictions - for example, bans on coining money and on interfering with contracts - on the exercise of state power, the states remained the primary locus of governing authority. Even the addition of a Bill of Rights, which was insisted upon by the Anti-Federalists, the champions of state power, did not change the situation, since it imposed restrictions only on the federal government.

Given the expansion of slavery and the denial of other rights in the Southern states in order to sustain that "peculiar institution," the record of the states in securing rights during the antebellum period was mixed at best. (Of course, the record of the federal government, which produced the Alien and Sedition Acts, fugitive slave legislation, and the Dred Scott decision, was little better.[5]) Following the Civil War and the recognition that not all states could be trusted to safeguard the rights of the newly free black citizens, the Thirteenth, Fourteenth, and Fifteenth Amendments were adopted, empowering the federal government to guarantee rights when the states failed to do so. That these amendments were designed to alter the roles of the state and federal governments in protecting rights is clear. Beyond that, however, scholarly debate continues as to whether the aim of the amendments was a constitutional revolution or merely an adjustment of the federal balance.[6] In any event, the U.S. Supreme Court's evisceration of the Thirteenth and Fourteenth amendments in *The Slaughterhouse Cases* (1873), *The Civil Rights Cases* (1883), and other rulings limited their immediate impact.[7] Because the federal government virtually abdicated its responsibility to protect rights, the primary responsibility reverted to state governments in the latter part of the nineteenth century.

Nonetheless, doubts about the states' commitment to protecting individual rights led to intermittent national action to secure rights. During the early part of the twentieth century, for example, the states' inability or unwillingness to deal with the abuses of child labor prompted national legislation and, after the Supreme Court invalidated the statutes, to congressional proposal of a constitutional amendment to address the problem.[8] The states' failure to protect adequately the rights of workers to organize led to the enactment of the Wagner Act in 1935. And the Southern states' record of racial repression launched the civil rights movement and prompted congressional and executive efforts to safeguard rights against violation by state and local officials or by private parties.

Yet the major innovation in protecting rights during the twentieth century has been the expansion in the role played by federal courts - and particularly the United States Supreme Court - through the process of constitutional litigation. Although examples of state initiatives exist - Iowa, for example, adopted the exclusionary rule prior to *Weeks v. United States* (1914), and Wisconsin required the provision of counsel to indigent defendants over a century before *Gideon v. Wainwright* (1963) - for the most part, state courts did little to stimulate the development of state civil liberties law.[9] Within the past half century, however, the U. S. Supreme Court and other federal courts have taken a leading role in extending rights protections through their efforts to develop the full implications of the Fourteenth Amendment. The Court has adopted the selective incorporation doctrine, under which provisions of the Bill of Rights become fully applicable to state governmental action, and has proceeded to incorporate most criminal justice guarantees of the Bill of Rights. In addition, rulings such as *Gideon v. Wainwright* and *Miranda v. Arizona* (1966) have given considerably broader scope to federal constitutional provisions than had previously been the case and have imposed new and often detailed requirements on the states. In effect, these rulings produced a federalization of legal standards for criminal justice. Litigants were encouraged to base their claims on federal constitutional guarantees and precedents and to ignore state law.

Beginning in the early 1970s, however, state declarations of rights reemerged as a source of constitutional protections. Prompted in part by Burger Court rulings, which either altered Warren Court decisions or directly encouraged a reliance on state constitutional principles, some state courts began to rely on their state bills of rights to provide greater protection than was available under U. S. Supreme Court rulings.[10] By the early 1990s, what had begun as a response by a handful of courts to specific Burger Court rulings had been transformed into a more general resuscitation of state civil-liberties law. This rediscovery of state bills of rights may mark another important shift in the state and federal roles in protecting rights. Instead of a single government bearing responsibility for protecting rights, the emergence of this "new judicial federalism" may promote complementary roles for state and federal authorities, providing the "double security" envisioned by Madison two centuries ago.

III

The complexities of the relationship between federalism and rights are particularly evident when one looks beyond the borders of the United States to the multiplicity and diversity of federal systems worldwide. While some of these federal (or confederal) systems long antedated the American federal system, many of those countries which instituted federal systems during the nineteenth and twentieth centuries have drawn on the American federal model, either implicitly or explicitly, in constructing their own federal systems. In some instances, too, the American federal experience has served a cautionary function. During deliberations over the Australian constitution in the late nineteenth century, for example, a major concern was whether the American

Civil War suggested that federal systems were inherently unstable.[11] Yet whatever the lessons other nations have drawn from American federalism, they have confronted a common set of problems. They, like the United States, have had to combine a respect for rights with the requirements of effective government and to apportion responsibility for defining and protecting rights between general and constituent governments.

Comparative analysis of federal systems highlights three points pertinent to discussions of federalism and rights. First, as noted at the outset of this essay, the past fifty years have witnessed a "federalist revolution." Since World War II, over a dozen nations - among them, Germany, India, and Nigeria - have established federal systems. Others - including Colombia and Denmark - have experimented with various quasi-federal arrangements, ranging from union to federacy to associated statehood. Still others have banded together in supranational confederal arrangements, best exemplified by the European Community. According to one estimate, "nearly 40 percent of the world's population now lives within polities that are formally federal; another third live in polities that apply federal arrangements in some way."[12] The implications of this development for discussions of federalism and rights are even greater than mere numbers might suggest. For this proliferation of federal arrangements has largely resulted from a concern for rights - or more particularly, from efforts to accommodate the rights claims of diverse groups residing within individual nations.

Second, nations may seek to accomplish quite different aims through federal union. In some countries - for example, Australia and Brazil - federalism serves the same purpose as it has in the United States, namely, to sustain a longstanding territorial diffusion of political power that cuts across differences in ethnicity, religion, and similar factors. To a considerable extent, the problems these federal nations face in reconciling federalism and rights mirror those confronted in the United States, even to the necessity of dealing with the claims of an indigenous population. But for most federal nations, these arrangements serve a different purpose. Canada, India, Nigeria, and a host of other nations have chosen federalism as a way of recognizing and accommodating ethnic and cultural differences within their populations, differences that correspond with rather than crosscut regions. When territorial divisions correspond with societal cleavages, this places particular strains on federal systems. Nations must be careful that their recognition of group rights and the devolution of power to constituent units does not so reinforce group attachments that it undermines allegiance to the larger political entity of which those constituent units are a part. They must also ensure that the recognition of group rights does not come at the expense of individual rights, that the devolution of power does not become a vehicle for the oppression of minorities within the constituent units.

The difficulties in achieving a proper federal balance in such circumstances led at least one early commentator, Alexis de Tocqueville, to conclude that federal systems would succeed only when territorial divisions crosscut, rather than reinforced, societal cleavages.[13] To some extent, recent events - the dissolution of Yugoslavia, the political turmoil in Nigeria, and the endemic regional crisis in Canada - support this judgment. Yet the use of federalism to reflect cleavages has not always produced such dire results. From an academic perspective, what this diversity of outcomes suggests is the need for sustained research on why some such federal systems have flourished while others have failed. In addition, researchers must consider whether federalism or other factors are decisive in determining the success of efforts to integrate diverse groups into a single nation.

Finally, comparative analyses of federalism underscore the diversity of federal forms and arrangements. Presumably, at some point researchers should be able to assess the strengths and weaknesses of various forms of federalism and pinpoint the circumstances under which each is most advantageous. Yet at present, because so few comparative studies of federalism have been undertaken, scholars' aims must be less ambitious. They need to look in detail at the operation of various federal systems and examine how successful they have been in protecting rights. They also need to identify the factors that have contributed to their success or failure in this endeavor.

IV

The essays in this volume were first presented at an international conference on federalism and rights, sponsored by the Center for the Study of Federalism and supported by National Endowment for the Humanities. They include the perspectives of both academics and practitioners, from the United States and abroad, on the relationship between federalism and rights. Although most authors focus on the American experience, because it has had such influence throughout the world and is so widely misunderstood, others address theoretical issues relating to federalism and rights or trace the experience of other countries in attempting to reconcile federalism and rights.

The first set of essays in this volume offers theoretical perspectives on federalism and rights. In the initial essay, Daniel Elazar focuses on the primary task confronting contemporary political leaders, namely, the creation and nurturing of democratic societies. For Elazar, federalism and the protection of individual rights are necessarily interrelated because they are - together with the idea of a civil society - the three pillars on which successful democracies rest. In asserting that federalism is essential to democracy, Elazar understands federalism broadly, not as a particular political arrangement but as a perspective on political life that diverges from both simple majoritarianism and parliamentary democracy. In the political realm, democracy requires a sense of political partnership and the operation of political choice through discussion and deliberation. It must accommodate diversity within the populace arising both from individual differences and from primordial ties and must prevent the development of a permanent majority ruling over a permanent minority. In the social realm, democracy requires the creation of a sphere within which private and public non-governmental activities can develop and flourish. Federalism, with its emphasis on power sharing and its refusal to reify the state, obviously contributes - along with the recognition of individual rights and the idea of a civil society - to the creation of a democratic political-social order. Yet if democracy is to flourish, it also requires a proper balance among the three pillars that support it. In recent decades the threat to this balance, Elazar asserts, has come from an overemphasis on individual rights and a depreciation of both federalism and the idea of a civil society. In seeking to redress the balance and achieve an appropriate relationship between private and public concerns, he proposes a reinvigoration of the notion of "federal liberty." This concept stresses that the fundamental right is that of establishing the sort of society in which one will live and of determining the obligations one will undertake; and in so doing, it seems to offer a means of reconciling individual rights and public group concerns.

Dick Howard's essay assesses the arguments which historically have been advanced for and against federalism. What is striking about his listing is that proponents of federalism seldom expressly champion it as promoting civil liberties, whereas opponents often emphasize the variations in rights that federalism countenances as among its major disadvantages. Yet in another sense, a concern for rights pervades the arguments for federalism. According to these arguments, the most important right is the right of self-government, and proponents insist that federalism is crucial to ensuring effective self-government. It promotes self-government first of all by ensuring that important choices are made at a level where citizens can feel a sense of political efficacy, and by encouraging community so that citizens can feel comfortable in voicing their opinions and acting upon them. It also fosters self-government and choice by encouraging pluralism, by allowing communities to devise their own goals and experiment with their own ways of achieving them. The expectation of federalism's proponents is that on balance this local autonomy will promote the security of rights. While opponents of federalism emphasize the dangers of local tyrannies, its proponents view concentrations of power as the primary concern. Thus, for proponents of federalism, the devolution of political power both secures the right of self-government and is instrumental to the protection of other rights.

Historically, legal scholars and jurists in the United States have made important contributions to our understanding of the relation between federalism and rights. Thus, one might have expected contemporary constitutional theory, with its preoccupation with the protection of rights, to explore that relationship in depth. Yet in his essay Gary Jacobsohn argues that constitutional theorists have not done so, largely because they have not taken federalism seriously. Although these theorists have differed in their assessments of federalism, Jacobsohn insists that these differences derive less from analyses of federalism than from disagreements over how rights are to be defined and protected. Leading non-interpretivist scholars, such as Ronald Dworkin and Michael Perry, have defined rights in universal terms and have therefore disparaged the notion that the particularism of federalism serves the cause of rights. Interpretivist theorists and judges, such as Robert Bork, have viewed rights as determined by popular mandate and thus have not demanded a uniformity of rights across jurisdictions. Yet they too have conceived of rights largely in terms of a freedom from regulation and have therefore not explored federalism's contribution to self-government. Even theorists wedded to the tradition of civic republicanism, which emphasizes the right to self-government, have substituted notions of group representation for geographically based federalism. As a result, Jacobsohn concludes, contemporary constitutional theorists have too quickly dismissed federalism as unimportant to the attainment of a regime of liberty.

A second section of this volume deals with the relation between federalism and rights in the United States. Jean Yarbrough's essay, which opens this section, explores the conceptions of federalism and of rights prevalent during the American Founding. Yarbrough rejects the portrayal of the Anti-Federalists as proponents of classical republicanism, maintaining that the Federalists and Anti-Federalists shared a common understanding of rights. Their disagreement centered rather on the likely source of threats to rights. Federalists distrusted local, factional majorities, while Anti-Federalists feared a powerful national government that might overreach its powers and violate rights. The system of federalism enshrined in the United States Constitution anticipated some of the Anti-Federalists' concerns by guaranteeing a constitutional status for state governments, a necessity if they were to check federal encroachments. Even those founders who initially adopted a nationalist position, such as James Madison, eventually concluded that the federal features which they had initially opposed were necessary to safeguard rights. In recent years, Yarbrough recognizes, this connection between federalism and rights has been severed by the nationalization of rights protections. Yet she questions whether this development, which she believes cannot be supported by any reasonable interpretation of the Fourteenth Amendment, has in fact made rights more secure.

In contrast to Yarbrough, Michael Zuckert denies that James Madison was ever a thorough-going nationalist. Rather, Madison championed a new and distinctive form of federalism which did not displace the states as the primary locus of governing authority but empowered the national government to intervene to check unwise or unjust measures in the states. Unfortunately, the Constitutional Convention did not fully endorse Madison's solution for protecting rights against state violation. While his fellow delegates inserted into the Constitution various prohibitions, such as the contract clause, to deal with the states' most egregious violations of rights, they rejected Madison's oft-repeated call for a congressional veto over all state laws. Moreover, the First Congress refused to support Madison's proposal to secure basic rights against state as well as national violation. Zuckert maintains that not until after the Civil War, in the Reconstruction amendments, did a modified version of the sort of "corrective federalism" espoused by Madison find constitutional expression. Even then, however, the Supreme Court, motivated by an attachment to antebellum federalism, read those aspects of corrective federalism out of the Constitution in *The Slaughterhouse Cases*. Only in the 1960s, through the gradual incorporation of the various guarantees of the Bill of Rights, did the Court eventually establish the national superintendence over state violations of rights that Madison had originally favored. Yet this new corrective federalism diverged from Madison's in important respects: oversight authority was lodged in the Supreme Court, rather than Congress, and the states had lost their primacy in policy making.

In campaigning for the ratification of the Constitution, Madison emphasized that American federalism provided a double security for rights, because both national and state governments could act to protect them. Even the development during the 1960s of a national superintendence over rights has not eliminated this dual protection of rights. Indeed, according to Justice

William Brennan, among the most significant constitutional developments in recent years has been the "rediscovery" of state guarantees of rights, a phenomenon known as the "new judicial federalism."[14] In her essay Judge Dorothy Beasley explores the legal principles that undergird the dual system of rights protection in the United States. Although the application of these principles remains complex and controversial, Judge Beasley insists that the development of state civil-liberties law encourages valuable experimentation in the "little laboratories" of the states and ensures that the scope of rights protections reflects the diverse perspectives of the various states. Her discussion of the right to privacy illustrates how the dual system of rights protection promotes judicial creativity: state judges, relying on express guarantees in their state constitutions, have developed an impressive body of privacy law. She also recognizes that the division of responsibility for protecting rights serves an important educative function, as state and federal judges learn from each other's interpretations of their constitutional guarantees.

Like Beasley, Talbot D'Alemberte finds inspiration in Justice Brennan's vision of a revived state commitment to the protection of rights. Yet countering this vision, he notes, is another vision of federalism, one which views invocations of federal principles as a tactic used to defeat rights claims. The transfer of responsibility from nation to state threatens rights, however, only if state authorities are either disinterested in protecting rights or incompetent in doing so. D'Alemberte thus concludes that those who share a principled attachment to federalism and to rights must become concerned with reforming state institutions so that they can effectively safeguard rights. With this in mind, he identifies two areas of particular concern. First is the states' woefully inadequate provision of counsel for indigent defendants, particularly in capital cases. This failure to accord capital defendants their right to effective assistance to counsel, he notes, encourages *habeas corpus* challenges to state convictions, thereby undermining respect for state courts, and raises questions about the states' willingness to vindicate basic rights. Second is the vulnerability of state judges to majoritarian forces, which interfere with their ability to protect rights. To combat this, D'Alemberte champions merit selection of state judges as a way to increase the independence - and hence the fearlessness - of state judges.

The essays in the final section of this volume examine the interplay of federalism and rights beyond the borders of the United States, in both national and supranational contexts. Probably the leading example of supranational federalism is the European Community. Although the treaties that created the

European Community never characterized it as a federal arrangement, over time the Community has developed federal features that distinguish it from other international organizations. According to Judge Koen Lenaerts, the development of federal features in the European Community derives in large measure from the EEC Treaty's recognition of entitlements as rights which citizens of member states could claim against member states other than their own. The recognition of individual rights under the Treaty, according to Lenaerts, has helped to vindicate the authority of Community law; for litigation by private parties, concerned for their own rights, has ensured effective compliance with that law. In addition, the obligation of protecting individual rights under Community law has promoted the development of legal mechanisms for extending the Community's supervisory authority over member states. For example, the European Court of Justice has required changes in the procedural law of member states and even the creation of new causes of action to vindicate rights under Community law. Thus, Lenaerts concludes that the European Community has become more federal (and less confederal) through its involvement in protecting rights, while the recognition of those rights owes much to federal features inherent in the constitutional structure of the European Community from the very outset.

Most countries that have adopted federal systems have done so to protect group rights, to accord ethnic or religious groups within their borders a measure of autonomy and therefore the opportunity to develop and express their group identities. Irwin Cotler analyzes the extraordinary constitutional changes that Canada has introduced - or attempted to introduce - over the last decade or so in an effort to counter secessionist sentiments and to create a more viable federal system. The constitutional revolution in Canada began in 1982 with the adoption of the Canadian Charter of Rights and Freedoms. Before its adoption, constitutional analysis even in rights cases revolved around the distribution of power between the federal and provincial governments. By constitutionalizing and judicializing rights protection, the Charter promoted the development of a Canadian rights consciousness and the proliferation of civil-liberties litigation that arguably made individual rights more secure. However, the Charter was also designed to enhance national unity by giving appropriate recognition to the multicultural character of the population and by safeguarding diversity and pluralism, and in this it failed. The Charter did include special protections for aboriginal and minority-language rights among its provisions, but these safeguards did not eliminate group concerns. Both the aboriginal people and the Quebecois continued to press for greater autonomy, while new groups (for instance, the western provinces) began to advance their own distinctive claims. This led to further constitutional efforts to redress grievances and reconcile marginalized groups. The most recent of these efforts was the Charlottetown Accords, which guaranteed Quebec a minimum level of representation in the federal government, transferred powers to Quebec and to other provincial governments, and recognized the aboriginal people as a third order of government alongside the federal and provincial governments. These efforts, however, alienated many Canadians, and despite extraordinary support from the major political parties, government officials, and nearly all elite groups, the Charlottetown Accords were defeated at the polls. Cotler concludes that the viability of the Canadian federal system remains in doubt.

NOTES

1.   Daniel J. Elazar, *Exploring Federalism* (Tuscaloosa: University of Alabama Press, 1987), p. 6.

2.   For example, in *Federalism: Origin, Operation, Significance* (Boston: Little, Brown, 1964), p. 245, William H. Riker contended that "the abstract assertion that federalism is a guarantee of freedom is undoubtedly false. ...If freedom is interpreted in a majoritarian way, then the assertion is invariably false, for federalism is an impediment to freedom. If freedom is interpreted in a minoritarian way, then either federalism has nothing to do with freedom or federalism is again an impediment to freedom." For more general support for Riker's assertions, see the authors surveyed in Gary Jacobsohn's essay in this volume.

3.   William Blackstone, *Commentaries on the Laws of England*, vol. I, ed. Stanley Katz (Chicago: University of Chicago Press, 1977), p. 125.

4.   See Michael P. Zuckert, "Toward a Corrective Federalism: The United States Constitution, Federalism, and Rights," in this volume.

5.   See generally Thomas D. Morris, *Free Men All: The Personal Liberty Laws of the North, 1780-1861* (Baltimore: Johns Hopkins University Press, 1974); and Paul Finkelman, *An Imperfect Union: Slavery, Federalism, and Comity* (Chapel Hill: University of North Carolina Press, 1981).

6.   Michael Zuckert's essay in this volume offers an interpretation of the meaning of the Fourteenth Amendment. For alternative accounts, see Raoul Berger, *Government by Judiciary: The Transformation of the Fourteenth Amendment* (Cambridge: Harvard University Press, 1977); Michael Kent Curtis, *No State Shall Abridge: The Fourteenth Amendment and the Bill of Rights* (Durham, N.C.: Duke University Press, 1986); and Earl M. Maltz, *Civil Rights, the Constitution, and Congress, 1863-1869* (Lawrence: University Press of Kansas, 1990).

7.   *The Slaughterhouse Cases*, 83 U.S. 36 (1873), and *The Civil Rights Cases*, 109 U.S. 3 (1883). For an overview of these developments, see William E. Nelson, *The Fourteenth Amendment: From Political Principle to Judicial Doctrine* (Cambridge: Harvard University Press, 1988).

8.   The Supreme Court struck down congressional efforts to regulate child labor in *Hammer v. Dagenhart*, 247 U.S. 251 (1918), and in *Bailey v. Drexel Furniture Company*, 259 U.S. 20 (1922).

9. See *State v. Sheridan*, 96 N.W. 730 (Iowa, 1903), preceding *Weeks v. United States*, 232 U.S. 383 (1914), and *Carpenter v. Dane*, 9 Wis. 249 (1859), preceding *Gideon v. Wainwright*, 372 U.S. 335 (1963). For an overview of state civil-liberties litigation in the nineteenth and early twentieth centuries, see G. Alan Tarr, "The Past and Future of the New Judicial Federalism," *Publius: The Journal of Federalism*, 22 (Spring 1994): 64-69.

10. For an overview of this "new judicial federalism" and representative cases, see Robert F. Williams, *State Constitutional Law* (Mineola: Michie, 1993). For a useful bibliography of the literature analyzing the reemergence of state civil-liberties law, see Earl M. Maltz, Robert Williams, and Michael Araten, "Selected Bibliography on State Constitutional Law, 1980-1989," *Rutgers Law Journal*, 20 (1989): 1093-1113.

11. See Brian Galligan, *Politics of the High Court: A Study of the Judicial Branch of Government in Australia* (St. Lucia: University of Queensland Press, 1987), p. 49.

12. Elazar, *Exploring Federalism*, p. 6. The examples in this paragraph are drawn from Elazar's volume; see Chapter 2, especially p. 60, Figure 2.4.

13. Alexis de Tocqueville, *Democracy in America*, ed. J. P. Mayer (Garden City: Doubleday and Co., 1969), pp. 167-168.

14. Justice William J. Brennan, Jr. makes this point in two articles: "The Bill of Rights and the States: The Revival of State Constitutions as Guardians of Individual Rights," *New York University Law Review*, 61 (October, 1986): 535-553, and "State Constitutions and the Protection of Individual Rights," *Harvard Law Review*, 90 (January, 1977): 489-504.

CHAPTER 1

FEDERALISM, DIVERSITY, AND RIGHTS

Daniel J. Elazar

THE THREE PILLARS OF MODERN DEMOCRACY

Three of the most important inventions of modern democratic government are federalism, the protection of individual rights, and the idea of civil society. The whole philosophic and political revolution that began in the seventeenth century and reached its highest points in the late eighteenth century in two different sets of events, the American Revolution and the subsequent constitutional experience of the United States and the French Revolution and subsequent Bonapartist experience of France and Europe, reflects these three inventions. The first, the American revolutionary experience and its extensions, generated practical ways to achieve the proximate ends of federalism, secure individual rights, and foster the idea of civil society. The French revolutionary experience, and its fall-out throughout Europe and ultimately the rest of the world generally sought democracy in the opposite direction and was far less successful. It was - and is - the proper combination of the three that makes true democracy possible.

Federalism

Federalism in this context is more than simply intergovernmental relations.[1] It is even more than the linking of constituent entities into larger wholes to maintain both self-rule and shared-rule. The political theory of federal democracy holds that the way of democracy is constitutionalized partnership and power sharing on a non-centralized basis through discussion and deliberation. It is not simply to make decisions by counting a simple majority of 50 percent plus one on all issues, allowing the simple majority to have its way, but to create a balancing of interests, voices and diversity in such a way that there is no permanent majority but rather that all majorities are aggregates of the various minorities that express their interests. People have more than one interest and therefore are part of different minority and majority coalitions at different times.

Federalism is a form of democratic republicanism that accommodates the diversity inherent in a democracy and a response to both Jacobin (or simple majoritarian democracy) and Westminster (or parliamentary democracy) that rejects both the premises and practical consequences of both as effective means of giving democratic expression, but which offers an alternative teaching about democracy and what democracy should be. Federal democracy as we know it is a teaching that was first articulated effectively and eloquently by the founders of the United States. It emphasizes constitutionalized pluralism and power-sharing as the basis of truly democratic government. It sees a democratic polity as one built upon a matrix of constituent institutions that together share power, not through a single center but in a multi-centered or noncentralized way. This is very different from Jacobin democracy which sees the state organized in the name of the general will as a power pyramid with those on the top as the ones who give expression to the general will. Ultimately, however, the decision as to who or what is on top, and who or what is on the bottom, is made by those who are on top. Under that model, by the very nature of things, the people often find themselves not just on the bottom of the pyramid but really underneath it. It is also different from the kind of club-like atmosphere of parliamentary democracy where, in a center-periphery model, power is concentrated in the elite club or clubs and everyone else is in the periphery. In effective parliamentary democracies, the periphery interacts with the center and to some extent influences who is in the center, or at least who is in one or another of the clubs in the center, but the peripheries still are the peripheries and the center is still the center.

Rights

Of the protection of individual rights little needs to be said to define them at this point since that is perhaps the most widely recognized and emphasized aspect of contemporary democracy. It is a subject worthy of considerable discussion. I will return to what constitutes rights, especially individual rights, and how they are best protected and expressed, but the idea of individual rights is so universal and so much a part of the understanding of democracy in the twentieth century that it hardly needs elaboration in a general discussion like this.[2]

The Restoration of Civil Society

The ideal of civil society holds that every political-social order has to have both governmental and private spheres and that government does not have the authority to intervene in every aspect of the social order.[3] Private is private. The private sphere is authentically private in that it is originally private by virtue of individual and natural rights and therefore is independent of government intervention in most ways, except where a limited public good is defined. The idea of civil society, as we have been reminded recently by those who revived its public discussion in the former Communist bloc as a weapon against totalitarianism, stands in diametric opposition to the idea of the totalitarian state. The totalitarian state allows no private sphere except perhaps by the grace of its leaders as rulers, and even that, like all matters of grace, always has the possibility of graciousness being revoked.

As the totalitarianism of Communist rule was challenged and eliminated, the challenge was framed by the locals as the idea of reviving civil society in the Communist-ruled lands. At the time, that was an idea much neglected, even forgotten in the West two and three centuries after the idea reached its highest development and served as the foundation of Western democratic republicanism. These two spheres, the governmental and the private, are linked in a very important way by a third, a public nongovernmental sphere. This third sphere is necessary if the civil society is to be republican civil society. Indeed one can visualize civil society as a stool resting upon three legs. One leg consists of the governmental institutions framing the society, the second is the private sphere, and the third, the public nongovernmental sphere consisting of the voluntary public cooperative institutions and activities that make it possible for civil society to function beyond simply protecting the individual and, at the same time, to do so without turning to government with its coercive powers as the whole matter of the public realm.[4]

The United States, which has been a preeminently successful civil society throughout most of its history, has been successful precisely because it has had a very large public nongovernmental sphere which is not private in the sense that it is not the personal property of individuals, and is not statist or governmental; it is public and voluntary, in which people come together freely to cooperate. Indeed it is clearly an element of American political philosophy that government is an intervener of last resort.[5] Americans have encouraged the private and public nongovernmental spheres to undertake whatever tasks are deemed necessary to be undertaken and only then, if that is not sufficient or if for some reason of equity, government is empowered. This is not the same as the distinction between civil society and the state; in federal democracies and in federal democratic theory there is no reified or separable "state." A civil society is a comprehensive association of associations and individuals. It organizes its governmental institutions and establishes other public institutions by the consent or the coming together of its citizens. Those institutions are fundamentally based on the network of public and private associations, and thus, rest on multiple separations of powers not united into a single coercive institutional power known as the state.

Until the New Deal, public nongovernmental institutions continued to be considered the primary repositories of collective activity; government, while important, was still limited or distant. Until the 1960s, government came to be considered a primary player, but primarily as a "backstop" to public nongovernmental institutions: that is to say, government was free to act but always couched its actions by justification based on the inability of the public to count on nongovernmental institutions to act appropriately, well, or completely. The Great Society brought a sea change in government, particularly the federal government, which became more assertive, pushing private and public nongovernmental institutions into a backup role. A decade later, the public affairs debate rediscovered those institutions and began referring to them as "mediating institutions." Although this rediscovery was for the good, relegating those institutions to that new role reduced them in importance and scope. That is more or less where we stand today, although, in recent years, we have begun to pull beyond that, to once again see those institutions as having an independent standing and role of their own and not merely to serve as bridges between the governmental and the private.

Most of republican civil society will be in the private sphere, yet at the same time, no society can exist without civil or political organization, with the authoritative allocation of values, tasks, resources, and responsibilities. The idea of proper government for a civil society, as it was framed by the seventeenth and eighteenth century founders of the modern epoch, views government as limited, but a necessity all the same. We have to look back to the seventeenth and eighteenth centuries to understand how they saw government both as limited and necessary, because the West lost that understanding in the nineteenth century. The nineteenth century was the century in which the ideologies of the automatic society were ascendant. No matter what ideology was prominent in the nineteenth century - laissez faire capitalism, Marxism, anarchism, Comptear sociology or whatever - all of them believed in the automatic society; namely, that all humans had to do to perfect society was to find the key to the march of history - the unrestricted market, the proletariat, the good nature of human beings, the immutable laws of society, or the like - to strip away all those fetters that prevented the automatic society from operating. Then, in the view of each, we would have the utopia of peace and justice, security and equality for which we all were searching.

In the twentieth century, we have painfully relearned that there is no such thing as an automatic society. Even in the best of societies there will be that five or ten percent who will not follow the rules and must be controlled by force if necessary, or, on the other hand, that there exists an irreducible desire in all humans for individual freedom that does not admit of elimination even by the greatest coercion. This means that all societies must be framed by government - limited government, properly organized government - but by government with its coercive powers that can protect the many against the few, if not the few against the many. In truth both are in need of protection at one time or another.

Thus, the idea of civil society has dual meanings: (1) that for society to exist there need be government as a framing institution that will (2) frame its civil society in which private and public nongovernmental as well as governmental activities can develop and flourish. The revival of this understanding is critical for understanding any process of building and improving the political-social order on which we all are dependent and in which we are all involved.

DIVERSITY: INDIVIDUALS AND GROUPS

Diversity is a perennial issue that many assume has changed form over the years of the modern and postmodern epochs. Individualism advanced to seemingly replace primordial or communal ties. In the modern epoch, at most, individual diversity was modified by the existence of associations or interest groups that for the most part were not treated as multi-generational even if they were. Even religious groups were treated as associations of those who were members at the time and not transcendently binding or as multi-generational. The reigning idea of the modern world was to move toward this kind of diversity and away from the primordial or communal diversity that had embraced so much of the world, perhaps all of it, throughout previous epochs.

Today we know that primordial and communal ties have continued to survive throughout the world to a greater or lesser extent. In the United States perhaps they have been diminished more than any place else. However, even in Western Europe where the idea of civil society was born, we see primordial groups that continue to survive and develop. As we move eastward and southward we see primordial groups that not only survive but are involved in deadly conflict with each other when and where the opportunity presents itself.

In the most extreme form then, the primordial ties of many ethnic, religious, and national communities lead to communities that are willing to fight for their existence and demands in the most bloody way. At times these groups require the restructuring of civil society, redefining human rights and reshaping the ties of federalism that they have extensively embraced. The problem of the civil society, then, is a problem of providing not only for the protection of individuals and the protections of the rights of association, but also the problem of dealing with the realities of group rights, primordial and communal, that are part of the realities of human existence. Here we find the beginnings of the convergence and the tensions between federalism and rights that are all too real in this world.

FEDERALISM AND RIGHTS

Even where such major problems have not developed, at times there appear to be contradictions between the requirements of federalism and those of individual rights - the question of slavery and civil rights for blacks in the United States for example, led to clashes of major proportions. We are now witness to such things in other parts of the world, but even where clashes have not reached such intensity, conflicts between a federalism based upon primordial groups and individual rights demands have led to other forms of conflict. There is a certain way in which federalism tends to support group rights, whether they be associational and not multi-generational or whether they be primordial and communal and multi-generational.

Rights ideas developed parallel to federalism and simultaneously with it, to end up after passing through various interpretations as the pursuit of individual rights at all costs, even in opposition to the principles of federalism. Yet there is another way in which the combination of the two tends to serve the larger interest of civil society. Throughout most of American history, I would argue, federalism and rights have not been in tension but have actually complemented each other in the development of a more successful, a more democratic, a more peaceful, a more just, and a more progressive civil society.

Nevertheless, the once real and now the apparent contradictions between the two require reconciliation. The real has now passed. It revolved around the slavery issue and the civil rights of nonwhites. With all of the problems that may still exist, they are not problems of federalism. For the first time in American history race is no longer a federalism issue in the United States. With regard to the second, the beginning of that reconciliation is in the recognition that there are at least two ways to deal with diversity - as the diversity of individuals and as the diversity of groups; and that there are at least two ways of dealing with rights - as standing in and of themselves or as related to responsibilities or obligations; and two ways of dealing with federalism - through federation, a modern invention in which the federal government is the national government that acts directly on the citizens even though they are also citizens of the constituent units, or through confederation, a form of federalism that had disappeared in the modern epoch but has now been revived in the post-modern, in which the constituent units are nations that preserve powers of full equal supremacy with the general government which is subordinate to them in some critical ways and has to work through them to reach their citizens.[6]

Just as federation essentially eliminated confederation as an option in the modern epoch, when the nation-state was the ideal model of comprehensive political organization, so, too, in the post-modern epoch, as the modern states system is being subsumed within new transnational networks, new forms of confederation are emerging to function side-by-side with federations. The existence of at least two possibilities in each of these three cases does not mean that they are dichotomous. In most cases, successful civil societies have kept them from being dichotomous and have drawn from each to develop some kind of synthesis that is helpful to the achievement of societal goals. In our time we are trying to renew that synthesis which has to be rebuilt for each generation and for each epoch. One of the most visible ways in which we are trying to rebuild it is through both federation and confederation. The European Community, now Union, began as a league, moved to become a confederation and just now postponed or deterred the possibility of becoming a federation. Two hundred years ago, the United States abandoned the Articles of Confederation in favor of the federal Constitution of 1787; nevertheless, the United States has confederal features which have survived at least until our times. U.S. political parties have been state-based and linked through confederal connections which have served to limit the tendencies of the federation to move toward a kind of national union that would eliminate noncentralization and require the concentration of power in the federal government. In recent years, we have seen some of the federalist institutions diminished after two centuries. As a result we have seen new concentrations of federal powers that are problematic, in terms of the generally American accepted views of what American civil society should be like.

In the interim, we have seen a triumph of rights thinking at the expense of both federalism and group diversity. Individual rights, once called natural rights, then civil rights and now human rights, have come to be considered in many quarters as "trumps" that overcome all other constitutional concepts and institutions, including the concept of the public good.[7] Those of this school hold that if an individual rights claim is raised, all other claims must stand aside. This raises serious questions. Is it possible to have a public good that is not simply a matter of confirming the precedence of individual rights? This, in turn has led others to a reconsideration of the rights ideology in an effort to balance it with some sense of responsibility or obligation that will have standing similar to the idea of rights.[8] In the United States in the last decade or so, we have seen powerful forces among both liberals and conservatives who are talking about responsibilities in civil community and the rebuilding of civic republicanism, and using words that suggest that there is a public good which has to be considered along with individual rights in one way or another, for the health of civil society.

FEDERAL LIBERTY

Here we come to the other and often forgotten dimension of federalism that deals not only with the constitution of governmental structures and functions, but with the idea of the public good in civil society - what was known in the early days of the modern epoch as federal liberty. Federal liberty was originally a concept of Reformed Protestantism, particularly American Puritanism at the time of the Reformation. It received its most effective formulation by John Winthrop in the 1630s when he was the governor of Massachusetts Bay Colony. Subsequently, it was secularized and redefined at the time of the American Revolution, principally by James Wilson, one of the founding fathers, of Scottish background, to involve the federal liberty of those who have consented together to form a civil society.[9]

Originally the Puritans had understood federal liberty as a product of the linking of humans with God through covenant. The term federal is derived from the Latin *foedus* which means covenant. It, in turn, is derived from the Hebrew *brit* and the biblical understanding of covenant. Federal liberty meant that every human being has the liberty to live up to the terms of the covenant to which he or she had consented. In its original form, that was the covenant with God. For Wilson, that was a covenant or compact among the states and among the citizens of the states to establish a certain kind of viable civil society that would be democratic and republican.

Every individual has the right to enter into the covenant but, once he or she does, then the definition of liberty is based on it, as they have collectively defined it through the federal pact. That constitutes federal liberty. Federal liberty offers a theory of proper relationships between rights and obligations that can preserve the gains of the modern and postmodern movements for human rights that have been so significant and so important for us all, while anchoring those rights in a set of obligations that will preserve the public good and recognize the idea that there is a public that collectively has a certain standing in the matter. Postmoderns would do well to return to these roots of federalism found in the concepts of federal liberty to see if they can find ways to overcome the excesses of contemporary rights thinking while preserving the gains and great advantages that accrue to us all by allowing and encouraging the development of rights and new ways for protection of rights. In this way, the synthesis between federalism and rights can be used to achieve an appropriate relationship between private and public concerns, between individual protections through rights thinking and public group needs through federalism. Bringing the two into a harmony again, this time through workings of the political system and not only in the conceptualization of civil society, is the great task before us.

NOTES

1. Samuel H. Beer, *To Make a Nation: The Rediscovery of American Federalism* (Cambridge: Harvard University Press, 1993); and Daniel J. Elazar, *Exploring Federalism* (Tuscaloosa: University of Alabama Press, 1987).

2. See the special issue of *Publius: The Journal of Federalism*, "Rights in America's Constitutional Tradition," 22 (Spring 1992).

3. Alan Seligman, *The Idea of Civil Society* (New York: The Free Press, 1992).

4.   Alexis de Tocqueville discusses this in detail in his *Democracy in America*, especially in the sections on voluntary associations.

5.   This is documented in depth in Daniel J. Elazar, *Cities of the Prairie* (New York: Basic Books, 1970); Daniel J. Elazar, ed., *Cities of the Prairie Revisited* (Lincoln: University of Nebraska Press, 1987); and other publications from the Cities of the Prairie Project of the Center for the Study of Federalism.

6.   Murray Forsyth, *Unions of States* (Leicester: University of Leicester Press, 1981); and Ivo Duchacek, "Consociations of Fatherlands: The Revival of Confederal Principles and Practices," *Publius: The Journal of Federalism*, 12 (Fall 1982): 129-177.

7.   Ronald Dworkin, *A Matter of Principle* (Cambridge: Belknap Press, 1986), Chapter 19.

8.   G. Alan Tarr, "Constitutional Theories and Constitutional Rights," *Publius: The Journal of Federalism*, 22 (Spring 1992), p. 99.

9.   Daniel J. Elazar, *The American Constitutional Tradition* (Lincoln: University of Nebraska Press, 1987), pp. 167-168.

CHAPTER 2

DOES FEDERALISM SECURE OR UNDERMINE RIGHTS?

A. E. Dick Howard

Federalism comes in many shapes and sizes. The number of constituent units may vary—from two in the former Czech and Slovak Federal Republic to fifty in the United States. The units may vary enormously in size and wealth; contrast Canada's rich Ontario and its poor maritime provinces. The degree of centralization may vary so much that a federation may resemble a unitary state, or it may appear to be a confederation. A federation may opt for a presidential system (as in the United States) or for that of a parliament (as in Canada). The means for resolving disputes between the federal government and its constituent units differ; the United States has its Supreme Court, Germany looks to its Constitutional Court. There are as many faces to federalism as there are notions about the ideal marriage.

Despite such a menu for federations, it is possible to suggest some generalizations. I propose in the pages that follow to consider some of the benefits that may be said to flow from federalism as well as some of the limitations or disadvantages. In doing this, I suggest that one think, not simply of formal federalism, but of a cluster of related values—federalism, localism, pluralism, diversity. Federalism as a constitutional arrangement has both advantages and disadvantages that go with formalizing the federal structure.

But some of the pros and cons of federalism remain relevant where, short of a formal federal system, it is proposed to have a generous measure of devolution, regional autonomy, home rule, subsidiarity, or some other way of institutionalizing pluralistic laws and policies.

THE VALUES OF FEDERALISM

Restraints on the Concentration and Abuse of Power

It is inevitable that government entails the use of power. Indeed, the idea of law itself turns on the assumption that there are circumstances when, in the pursuit of some social value, an individual must be forced to do that which otherwise he would not do or to refrain from that which otherwise he would do.

It is equally inevitable that to create government with the power over the lives of individuals is to invite abuse of that power. It is no accident that we quote Lord Acton as often as we do.[1] One of the great challenges of constitutional democracy is how to give government sufficient power to do its job while at the same time creating restraints on the abuse of that power. What troubled the barons at Runnymede—could the king be trusted to keep his promises—troubles us still.

Philosophers, constitution-makers, judges, and others have sought various ways to restrain government's power in order to protect individual liberty. The drafters of the first American state constitutions, remembering royal power, looked to popular government to safeguard liberty.[2] Chief Justice John Marshall invoked judicial review.[3] But no device is more important—or more imbedded in the American experience—than the use of structural devices, dispersing power in order to guard against its abuse.

One structural device is the separation of powers - the creation, at the level of the federal government, of three branches, each having its own independent source of authority in the Constitution. Equally fundamental in the American scheme of things is federalism. James Madison drew the intimate connection between federalism and the separation of powers:

> In the compound government of America, the power surrendered by the people is first divided between two distinct governments, and then the portion allotted to each subdivided among distinct and separate departments. Hence a double security arises as to the rights of the people. The different governments will control each other, at the same time that each will be controlled by itself.[4]

Alexander Hamilton saw similar virtue in having competing bases of government power:

> Power being almost always the rival of power, the general government will at all times stand ready to check the usurpations of the state governments, and these will have the same disposition toward the general government. The people by throwing themselves into either scale, will infallibly make it preponderate. If their rights are invaded by either, they can make use of the other as a means of redress.[5]

The dynamics of contemporary politics justify concern about the dangers of powers being used in an irresponsible way at the federal level. If responsible government assumes that decisions will be made in some way by which decision-makers are ultimately accountable to the people, then there is ample reason to be concerned about the by-passing of the democratic process by the "triangle of power"—the making of public policy by federal bureaucracies, congressional committees, and interest groups.[6]

The Educational Value of Civic Participation

Alexis de Tocqueville, a great admirer of American democracy, saw the educational dimension of citizens' intimate participation in local government. The townsperson, he said,

> takes part in every occurrence in the place; he practises the art of government in the small sphere within his reach; he accustoms himself to those forms without which liberty can advance by revolutions; he imbibes their spirit; he acquires a taste for order, comprehends the balance of powers, and collects clear practical notions on the nature of his duties and the extent of his rights.[7]

Highly centralized regimes employ prefects or other officers, armed with the writ of the capital, to put laws into effect. Executing such laws is a relatively solitary experience of commands being given by one party and being obeyed by another. That the central government is elected in a democratic fashion may soften the experience (although not if the voice giving the commands is that of the all-powerful people, as in revolutionary France), local execution of laws made at the center does not invite much by way of dialogue. It is deliberating together—face-to-face debate over the issues of the moment - that makes for reflection. The essence of being a citizen is to have the opportunity, not simply to vote for those who make the laws, but also to have a voice in how decisions are to be fashioned, what choices to be made. Local government can thus become a classroom for those who take part in it.

Mark Tushnet makes the useful point that it is in the give-and-take of local government and politics that citizens are most likely to realize the imperative that each must, to some extent, subordinate his or her self-interest if civic projects are to take place at all.[8] Pundits and voters alike decry "gridlock" at the federal level. Likewise they deplore the excessive power of special interests. Yet the American people, in election after election, have tolerated divided government, the White House in the hands of one party, Congress in the hands of the other. And special interests continue to flourish, whatever the cost to the common good.

State and local governments can, of course, also see failure to lay aside partisanship or selfish interests bringing about deadlock. The inability of California's governor and legislature to agree on an approach to that state's troubled economy brought about a budget impasse, in which the state was reduced to issuing IOUs which banks, in turn, would not honor.[9] The cost of such paralysis at the state or local level is, however, sooner obvious to the ordinary citizen than is deadlock at the national level, where politicians seem to hope to postpone indefinitely the day of reckoning that surely must come because of the mounting federal debt. The pain inflicted when a municipality does not collect the garbage is the kind of cost that quickly engages the attention of even the most acquiescent of citizens.

A Sense of Community

An insistence on individual rights tends to emphasize an atomistic view of society. Indeed one of the great contributions of western constitutionalism has been to give a special place to human rights. The Bill of Rights to the United States Constitution is, above all, a list of "negative" rights, that is, limitations on government action.

There is, however, another important strain to constitutional thinking, one that stresses shared or community values. If the Bill of Rights reflects an individualistic ideal, then the early American state constitutions remind us of the notion that republicanism connotes also the inculcation of a sense of community or shared values.

George Mason's 1776 Declaration of Rights for Virginia included, of course, protections for individual liberty, such as bans on general warrants and on cruel and unusual punishments.[10] But Mason's declaration also carried the language of aspiration: "That no free government, or the blessings of liberty, can be preserved to any people, but by a firm adherence to justice, moderation, temperance, frugality, and virtue, and by frequent recurrence to fundamental principles."[11]

A centralized government does not necessarily make republican virtues and a sense of community impossible. But such is human nature that distance tends to strain one's sense of benevolence and empathy. It almost seems axiomatic that, when newspapers or television report human disasters or misfortunes, the further the distance to the unhappy scene, the greater must be the toll in human life or suffering for the item to be reported - certainly, to be covered in detail. A neighbor's house burns, and it makes the evening news, but it takes a typhoon or a volcano's eruption for a disaster halfway around the world to reach our attention.

Ideally, of course, individuals should have the same concern for their fellow human beings wherever they live. Such phenomena as missionary movements and the Peace Corps remind us that human compassion does not stop at national boundaries. But if it is civic virtue one wishes to instill—as the American founding generation hoped—one must begin with that which is closest at hand.[12] Edmund Burke, in his *Reflections on the Revolution in France*, put it this way: "To be attached to the subdivision, to love the little platoon we belong to in society, is the first principle (the germ as it were) of public affections. It is the first link in the series by which we proceed towards a love to our country, and to mankind."[13]

Federalism encourages the need to pay special attention to those people whose problems are closest at hand. And there is plenty of work to do near to home; what community has not seen the "not in my backyard" sentiment surface when it comes to shelters for the homeless or residences for the mentally retarded?

The Pluralistic Society

Closed societies seek uniformity—one party, one theology, one road to sacred or secular salvation. The open society allows individual idiosyncrasies to flourish. Individualism has its practical advantages, especially in the economic sphere; progress and invention are encouraged where individual enterprise and initiative are encouraged. There is also a deeper value in pluralism; it permits the human spirit to flower and express itself.

Local communities can often stifle individualism and self-expression. Many of the small towns that dotted nineteenth-century America were anything but models of pluralism. But social mobility offers a way out of such places. And, at the larger geographical level, federalism and localism serve as a counter to uniformity. In the United States, state and local boundaries are to some extent arbitrary. The states' very existence, however, are reminders that mores and attitudes do differ from one part of the country to another. The federal Constitution and laws place limits, of course, on the extent to which local preferences may prevail.[14] But the fact of federalism's existence encourages diverse attitudes to manifest themselves.

Federalism counters another kind of monopoly—that of political power and political parties. Disparate units having governmental powers offer arenas in which parties and factions finding themselves in the minority on the national stage can have local bases from which to compete and hope that, with luck, they can become majorities in the country at large.

The American states have frequently offered just such opportunities for political figures to hone their skills and marshal their troops for runs at national office. Woodrow Wilson in New Jersey, Franklin Roosevelt in New York, Jimmy Carter in Georgia, Ronald Reagan in California, Bill Clinton in Arkansas - all were state governors before being elected to the presidency.

Local Solutions to Local Problems

Federalism has its practical side. Many problems require no uniform solution throughout a country. Local circumstances, local traditions, even local tastes may suffice. Consider the Supreme Court's approach to cases in which a state law or regulation is challenged by a party claiming the ordinance to be a burden on interstate commerce. From the early cases onward, the Court has actively policed such state enactments, lest they interfere with the free flow of commerce. Yet the Court understands that local conditions may call for a local formula.

A case in point is Justice Curtis' 1851 decision in *Cooley v. Board of Wardens of the Port of Philadelphia*.[15] Cooley objected to a Pennsylvania law requiring ships entering or leaving the port of Philadelphia to engage a local pilot to guide them through the harbor. Justice Curtis had no doubt that Pennsylvania's statute was a regulation of commerce. He postulated that some subjects would, of course, require a single uniform rule, but that there were others - he thought pilotage to be such a case - "imperatively demanding that diversity, which alone can meet the local necessities of navigation." Congress (which had deferred to the states on the subject of pilotage) was entitled to conclude that there was "no doubt of the superior fitness and propriety, not to say the absolute necessity, of different systems of regulation, drawn from local knowledge and experience, and conformed to local wants."[16]

States as Laboratories

Justice Louis Brandeis coined the now familiar metaphor of the states as laboratories when, in a 1932 Supreme Court opinion, he said, "It is one of the happy accidents of the federal system that a single courageous state may, if its citizens choose, serve as a laboratory, and try novel social and economic experiments without risk to the rest of the country."[17]

Some observers might question whether the American states have lived up to Justice Brandeis' attractive portrait. At mid-twentieth century, the ideal of democracy was submerged by glaring malapportionment in state legislatures. State courts delivered opinions that often failed to command the bar's respect, and criminal justice in the states too frequently failed to meet minimum levels of fairness and due process.

Today the states are far stronger and more responsible entities than they were in the 1950s. Some of the reforms were mandated by federal law. The Supreme Court's reapportionment decisions, requiring that representation be based on population, brought about significant changes in the composition of state legislatures. Civil rights laws, notably the Voting Rights Act of 1965, removed many of the most serious barriers to voting.

Other reforms came from the states themselves. During the 1960s and 1970s, a number of states rewrote their constitutions, replacing archaic charters that often resembled a statute book with constitutions encouraging responsible and responsive government. State governors now can exercise greater leadership, executive branches have been overhauled, legislatures are better staffed, and state courts are more professional.

Even before these structural reforms took place, the states were the locus of much innovation - spawning ideas that often led to imitation at the federal level. When Wyoming became a state in 1890, it was the only state in which women could vote - anticipating the Nineteenth Amendment, which became effective in 1921. Wisconsin pioneered unemployment compensation, while Massachusetts led the way in establishing minimum wage laws for women and for minors.[18] Budget techniques turning on program performance, including the idea of "zero-base budgeting," were tried out by state governments before being adopted by the federal government.[19] The list of state innovations is a long one. Indeed, as Congress debates proposals ranging from no-fault insurance to containing the cost of hospital and health care, proponents and opponents alike are sure to cite the experience gleaned - both successes and mistakes - from the state capitals.

It is important to note that competition among the states can lead to the lowering of standards. Harry Scheiber gives Delaware's corporation laws and Nevada's divorce laws as classic examples of minimal legislation designed to give in-state industries the advantage over those in other states.[20] Competition among states may actually stifle innovation, especially where states fear that attempts to deal with a social problem may cause industries to locate in states with fewer benefits or less regulation.[21]

A Continuing Referendum on Fundamental Principles

Any allocation of power among levels of government - whether through formal federalism or through some other device - introduces ambiguities into the processes of government.   Students of American state and local government know the often byzantine quality of the impact of Dillon's Rule.[22] And beginning with the earliest decisions of the United States Supreme Court, federalism as a constitutional principle has produced thousands of pages of judicial opinions seeking to strike some balance between national and local interests.

Americans have never ceased to debate - and to reinterpret - the meaning of "federalism." One is reminded of the old saw about a violin's being defined as a small viola, and a viola's being defined as a large violin. What does it mean to believe in "federalism" or to call oneself a "federalist"? When the Articles of Confederation were still in force, those who, like James Madison, saw themselves as being "federalists" were advocates for greater powers in the central government. Indeed, the Virginia plan at the Philadelphia convention called for a national legislative veto over state legislation that might impinge upon national interests.[23]

In the third century of the federal union, however, to speak of "federalism" or to speak of oneself as a "federalist" is usually to advocate more respect for the states as entities and more powers and functions to be entrusted to state and local governments. Thus, dissenting from the Supreme Court's decision in *Garcia v. San Antonio Metropolitan Transit Authority*, Justice O'Connor declared that the Court "cannot abdicate its constitutional responsibility to oversee the Federal Government's compliance with its duty to respect the legitimate interests of the States."[24]

Federalism has a dual purpose. It aims at achieving unity while also preserving diversity. Any state that is federal in character must reconcile local preferences and wider demands. Pursuing competing ends often produces tension and conflict. The result is a dialogue, a dialectic about the allocation of power. Some of the dialogue goes on between levels of government - in Congress, where states' interests may be invoked during debate on legislation, and in the courts, as when state laws are attacked as being burdens on interstate commerce or as being preempted by federal legislation - and in other forums.[25]

The conversation about basic principles goes on among the people as well. In a federal system, a citizen has allegiance to more than one level of government; in the United States, one is a citizen of both state and nation. Ordinary people are drawn into the unending debate over federalism. Do the individual states tend to promote individual liberty, or to undermine it? In such debates, abstractions quickly yield to specifics, and citizens, especially when they vote, must make choices. In mulling the uses of federalism and localism versus central solutions, the citizen may hear the echo of the founders' debates. Indeed, Daniel Elazar, one of the great American students of federalism, maintains that, by generating questions that require continuing public attention, "federal arrangements may be sufficiently justified for this reason alone."[26]

Accountable Government

A hallmark of democratic government is that those who are elected to public office are accountable to those who elect them. It is equally important to a healthy polity that citizens feel that sense of accountability. Accountability begins with elections, but it does not end there. Representative government requires that the connection between the governors and the governed not simply take place on election day; there must be the continuing opportunity for citizens to tell office-holders just what is on their minds.

The more local the government, the greater the opportunity for communication between those in office and those who put them there. Proximity tends to increase accountability by enhancing access. Jack Kilpatrick, with his usual flair for words, paints this picture:

> The county commissioner dwells low on Olympus, and the local alderman is accessible in ways that United States Senators and Cabinet Secretaries are not accessible. When a citizen of Virginia travels to the Capital at Richmond, he travels with a sure sense of participation and community; he speaks to the committees of the General Assembly, supporting or opposing particular legislation, as a fellow-citizen in the community of four million that is Virginia. When he travels to the Capital at Washington, by contrast, he feels insecurity gnawing at his vitals. He finds the palace ringed by the glossy castles of potent baronies - the Machinists, the

Mineworkers, the Educationists - and the marbled catacombs of the Senate Office Building are filled with total strangers. In this distant opulence, he stands subdued.[27]

The Right of Choice

Of all the values implicit in federalism, none is more fundamental to self-government by a free people than is the right of choice. We may place high values on many interests - the wish to be left alone, the hope for economic prosperity, the opportunity for self-expression. All of these are aspirations that one recognizes as highly valued in most democratic societies. But federalism reminds us of the core value in democratic government: the right to become involved in the public life of a polity.

The touchstone of a democratic government is consent. Alexander Bickel declared that "coherent, stable - and morally supportable - government is possible only on the basis of consent, and...the secret of consent is the sense of common venture fostered by institutions that reflect and represent us and that we can call to account."[28]

In the American constitutional system, the right of individuals to participate in the process of making political choices is reinforced by a cluster of fundamental rights, among them free expression, criticism of public officials, voting, and equality of representation. It is inescapable that state and local governments have often trampled these very rights. State and local laws and ordinances have often operated to deny the vote on grounds of race, to foreclose public forums to disfavored views, or otherwise to oppress racial, religious, or other minorities.

The remedy for wrongs like these lies in judicial enforcement of such constitutional guarantees as the Fourteenth Amendment's equal protection clause and Congress' use of its constitutional powers, such as those conferred by Section 5 of the Fourteenth Amendment. Guarding against abuses of individual rights by states and localities does not, however, mean that we should abandon the place that the right to make political choices must have in the constitutional galaxy. Federalism reinforces this right of choice - and does so at levels of government closer to the people, where choices are more likely to have immediate and perceptible impact. Democratic government is healthier when people can see that how they vote, and what their representatives do, actually matters.

THE OTHER SIDE OF THE COIN

Any fair assessment of federalism must include its costs and disadvantages. Some of these are discussed below.

The Tyranny of Small Places

In the best of all possible worlds, small communities would always be the classrooms for democracy, citizen education, and civic virtue which this essay portrays them to be. History reminds us, however, that life in small towns is not always so gentle. Community life in seventeenth century Massachusetts was one of conformity, in which magistrates imposed their understanding of God's law regardless of complaints that rights under Magna Carta and other English laws were being overridden.[29] In our own time, one has but to read the pages of the U.S. Supreme Court Reports to realize how often it is that violations of individual liberties have been perpetuated by states and local governments.

In the post-Reconstruction era, it was southern states, defeated in war but defiant in peace, that imposed Jim Crow laws whose unmistakable purpose was to reduce the recently freed slaves to as near a condition of servitude as possible. The same states enacted restrictive suffrage laws aimed squarely at disenfranchisement of as many blacks as possible. And states and localities fought the civil rights movement of the 1960s with every legal tool (and some not so legal) they could muster. In the era of "Massive Resistance," calls for "states' rights" were often thinly veiled appeals to racism.

The problem is not confined to one region. Every section of the United States has its unhappy examples of state and local laws being used to the disadvantage of racial, religious, or other minorities. It was Boston where in an earlier time one saw "Irish need not apply" signs, and it was California that enacted laws against Japanese ownership of land.

Entrenched rights, available against state and local laws, are important to all citizens. They are, however, especially likely to be invoked on behalf of minorities. Much First Amendment law, for example, has been made in cases where some unpopular group like the Jehovah's Witnesses has run afoul of a local ordinance or regulation.[30] In the United States, since the adoption of the Fourteenth Amendment it is just such minorities who have put their greatest hopes in national laws and federal courts to combat discrimination tolerated or even fostered by state and local governments.

Local constituencies are often more homogeneous and cohesive than is the country at large. Thus a town, city, or even state may be more susceptible to being captured by some powerful local majority (economic or social) and to neglect or oppress local minorities. Charles Fried describes how at local levels a few determined activists - much in the manner of the left wing of Britain's Labour Party - seize political power by going to a few meetings and staying to the end when the key vote is taken.[31]

Reminders of the opportunities for seizing and abusing power in states and localities offer an important antidote to a sentimental attachment to some mythical notion of unalloyed local democracy. But, as students of federalism will remind us, such anecdotes must stand alongside the harsh realities of the ways in which interest groups, lobbyists, and political action committees distort the democratic process at the national level in the United States. Indeed, many interest groups would rather try and work their will with a single level of government in Washington than be forced to compete in fifty state legislatures and state capitals.

Varying Rights and the Perception of Injustice

The idea of justice connotes consistency in the law, the notion that all citizens should enjoy the same rights. Ronald Dworkin, in his *Law's Empire*, equates the principle of consistency with "a single and comprehensive vision of justice." Dworkin's theory of integrity in the law "requires government to speak with one voice, to act in a principled and coherent manner toward all its citizens, to extend to everyone the substantive standards of justice and fairness it uses for some."[32] In a similar vein, John Rawls, in *A Theory of Justice*, claims an equal intrinsic value for each citizen and concludes that the "citizens of a just society ought to have the same basic rights."[33]

No precept has done more to reshape the face of American federalism than has the principle of equal justice. The framers at Philadelphia left the issue of slavery to fester until it was resolved by force of arms in the Civil War. The most sweeping of the Reconstruction amendments was the Fourteenth, which in time brought about a fundamental shift in the nature of the federal union. Section 1's due process and equal protection clauses are at the foundation of much of the federal judiciary's modern jurisprudence. Section 5 serves as the basis for important congressional civil rights legislation, such as the Civil Rights Act of 1964.

The Warren Court brought its egalitarian instincts to bear upon a range of state laws. In a series of opinions, the Court used the Fourteenth

Amendment's command of due process of law to apply to the sta
the procedural requirements of the Bill of Rights, such as the right ᴡ ᴄounsel
and the privilege against self-incrimination.[34] The justices drew upon the
equal protection clause to require desegregation in public education and to
mandate that state legislatures be apportioned on the basis of population.[35]

Appointments to the Supreme Court by Presidents Reagan and Bush have
markedly changed the face of that tribunal. It is a decidedly more conservative
place than it was in the days of Earl Warren. Yet, even while many doctrines
put in place by the Warren and Burger Courts will now undergo scrutiny and
revision, it is hard to imagine the new majority on the Court disturbing such
egalitarian landmarks as one person, one vote, strict scrutiny of laws weighing
more heavily on blacks than on whites, and decisions "incorporating"
provisions of the Bill of Rights.

The staying power of such decisions - many of which provoked sharp
dissent and controversy at the time of their writing - illustrates the power of
the notion of justice as equality. Proponents of federalism who suppose that
rights should be permitted to vary among the units of a federal system must be
prepared to reckon with the power of this concept of justice.

It is not just jurists who may be offended by the notion that rights might
vary from one political unit to another. Uniform norms may also square better
with the laity's sense of what rights are about. The ordinary person is not
surprised to find that speed limits may vary from one state to another. But it
might be harder to explain to that person that rights can vary from one part of
the country to another. The more mobile the population - as is certainly the
case in the United States - the more surprised the ordinary citizen is likely to
be if told that one's protection against overreaching police conduct might not
be the same in Georgia as it would be in California.

A Sense of Nationhood

A common set of laws, including uniform notions of rights, may aid in
building a sense of nationhood. It may fairly be argued that the first genuine
national debate in the United States was the contest, in 1787-88, over
ratification of the Constitution. Until that time, politics had a distinctly local
flavor.[36] After that time, political parties - the precursors of the parties we
now know - emerged.[37] It is plausible to argue that, rather than the American
nation's creating the Constitution, the Constitution created the nation.

More generally, one may suppose that uniform laws, uniformly
administered, could foster a sense of common ties among people who may

otherwise be divided by race, religion, or other barriers. This may have been one of the corollaries of the extension, in ancient times, of Roman citizenship to the multitude of peoples who lived within the Empire. In the modern era, codification (along the lines of the Code Napoleon) and centralized administration (as from Paris) are natural handmaidens of an effort to create a single people. The idea of a "political community" may be said to rest on an assumption by people who "accept that their fates are linked in the following strong way; they accept that they are governed by common principles."[38]

Federalism, of course, rests on a somewhat different assumption: that it is possible to have various political communities, each enacting and enforcing its own laws, within a larger political community. Whether there will be relative equipoise depends on the politics and social fabric of a given country. Sometimes the tendency will be to centralization, as in the history of American federation. Sometimes, centrifugal forces will prove irresistible, as in the breakup of Yugoslavia.

The Practical Advantages of Uniformity

A common body of law does have its advantages. Consider, for example, the task of judges and lawyers in interpreting constitutional law. A lawyer's brief may invoke both state and federal constitutions in alleging the invalidity of a governmental action. In such a case the judge must have a sure grasp of two sets of constitutional principles, which may overlap but which often differ.

Uniformity of the laws may make it easier for government officials to apply the law. Police officers, for example, need to have at least a working knowledge of the constitutional restraints on unlawful searches and seizures. It is hard enough for the ordinary law enforcement officer to understand the intricacies of judicial interpretation of the Fourth Amendment to the United States Constitution. Matters become even more complicated when a state's constitution lays down a different (that is, more restrictive) standard.

The advantages of a single system of law do not, by themselves, add up to a sufficient reason to reject federalism. Uniform laws, whether in a unitary or a federal system, are, after all, not by that token easy to understand or apply But the added complication of different sets of laws that one finds in a federal system is simply one of the costs to be weighed in deciding whether, and in what measure, a country should be federal.

CONCLUSION

What scorecard would one give to federalism, especially as judged from the perspective of its use and history in the United States? And what place might federalism have in other places, such as Central and Eastern Europe?

American federalism has had its dark chapters; its association with the unhappy story of race and discrimination is one of those chapters. It has had, at the same time, its rewards; to the extent that it has helped promote pluralism, experimentation, and limits on undue concentration of power, federalism has been a benign force in American history.

As we follow the sad and often tragic events unfolding in Central and Eastern Europe and in the former Soviet Union, we know that federalism is no assurance of a more tolerant or enlightened society. Thomas Masaryk's hopes for Czechs and Slovaks to become one people, with a unified vision, has foundered on the shoals of national feelings. The Yugoslav federation lasted as long as Communist power held it together; different winds brought dissolution, war, atrocities, and "ethnic cleansing" of a kind we had hoped after the end of World War II never to see again.

Even so, the values that federalism seeks to foster are important if disparate national and ethnic groups are to live in conditions of democracy, freedom, prosperity, and peace. Some brand of federalism - or its cognates, such as devolution or regional arrangements—may give the breathing space necessary for otherwise unfriendly people to co-exist in circumstances of relative peace. Daniel Elazar has commented on "cultural cleavages" reflecting the aspirations of separate peoples, each "clamoring for its place in the political sun."[39] Creative thinking is required to accommodate such potentially explosive forces.

In their 1990 meeting at Copenhagen, the states of the Conference of Security and Cooperation in Europe pledged their commitment to seeing "pluralistic democracy" flourish in Europe.[40] For the first time in a CSCE document, the participating states moved from their traditional concern with human rights to institutional questions such as free elections and an independent judiciary. Among the areas of particular interest in the Copenhagen Document is that of local government and decentralization.[41]

It is striking that about a quarter of the Copenhagen Document takes up the sensitive and thorny issue of the place of national minorities in a democratic society. The document explores not only devices to prevent discrimination, but also measures that would promote the exercise of their rights in community with other members of the group.[42]

The peoples of the post-Communist era face a multitude of problems - how to promote economic growth, how to build the infrastructure of democratic government, how to nurture civic values. They will need to create government with enough power to deal with troublesome social and economic problems, while hoping to curb power's abuses, remembering, as surely they do, the decades of lawless rule by a party accountable only to itself. In this quest, those who sift the lessons of other countries' experience might draw an idea or two from American federalism. Both time and distance separate the world of the American founders from that of post-Communist lands. But they are joined by a common concern for the human condition.

NOTES

1.   "Power tends to corrupt and absolute power corrupts absolutely." Letter to Bishop Mandell Creighton, April 3, 1887. See *Life and Letters of Mandell Creighton* (1904), I. 372.

2.   See Willi Paul Adams, *The First American Constitutions: Republican Ideology and the Making of State Constitutions in the Revolutionary Era* (Chapel Hill: University of North Carolina Press, 1980), pp. 129-149.

3.   *Marbury v. Madison*, 1 Cranch (5 U.S.) 137 (1803).

4.   *Federalist* No. 51.

5.   *Federalist* No. 28. "In short," remarks Daniel Elazar, "federalism is designed to prevent tyranny without preventing governance." Elazar, *Exploring Federalism*, p. 29.

6.   See Richard B. Stewart, "Federalism and Rights,"" *Georgia Law Review*, 19 (1985), p. 918. See also C. Wright Mills, *The Power Elite* (New York, 1956), p. 8.

7.   Alexis de Tocqueville, *Democracy in America*, trans. Henry Reeve (New York, 1900), I, p. 67.

8.   Mark V. Tushnet, "Federalism and the Traditions of American Political Theory," *Georgia Law Review*, 19 (1985), p. 989.

9.   After California's 36th day without a state budget, the Bank of America, California's largest bank, stopped accepting the state's IOUs. Wells Fargo Bank and Union Bank, the state's second and fourth largest banks, had previously said that they would stop honoring the IOUs. *New York Times*, August 6, 1992, p. A14, col. 1.

10.   Sections 9, 10.

11.   Section 15. Mason's Declaration of Rights, with some additions and changes effected over the years, appears today as Article I of the Constitution of Virginia.

12.   See Michael W. McConnell, "Federalism: Evaluating the Founders' Design," *University of Chicago Law Review*, 54 (1987), p. 1484.

13.   Edmund Burke, *Reflections on the Revolution in France* (Chicago: University of Chicago Press, 1955), pp. 71-72.

14.   Daniel Elazar believes that it is "the dual possibility of state protection and federal intervention that has made federalism in the United States a major bulwark of pluralism." Elazar, *Exploring Federalism*, p. 101.

15.   12 How. (53 U.S.) 299 (1851).

16.   12 How. (53 U.S.) at 320.

17. *New York Ice Co. v. Liebermann*, 285 U.S. 262, 311 (1932) (Brandeis, J., dissenting).

18. Justice O'Connor cites these and other examples in her dissenting opinion in *FERC v. Mississippi*, 456 U.S. 742, 788-89 (1982).

19. See Lewis B. Kaden, "Politics, Money, and State Sovereignty," *Columbia Law Review*, 79 (1979), p. 855.

20. Harry N. Scheiber, "American Federalism and the Diffusion of Power: Historical and Contemporary Perspectives," *Toledo Law Review*, 9 (1978), p. 621.

21. See Michael H. Schill, "Intergovernmental Takings and Just Compensation: A Question of Federalism," *University of Pennsylvania Law Review*, 1376 (1989), p. 870.

22. Dillon's Rule, first advanced in the nineteenth century, strictly construes the powers given local governments under state law. See John F. Dillon, *Law of Municipal Corporations*, 2d ed. (New York, 1873), vol I, p. 173; *Clark v. City of Des Moines*, 19 Iowa 199, 212, 87 Am. Dec. 423 (1865).

23. For the text of the resolutions proposed by Governor Edmund Randolph at the Philadelphia convention on May 29, 1787, see *Papers of James Madison*, vol. 10, pp. 15-17.

24. *Garcia v. San Antonio Metropolitan Transit Authority*, 469 U.S. 528, 581, (1985) (O'Connor, J., dissenting).

25. Robert Goldwin notes that the federal system is "a kind of school for statesmen; to do their work well they must seek out and study, again and again, the underlying principles of our form of government." Robert A. Goldwin, ed., *A Nation of States: Essays on the American Federal System* (Chicago: University of Chicago Press, 1964), preface.

26. Elazar, *Exploring Federalism*, p. 85.

27. James Jackson Kilpatrick, "The Case for States' Rights," in Goldwin, *A Nation of States: Essays on Federalism*, p. 102.

28. Alexander M. Bickel, *The Least Dangerous Branch*, (Indianapolis: Bobbs-Merrill, 1962), p. 20.

29. A. E. Dick Howard, *The Road from Runnymede*, (Charlottesville, 1968), pp. 35-52.

30. See, *e.g.*, *Cantwell v. Connecticut*, 310 U.S. 296 (1940).

31. Charles Fried, "Federalism - Why Should We Care," *Harvard Journal of Law and Public Policy*, 6 (1982), p. 2.

32. Ronald Dworkin, *Law's Empire*, pp. 134, 165.

33. John Rawls, *A Theory of Justice* (Cambridge, 1971), p. 61. See also H. L. A. Hart, *The Concept of Law* (Oxford, 1961), pp. 156-60, 190-92.

34. *Gideon v. Wainwright*, 372 U.S. 335 (1963); *Malloy v. Hogan*, 378 U.S. 1 (1964).

35. *Brown v. Board of Education*, 347 U.S. 483 (1954); *Reynolds v. Sims*, 377 U.S. 1362 (1964).

36. See Robert C. Murphy and Edward C. Papenfuse, "Maryland and the Constitution: Changing Perceptions of Home Rule and Who Should Rule at Home," to be published in a forthcoming volume of essays on the contributions of the original thirteen states to American constitutionalism (Conference of Chief Justices, Williamsburg, Virginia).

37. See generally Richard Hofstadter, *The Idea of a Party System: The Rise of Legitimate Opposition in the United States* (Berkeley: University of California Press, 1972).

38. Dworkin, *Law's Empire*, p. 211.

39. Elazar, *Exploring Federalism*, p. 101.

40. Document of the Copenhagen Meeting of the Conference on the Human Dimension of the CSCE (Copenhagen, 1990), Preamble.

41. "Conference on the Human Dimension," paragraph 26.
42. See "Conference on the Human Dimension," part 4.

CHAPTER 3

CONTEMPORARY CONSTITUTIONAL THEORY, FEDERALISM, AND THE PROTECTION OF RIGHTS

Gary Jeffrey Jacobsohn

The field of constitutional theory is today, as it has been in the past, a battleground on which the struggle to determine the meaning and scope of our rights is being waged. It is not the crucial battleground - lacking both general visibility as well as the certainty that it will have much bearing on the outcome of the struggle - but it is probably the most contested terrain within the jurisprudential field of vision. In this essay I will endeavor to survey this terrain where it traverses the historically fertile ground of federalism. While recognizing that the intersection of rights and federalism has provided many of the most notable constitutional landmarks in American history, I will confine myself to a discussion of the contemporary scene. It is a scene that fits very well the evolution of constitutional theory, in which contests over the domain of legally protected rights have typically been the animating force behind efforts to establish the primacy of one level of government or another.

Thus Alexander Hamilton's observation in *Federalist* No. 28 expresses very well not only the rights enforcing practical possibilities of federalism's checks and balances, but also one of the more important story lines of constitutional jurisprudence in addressing questions of individual and group rights. However, in this theoretical setting we are speaking more accurately of invasions upon differing *definitions* of rights, so that the issue of federalism as it appears in constitutional theory is a substitute for (or variant of) the question of how rights are properly to be derived and defined. Should the Supreme Court, for example, act as a national instrument of "noninterpretive review" in order to counter what some might consider a crabbed understanding of rights prevailing at the local level? Is a particular right expressive of some profound moral truth, such that any experimentation in the laboratories of state policy making must be strictly monitored in accordance with uniform definitional standards? What avenues of redress are available at the state level to mitigate the confining effects of a Supreme Court newly wedded to a more narrowly conceived judicial philosophy? How can a more communitarian or group-oriented conception of rights exploit the federal solution to neutralize the hegemonic impulse of the more orthodox constitutional bias in favor of individualism and autonomy?

These questions link up with familiar debates in constitutional theory over such matters as original intent, judicial activism and restraint, noninterpretive review, the trumping power of moral principles, and natural law. All bear directly on federalism and the question of rights. What is most apparent in the multiplicity of perspectives found under the rubric of contemporary constitutional theory is the extent to which doctrinal conclusions regarding federalism are ultimately expressive of the epistemological assumptions underlying a given theory of rights. Thus in the American context a theorist's philosophy of federalism creates structural possibilities for the realization of deeper philosophical commitments. In some instances this produces awkward political-constitutional alliances, as when we find, for example, people of radically different disposition on a question like abortion adhering to fundamentally similar views on the appropriate constitutional relationship between the national and state governments. Jurisprudential commitments pertaining to the derivation of rights are doubtless only part of the explanation for this convergence, although in what follows they will receive nearly all of my attention.[1]

The jurisprudential perspective on rights and federalism that is either explicit or implicit within the spectrum of modern constitutional theory reveals a predominant, almost pervasive, inhospitability to the idea of federalism, at least as that term entails a connection between liberty and decentralization. More specifically, those arguments that see in the structure of federalism an opportunity to realize the public rights flowing from membership in self-governing community are given low priority in most of the prominent works of contemporary constitutional theory. Instead, a philosophically driven compulsion for a uniformity of rights on the one hand, and a desire to respect the integrity of diverse group experiences on the other, have joined with a characteristically modern conception of the role of the federal judiciary to render federalism essentially unimportant to the attainment of a regime of liberty.

COHERENCE, CONSISTENCY, AND FEDERALISM: THE ASPIRATIONAL IMPLICATIONS OF RIGHTS

An assessment of Justice Brennan's views on federalism concluded that "nationalism was simply the medium through which constitutional law had come to its natural focus on individual rights."[2]

Constitutional government had as its *raison d'etre* the preservation of the rights of the individual, which meant for Justice Brennan that interpretation of the fundamental law should at all times manifest a commitment to that underlying purpose. In such a purposive jurisprudence the federal allocation of power is a structural attribute of the Constitution that in a positive sense should reinforce the cause of rights, and in a negative sense ought not obstruct its realization. The question of whether a consequential right guaranteed by the federal government can be violated by a state is a historical question. The history that best comports with the aspirational view appears in Justice Brennan's writing: "The passage of the Fourteenth Amendment fulfilled James Madison's vision of the structure of American federalism."[3] Brennan's assumption was that rights granted at the time the Constitution was written represented only the initial step toward the realization of a deeper constitutional vision that could only be fulfilled through the medium of nationalism.

Madison's proposed amendments to the First Congress did indeed include a provision that no state shall violate freedom of religion, freedom of the press, or trial by jury in criminal cases. What eventually became the Bill of Rights, of course, did not include this restriction on the states. Thus Chief Justice Marshall's opinion in *Barron v. Baltimore*, establishing that these amendments applied only to the national government, can plausibly be seen as contradicting Madison's original vision of the structure of American federalism. But in jurisprudential terms Brennan's point transcends the particulars of the Bill of Rights' evolution; the decision in *Barron* would stand as a constitutional anomaly whatever the history surrounding Madison's involvement in the Bill's adoption. It is not simply that as an exponent of "contemporary ratification" Brennan can take liberties with historical details that illuminate the subject of original intent. Rather, the critical factor here is the conception of rights implicit in his constitutional vision, one that requires consistency in the application of standards of right conduct.[4]

We can see this most clearly in such theorists as Ronald Dworkin and Soterios Barber. For Barber,

> Marshall's theory [in *Barron*] remains problematic, for the general normative properties of the Constitution have to be taken into account in deciding between alternative interpretations of the framers' intentions, and Marshall's theory offends both the need for consistency among constitutional provisions and the aspirational aspect of the Constitution as a whole.[5]

Constitutional interpretation, then, calls for an invocation of the aspirational spirit of the document, entailing, as it were, a judicial effort to render the Constitution more true to itself. "Fidelity to the framers as framers would require that one try to resolve their contradictions in accordance with a theory of their highest values."[6] They may very well have had a theory of federalism that placed a high value on the virtue of diversity, but this, we are led to infer, did not express their *highest* value. Their highest values were bound up in a theory of rights from which derived the obligation to achieve philosophical coherence within the constitutional system as a whole. Since fundamental rights, rightly conceived, possess a universal dimension, it is basically incoherent to hold them applicable to one government but not another. For this reason, "nationalism is decidedly more plausible than states' rights as an imputation to the framers."[7] Or as Robert Post has written of Justice Brennan, "the issue was...not one of state *versus* federal power," but of "state *and* federal government versus the individual."[8]

Again, the precise historical circumstances surrounding both the adoption of the Bill of Rights and the passage of the Fourteenth Amendment are not the reason for this subordination of federalism to rights. It is therefore distinguishable from the position associated with Justice Black, whose famous incorporation argument leads to many of the same constitutional outcomes, but whose positivist constitutional theory displays an attitude bordering on contempt for the judicial application of normative philosophy. Justice Black may have been a great hero to civil libertarians, even if, jurisprudentially speaking, he did not take rights seriously. Thus he would never have been found acknowledging that the Constitution fuses legal and moral issues, by making the validity of a law depend on the answer to complex moral problems, like the problems of whether a particular statute respects the inherent equality of all men.[9]

The nationalizing thrust of his constitutional adjudication was philosophically neutral in the sense that it relied upon a particular reading of historical facts; a different account of the same data by, say, a Charles Fairman or a Raoul Berger would support a states' rights version of federalism.

Very different are the premises of Ronald Dworkin, who wants us "to treat ourselves as an association of principle, as a community governed by a single and coherent vision of justice and fairness and procedural due process in the right relation."[10] In *Law's Empire* he elaborates upon just what such an association of principle requires - first among which is an

adjudicative principle of integrity [that] instructs judges to identify legal rules and duties, so far as possible, on the assumption that they were all created by a single author - the community personified - expressing a coherent conception of justice and fairness.[11]

The fusion of constitutional law and moral philosophy that Dworkin appealed to in his earlier work culminates here in a clear message: as far as matters of principle (*i.e.*, rights) are concerned, it is the national community that embodies our commitment to achieve a just society.[12] "Integrity fixes is gaze on...matters of principle: government must speak with one voice about what these rights are and so not deny them to anyone at any time."[13] Echoes, in other words, of a Hamiltonian conception of sovereignty, albeit in the service of a Jeffersonian emphasis on guaranteeing individual rights.

There is a price tag for respecting the trumping power of rights.

If rights make sense at all, then the invasion of a relatively important right must be a very serous matter. It means treating a man as less worthy of concern than other men. The institution of rights rests on the conviction that this is a grave injustice, and that it is worth paying the incremental cost in social policy or efficiency that is necessary to prevent it.[14]

Dworkin's oppositional juxtaposition of principle and policy means that we may have to forgo the collective good associated with the latter in order to conform to the requirements of justice extending from the former. However, this tradeoff may be viewed very differently if one understands the process underlying the collective good in principled terms, as itself involving a fundamental right, the right of self-government. Federalism from this perspective acquires a more substantive meaning that elevates it as a constitutional value above the level implicit in predominantly structural and functional interpretations. It is, as will be spelled out more fully later, less directly concerned with an individualistically oriented "integrity of principle" than with the more communitarian-centered liberty embedded in a respect for jurisdictional and geographic integrity. As such, it may be seen to possess the jurisprudential weight attached to matters of principle in many prominent works of contemporary constitutional theory.

What is jurisprudentially at stake here is suggested in Dworkin's concluding observation that "law's empire is defined by attitude, not territory or power or process."[15] Attitude is "addressed to politics in the broadcast sense." It is "a fraternal attitude" intended to define law "for the people we want to be and the community we aim to have."[16] So what does this mean? Community is in this context territorially unbounded, reflecting our broadest political aspirations. The constitutional agenda set by the interpretive enterprise of a community of principle is very different from the principle of community expressed in the terms of a rights-oriented vocabulary of local prerogative. After all, "the Constitution does insist that each jurisdiction accept the abstract egalitarian principle that people must be treated as equals."[17] On the subject of abortion, for example, leaving the issue to be resolved differently by the individual states is unacceptably incoherent, as it offends the principle of equality rightly understood - which means for Dworkin, in the light of contemporary moral philosophy. Once the abortion right has been identified as fundamental, which is to say necessary to achieve the philosophical community's aspiration to equality, then divergent localist sentiment must not be permitted its particularistic expression in law.

Dworkin's constitutional jurisprudence, and especially its reliance upon contemporary moral theory, has been attacked from many points along the political spectrum. Most vituperative have been positivist original intent proponents on the right, who are also passionate defenders of federalism. But there is a version of original intent theory that is thoroughly nationalist in its constitutional theory, more often than not associated with conservative causes, and critical of Dworkin's argument for being insufficiently distinguishable from the positivists that Dworkin attacks. Its exponents stake their claim in the epistemology of the founders, finding in the framers' natural rights commitments a key to solving some of the most vexing problems in contemporary constitutional adjudication. "The Constitution was a means, an instrument for conveying, in a legal structure, the principles that marked the character of the American republic."[18]

The principles, as explained by Hadley Arkes, refer to those natural rights standards of right and wrong that existed antecedent to the Constitution, and that still provide us with a structure of moral understanding from which we can derive logically compelling constitutional outcomes. This same logic parallels "the decision in 1787 to replace a confederacy with a national government."[19] The existence of the national government symbolizes the constitutional commitment to the realization of moral principle. It means that "there is no subject in our law, no matter how local, that does not imply an understanding of the principles - the understanding of right and wrong - on which the law has been settled."[20] Whatever their differences, it is difficult imagining Dworkin in disagreement with Arkes when he says: "We may rightly prize the benefits of federalism, but the arrangements of federalism cannot supply a real principle, which marks off plausible zones of jurisdiction."[21]

There is, however, an important difference in emphasis between Arkes and Dworkin. Both can make a reasonable claim to be followers of Madison with respect to a theory of rights, but for Arkes it is the Madison of *Federalist* No. 10, whereas for Dworkin it is the Madison of the Bill of Rights. When Arkes discusses the role of the government in securing individual rights, he emphasizes the power and responsibility of the Congress to correct moral wrongs perpetrated at the local level by actors public or private.

> As the Founders understood, the national government would be more detached, far less dependent on the forces that were dominant in local politics. That disengagement put the officers of the national government in a far better position to intervene in the separate states, to protect minorities whose interests may be threatened, unjustly, by the majority that now controls the government and annexes to its own enthusiasms the force of law.[22]

To be sure, the Supreme Court should not be an idle spectator in the preservation of people's natural rights, but its prominence as an institutional guarantor of individual liberties is, for Arkes, much less pronounced than for someone like Dworkin, for whom the Court possesses a special counter-majoritarian mission.

Thus the same Madisonian reason that justifies federal intervention in the states to safeguard rights provides grounds for minimizing the need for an enumeration of rights in a written constitution. The large republic argument of *Federalist* No. 10 complements the nationalist logic that flows from the epistemological premises of the founders' commitment to natural rights. The point is that the national government should act decisively in the presence of a "wrong," meaning that it is morally obligated - and hence constitutionally qualified - to forbid that wrong universally. If, as Hamilton argued in *Federalist* No. 84, the Constitution is itself a bill of rights, then it follows that the institutions that speak for the people as a whole have the authority to pursue the rights-oriented implications subsumed in the spirit of the document. Arkes, unlike Dworkin, would argue that the moral imperatives of this spirit are the same as what they were in the late eighteenth century, and further that access to them is not the special preserve of the Supreme Court. On the other hand, the existence of a specific enumeration of rights has tended to enhance the role of the Court as the preferred guardian of our liberties, and with this enhanced role has come the misconceived notion that specialized knowledge is required to comprehend the content and scope of these liberties. In Dworkin's constitutional jurisprudence, this specialized knowledge refers to the esoteric world of contemporary moral theory. Arkes would therefore dispute much of interpretation that emerges from a fusion of this theory with constitutional law (on abortion for example), but he would be hard put to deny the nationalist implications contained therein. What counts as fundamental rights may differ, and what is deemed the appropriate agent for enforcement of rights may also differ. But to the extent that our rights are portrayed in transcendent, universal terms, they demand a consistency that can only be satisfied by constitutional nationalism.

THE ROLE OF THE COURT:
THE SEPARATION OF RIGHT AND STATE

The enhanced role of the Court expresses itself in a variety of doctrinal ways, depending on the particular part of the Constitution implicated in a given case. The belief that the Court has specialized knowledge into the substance of constitutional rights entails a denigration of the capacity and authority of competitive institutions to pronounce upon their definition and scope. This denigration will be especially severe where competition coincides with constitutional inferiority, namely in the policymaking branches at the state level. At least in the constitutional theory ascendant in the law schools, there is a functional separation of institutional responsibility, with the federal courts having a privileged status within the domain of rights, a domain bearing no principled connection to he structural regime of federalism. On the other hand, where the content of rights is portrayed as theoretically indistinguishable from the content of other policy on either epistemological or procedural grounds, there is not likely to be this jurisprudential wall of separation between the arenas of rights and federalism. This is especially the case among original intent theorists who strictly delineate law and morality.

Hadley Arkes, for example, has not been reluctant to accuse his fellow conservatives Raoul Berger, Robert Bork, and William Rehnquist of having joined the "modern heresy" of renouncing an "understanding of right and wrong that is universal in its reach."[23] As a result, their "positivism...will insure that, in jurisprudence, conservatism will be brittle and unworkable, and that on matters of moral consequence conservative jurisprudence will have nothing to say."[24] Maybe so, but with regard to questions of federalism and rights, their jurisprudence has had a great deal to say. Moreover, their views have hardly been confined to scholarly discourse, as the Rehnquist Court has on the whole been notably generous in its deference to states in determining the substance of constitutional entitlements - which is to say it has been loathe to follow the dominant trend prevalent in academic circles.

The direction taken by the Court can of course easily be explained in terms of electoral politics and the appointment process. But it also reflects the broader currents of relativistic thought in the society that have provided a comfortable niche for philosophical skepticism within constitutional theory, thus offering, in tandem with the rhythms of politics, a new judicial lease on life for federalism. Lino Graglia, for example, says that we should be grateful "if we can get the Court to stop its own dismantling of federalism by its constant discovery of new constitutional rights."[25] After all, "in a democracy, constitutional rights come only from the people."[26] Or, as Calvin Massey has aptly put it,

> If constitutional values lack fixed, or even ascertainable referents, there is no self-evident reason why a coterie of life tenants should select the constitutional values that eternally bind an entire society. If such values are utterly subjective, what valid argument can be made to deny the people's elected representatives the final word?[27]

Judges, in other words, who cannot or do not wish to defend in principled terms the objective superiority of a fundamental right (even one that is textually guaranteed against invasion by the federal government), they are in no position to require uniformity across jurisdictions with respect to how such a right is to be regarded.

Thus it makes sense for Robert Bork, as a self-proclaimed legal positivist, to assert that "federalism...is the only constitutional protector of liberty that is neutral."[28] Its neutrality inheres in its compatibility with a constitutional indifference toward competing moral standards, so that subnational jurisdictions cannot logically be forced, in the absence of a clear textual command, into compliance with a given rendering of the scope and substance of a right. Indeed federalism embodies the principle of neutrality; it is the institutional representation of the sovereignty of individual choice.

> If another state allows the liberty you value, you can move there, and the choice of what freedom you value is yours alone, not dependent on those who made the Constitution. In this sense, federalism is the constitutional guarantee most protective of the individual's freedom to make his own choices. There is much to be said, therefore, for a Court that attempted to preserve federalism, which is a real constitutional principle, by setting limits to national powers.[29]

By emphasizing that federalism is a *real* constitutional principle, Bork wishes to underscore the importance of a constitutional "freedom to escape"; although there is reason to question the *political* neutrality of such a right. What is noteworthy about this defense is that it tends to undermine the rootedness of community, which is surely one of the most treasured values secured by federalism. Thus the exercise of the freedom to escape comes with an appreciable cost, one that itself is subsumed in an important principle. In this respect the contemporary jurisprudential defense of federalism involves a significant departure from the tradition of rights and community associated with the framers. In addition, the availability of a right to escape, more so than most other rights, would seem to depend upon a person's socio-economic standing. In this sense the principle of federalism resembles the principle of the marketplace, with the states in effect engaged in a competition for citizens.[30] Utah's regulation of pornography is too restrictive for you? Move to Nevada. You don't like Pennsylvania's limits on abortion? Then relocate to New York. A similar message is contained in Richard Epstein's defense of "exit rights under federalism," where it is pointed out that "the antithesis of a well-functioning market is of course the monopoly of the government."[31] The Supreme Court, then, has a responsibility to minimize the monopoly over rights exercised by the federal government. This is essentially a formula for judicial self-restraint, since it is the Court itself, a national institution, that is best positioned to become both the principal abettor and the primary beneficiary of a constitutional monopoly.

More specifically, it is a formula for judicial self-restraint in permitting the states maximum flexibility and leeway in implementing their own conception of the scope of a constitutional right, or in denying the existence of a right where no explicit textual provision can be found. The idea is to prevent the occurrence of market failure. It needs to be distinguished from theories that rely on the *existence* of market failure to *justify* judicial intervention in the domain of the states. For example, John Hart Ely has described his approach to constitutional adjudication as being

> akin to what might be called an "antitrust" as opposed to a "regulatory" orientation to economic affairs. Rather than dictate substantive results, it intervenes only when the "market" - in our case the political market - is systematically malfunctioning.[32]

The approach allows for judicial intervention in pursuit of "representation-reinforcement," with the accompanying disclaimer that the Court is not imposing its own conception of fundamental values upon the democratic process. Such a disclaimer is necessitated by the same professed commitment to legal positivism that one find in Bork. So, Ely says,

> Our society does not, rightly does not, accept the notion of a discoverable and objectively valid set of moral principles, at least not a set that could plausibly serve to overturn the decisions of our elected representatives.[33]

Bork is lavish in his praise of Ely's attack on fundamental values jurisprudence (a "devastating critique"), but equally emphatic in his denunciation of Ely's antitrust approach. "The concept of market failure usually means no more than that the market is producing results the critic disapproves of on grounds that ultimately turn out to be moral or aesthetic."[34] Both in their own way are followers of Holmes (whose marketplace of ideas is traceable to the same positivist jurisprudential source); however for Bork, Ely's credentials are disputable on the grounds that his process orientation turns out to be an elaborate subterfuge to conceal Dworkin-like substantive moral commitments. In Ely's constitutional theory, the Court is but a "referee," engaged in the modest tasks of "clearing the channels of political change" and "facilitating the representation of minorities." But Bork (and others who have criticized Ely in similar fashion) finds this account of the judicial function grossly misleading, for it disguises the extent to which the Court will more often than not be on the side of one of the players in what is basically a political game. In the context of federalism it deflects attention from the serious threat posed by Ely's political market to the escape option in Bork's market. Thus the claim to be opening up the political process in reality serves to foreclose the constitutional freedom made possible by the structure of federalism.

Not always of course, as Ely's well-known critique of *Roe v. Wade* makes clear.[35] But as his effusive praise of the Warren Court also indicates, on most of the controversial individual rights questions on the recent judicial agenda,

Ely supports the trend toward greater national uniformity in the constitutional conceptualization of rights.[36] The doctrinal core of this conceptualization, and the inspiration for Ely's constitutional theory, is incorporated in the famous footnote of the *Carolene Products* case, around which there has developed in liberal jurisprudential circles an almost unique aura of reverence. The extension of special judicial solicitude to minorities unmentioned in the Constitution on the basis of their claims of political underrepresentation necessarily restricts the freedom of action of local communities.[37] The logical implication from this, that the rights of minorities (that is, not just racial minorities) are of dubious constitutional security at the sub-national level, is largely what makes Justice Stone's footnote so profoundly important.

Indeed, for Bruce Ackerman, it is a "transformative opinion," an opinion, in other words, that conveys the message contained in what is for him one of those historically rare exercises in popular sovereignty that ultimately amend the meaning of our fundamental law.[38] The New Deal, according to Ackerman, provided just such a constitutional moment, legitimating profound constitutional change without formal amendment, and *Carolene Products* provided the justification for the Supreme Court to complete the constitutional transformation. All together it was a "self-conscious act of constitutional creation that rivaled the Founding Federalists...in scope and depth."[39]

Ely might differ here, believing that the founders had, through several critical open-ended clauses, already delegated to future constitutional decision-makers the authority to protect unenumerated rights necessary to fulfill the procedural aspirations of democratic governance. But while the sources of Ely's and Ackerman's (and Dworkin's) commitment to the constitutional jurisprudence of *Carolene* may differ, the effects are similar as far as federalism is concerned. On this point the liberal jurisprudential legacy of the New Deal transformation is clear: federalism and rights are essentially separate domains, each requiring a different conception of the appropriate role of the Court in constitutional interpretation. How separate is revealed very clearly in the work of Jesse Choper and Michael Perry - the first a process theorist resembling Ely in some respects, and the second a fundamental values proponent in the tradition of Dworkin.

Choper goes so far as to suggest that "the assertion that federalism was meant to protect, or does in fact protect, individual constitutional freedoms has no solid historical or logical basis."[40] Questions of individual liberty involve issues of principle, whereas those of federalism concern considerations of practicality; hence the Court should be engaged in the former and detached from the latter, where, as an institution, it possesses no particular claim of competence. The nationalization of rights follows:

> In America, the federal Constitution, not the federal system, seeks to guarantee individual rights; and the federal judiciary, not the processes of state and local governments, provides the most effective method for their enforcement.[41]

Thomas Pangle has described the irony in the Anti-Federalists' championing of a Bill of Rights, the successful culmination of which added enormously to the power of the federal courts.[42] Choper accents this irony with a twist of his own in the distinction he draws between the federal Constitution and the federal system, suggesting a separation of law and politics that would doubtless have troubled many Anti-Federalists and Federalists alike in its seeming denial of the inextricability of rights and democratic politics. As Justice Frankfurter put it in his famous flag salute dissent, "the consent upon which free government rests is the consent that comes from sharing in the process of making and unmaking laws."[43]

Choper's advocacy of functional representation by the federal courts for members of minority groups, who unlike states and localities are not adequately represented in the deliberations of the political branches, is another aspect of this separation.[44] Its jurisprudential implications are highlighted in Michael Perry's argument for a functional justification of noninterpretive review in individual rights cases. This in turn is accompanied by an insistence that with regard to questions of federal-state power the Court must adhere to a strictly interpretive philosophy - that is to say, it must abjure a conscious policy-making role when federal action is challenged on federalism grounds. For example, "Unless the majority's decision [in *National League of Cities v. Usery*]...can be explained as a product of interpretive review, it is illegitimate."[45] Such is the radical separation of federalism and rights that Perry's chapter on federalism and separation of powers advises the reader that those whose interest in his book has to do with the question of rights may see fit to skip the chapter entirely.[46]

"Noninterpretive review in human rights cases enables us to take seriously...the possibility that there are right answers to political-moral problems."[47] This is Dworkin without Dworkin's controversial denial that supplying the right answer requires judicial discretion. The Supreme Court, in this account, is uniquely qualified to function as an instrument of moral growth, capable, in other words, of advancing the polity's collective morality by pursuing a principled vision of human rights. The success of this role hinges upon the nationalization of rights conjoined with its de-politicalization. Nationalization since, as Earl Maltz has pointed out, emphasizing the conflict between judicial and legislative competence leads to an expansive reading of the Fourteenth Amendment, extending, in other words, the already transformative reach of that amendment.[48] And de-politicalization because of the necessity to remedy the deficiencies of the political process in representing the rights of unpopular minorities, and to ensure that the untidy business of normal politics will not sacrifice enduring principle on the altar of short-term strategic gain. Or as David Richards, another "separationist" has put it,

> Judicial review is the natural culminating point of the architecture of America's experiment in Lockean constitutionalism because it is the most nearly adequate institutional embodiment of its supreme requirement: the impartial and independent judgment of the inviolable rights of the person that must be immune from political bargaining and compromise.[49]

Thus the separation of rights and federalism results, as in Dworkin, Arkes, and Ely, from the universalizing logic of principles (natural, philosophical, or structural) that resist geographic compartmentalization. The further distinction that is sometimes made with regard to a unique role for the Court depends on whether one views that national institution as having special purchase on the meaning of rights and/or whether one's particular understanding of rights (*e.g.*, representation-reinforcing) implies a critique of the enforcement capacity of the other branches. Again, the rejection of this separationist position has largely been undertaken by theorists like Bork, who espouse a version of constitutional positivism in which the derivation of rights by either democratic choice or textual provision requires neither nationalization nor the privileging of the federal judiciary. They resist the imposition of externally derived requirements that limit the political autonomy of self-governing local communities. But rather than focusing on the participatory nature of the rights involved, the emphasis has been thoroughly modern, namely upon a private liberty such as the right to escape. With that in mind, I turn finally to an alternative understanding that is both radical and reactionary in its conceptualization of rights and federalism.

THE TRANSVALUATION OF FEDERALISM

The strongest case for federalism has always been rooted in community. But because the case for community has been most cogently put as a challenge to individualism and personal autonomy, the connection between rights and federalism has become obscured.[50] Here is a typical view:

> To one who believes in the majoritarian notion of freedom, it is impossible to interpret federalism as other than a device for minority tyranny....To those who wish to enforce it, the plea for...maintaining the guarantees of federalism is simply a hypocritical plea for the special privilege to disregard the national majority.[51]

If one's response to this is to share in concern about minority tyranny but to counter with an even more passionate warning about *majority* tyranny, one might be making a good point while perhaps missing *the* point. As John Kincaid has observed, "The federal Constitution has come to be understood as the constitution of a national community of individuals."[52] Or as I have been emphasizing, prevailing constitutional and jurisprudential notions of individual liberty have contributed to an erosion in the moral authority of subnational jurisdictions to protect rights. Where rights are involved, local communities have become the problem, not the solution.[53]

However, as part of the "republican revival" in constitutional theory, we have seen in recent years expressions of disillusionment with the individualist premises of the national community, and with it an effort to recover some of the principles behind apparently discredited notions of federalism. Yet these notions have in turn been radically transformed, leaving us with a distinctly modern republican analogue to the older federalism. Whereas the more distant account united rights and structure in the interest of self-governing individuals acting as members of their community, some contemporary constitutional theorists - most notably Cass Sunstein - have appropriated this teaching and placed it in the service of an alternative constitutional agenda. In this agenda ascription replaces geography, and as with the theories already discussed, a particular epistemology of rights is at the core of the preferred solution.

The separation of rights and structure so prevalent in modern constitutional discourse has been incisively critiqued by the constitutional historian Akhil Reed Amar. He shows that "in the 1780's 'liberty' was still centrally understood as public liberty of democratic self-government - majoritarian liberty rather than liberty against popular majorities."[54] But it was not the "national majority" to which was exclusively entrusted this vital role. As Amar puts it, "What has been lost...is the crucial Madisonian insight that localism and liberty can sometimes work together, rather than at cross-purposes."[55] Amar's analysis of the Bill of Rights highlights the structural continuities between that document and the original Constitution, and in so doing he reveals a complementarity between rights and federalism that is often overlooked in discussions of the first ten amendments. Of course the Fourteenth Amendment, in codifying the political reality that states were also a great threat to liberty, shifted the emphasis of the Constitution away from public liberty to a more individualistic, less affirmative understanding of rights; but this fundamental adaptation should not distort our understanding of the political philosophy underlying the charter of 1789; nor should it require the total abandonment of this philosophy in the present.

> Like people with spectacles who often forget they are wearing them, most lawyers read the Bill of Rights through the lens of the Fourteenth Amendment without realizing how powerfully that lens has refracted what they see.[56]

Amar can perhaps be criticized for exaggerating the strength of the civic republican strand in early American constitutional thought and practice, but his examination of such constitutional provisions as the militia system and trial by jury are extremely important in directing our attention to the participatory dimensions of rights and their connection to the federal structure of the constitutional regime.[57] If the full meaning of the *public* character of rights goes unappreciated, then, as in Choper's account, the role of federalism in the protection of rights will go unacknowledged. But it is also important to note, particularly in light of Arkes' emphasis on the natural rights commitments of the framers, that the localist, self-governing dimensions of rights were not, at least as far as these framers were concerned, in principle incompatible with the logic of first principles of justice. To be sure, they recognized the destructive potential of passion and self-interest at the local level, but they were also impressed by the capacity for reasoned judgment that was, in their view, the possession of the common citizen. So, for example, men as different in their political views as Alexander Hamilton and Thomas Jefferson could enthusiastically support the practice of jury nullification (the right of jurors to decide questions of law as well as fact), because they agreed with Hobbes that "the law of nature addresses itself in its rules directly to the reasonable insight and understanding of every man [and] does not require proclamation [by judges]."[58] The accessibility of ordinary individuals to a shared natural rights tradition meant that the law of the juries would be both stable and just. Citizens who served on the jury could introduce into the administration of criminal justice the distinctive sense of their communities, while bringing this to bear upon their obligation to respect the principles of natural justice. There are many reasons for the subsequent delegitimation of the natural rights consensus of the framers' time. The binding character of the judge's instructions to the jury on questions of law came to fulfill the function of imposing a uniformity and order (that might otherwise not exist) upon a diverse group of citizens lacking common agreement concerning fundamental precepts of right conduct.[59]

The renewed interest in jury nullification that surfaced in this country in the 1960s and 1970s can be seen as a sort of preview of some of the republican constitutional theory of recent years, particularly as it pertains to federalism and rights. The latter-day proponents of what Roscoe Pound referred to as "jury lawlessness" envisioned a criminal justice system that would recognize the group reality of social experience. They saw jury nullification as a way of ensuring that this experience would manifest itself directly in the prevailing views of the community and would be (without the assistance of natural rights reasoning) the principal source of the jury's equitable and legal consideration. Unlike the earlier model of jury nullification, the logic behind this reformulated idea was premised on the phenomenon (as well as the intractability) of group difference rather than on any presumption of shared values. And it presumed a logic that had at that time not been fully developed theoretically, the logic of group rights.

For Sunstein, perhaps the most prolific of the new republican constitutional theorists, it is not the intractability of group difference that is at issue. Indeed, "republican thought is characterized by a belief in universalism," that is, "a belief in the possibility of mediating different approaches to politics, or different conceptions of the public good, through discourse and dialogue."[60] But it is a universalism that is in principle fundamentally alien to the universalistic theories of rights alluded to earlier. This is how Sunstein puts it:

> Republicans believe in rights, understood as the outcome of a well-functioning deliberative process....But republicans are skeptical of approaches to politics and constitutionalism that rely on rights that are said to antedate political deliberation.[61]

Rights, in other words, are historical achievements reflecting the particularity of the community discourse from which they originate.[62] Sunstein makes clear his opinion that this republican perspective is not a latter-day invention; rather it was vital to the American constitutional tradition at its outset. It is therefore erroneous, he claims, to understand that tradition as proceeding from an invocation of pre-political rights.[63] In this context, then, the institution of federalism makes a great deal of sense.

> One of the great strengths of the original constitutional system was its simultaneous
> provision of deliberative representation at the national level and self-determination at
> the local level, furnishing a sphere for traditional republican goals.[64]

The politicalization of rights (*i.e.*, rights as the product of the deliberative process) would appear to thrive under the regime of diversity that federalism provides. The impulse to nationalize rights is certainly not so compelling in the absence of the epistemological structure of the pre-political. The definition and scope of rights will therefore be reflective of a deliberative process that is in turn expressive of the character of the community. But how are we to understand the community? It is very different from the conceptualization seen earlier in Dworkin.

> At the time of the framing...geography was thought to define distinct communities
> with distinct interests; representation of the states as such seemed only natural. It
> would not be impossible to argue that racial and ethnic groups (among others) are the
> contemporary analogue to groups that were defined in geographical terms during the
> founding period.[65]

If we are to perpetuate the republican tradition under the circumstances of contemporary life it becomes necessary to imagine alternative constitutional structures, specifically the replacement of geography with group identity as the linchpin of the new republican solution. "Distinctly non-Madisonian institutions may be necessary to serve republican goals."[66] And so Sunstein asks us to consider the hopeful possibilities contained in proportional representation, "the functional analogue of the institutions of checks and balances and federalism, recognizing the creative functions of disagreement and multiple perspectives for the governmental process."[67]

Strictly speaking it is correct for Sunstein to say that "the basic constitutional institutions of federalism, bicameralism, and checks and balances share some of the appeal of proportional representation, and owe their origins in part to notions of group representation."[68] But there is a critical difference between the understanding of group representation prevailing at the founding and that which is assumed in this contemporary republican claim. Madison wrote in *Federalist* No. 10 of a political solution premised on a multiplicity of interests, but it was a solution that presumed a "permanent and aggregate interest of the whole." Sunstein's structural analogue is meant to ensure "that the process of deliberation is not distorted by the mistaken appearance of a common set of interests on the part of all concerned."[69] The difference is highlighted by Sunstein's favorable citation of the work of the feminist theorist Iris Marion Young, who, in her argument for "differential citizenship," seeks to demonstrate the superiority of an ascriptively defined group rights approach over the established constitutional principle that "the rules and policies of the state...ought to be blind to race, gender, and other group differences."[70] Her principal quarrel is with the belief that "citizenship transcends particularity and difference,"[71] but ultimately it is in this transcendence that one finds Madison's common interest. Or put another way, Madison also emphasizes group differences, seeing them "sown in the nature of man"; but the particularities that finally emerge are not incompatible with voluntary choice. Hence the reality of difference does not negate the more important unity embodied in human nature.

The substitution of ascriptive representation for geographically based federalism would do more than create a functional structural analogue to federalism; it would substitute a wholly different conception of rights for what has been the dominant American constitutional tradition. Other polities with a more vibrant tradition of cultural pluralism and autonomy, as well as a more urgent need to resolve the problem of ethnic conflict, may be in a better position to accommodate a federal solution that is driven by a commitment to group representation.[72] The flaw in the analogy as applied to the United States comes with the failure to discern in the very structure of federalism a specific model of rights. By representing communities geographically the framers were, to be sure, defining distinct communities with distinct interests, but the nature of the interests were such that people's rights were not linked to their deepest primordial attachments. It was a representation of diversity consistent with the underlying presupposition of American nationhood - that it was a set of political ideas rather than any particular ascriptive loyalty that gave substance to membership in the broader political community. Hamilton argued in *Federalist* No. 17 that "it is a known fact in human nature that its affections are commonly weak in proportion to the distance or diffusiveness of the object."[73] The fact that "a man is more attached to his family than to his neighborhood" also suggests that his passion is more likely to overwhelm his reason in defending the first in comparison to the second. This is consistent with Madison's teaching in *Federalist* No. 10 that economic interests were the safest and most reliable structure for controlling the effects of faction. Embodied in the geography of federalism was a constitutional conception of community whose reliance on groups did not lead to group rights, and was therefore not a threat to the rights of individuals. A republicanism tied to a politics of ascription is a questionable replacement for a federal solution that, when associated with the practice of territorial representation, encourages the development of inclusive, rather than exclusive, rights.[74] And its claims to the contrary notwithstanding, it provides an unfriendly constitutional environment for the enhancement of those deliberative processes that distinguish the rights of democratic citizenship.

CONCLUSION

Federalism is in may ways the Rodney Dangerfield of contemporary constitutional theory: it gets very little respect. Constitutional amendment, formal and informal, has, of course, paved the way for the erosion in federalism's once esteemed place in American jurisprudence. This erosion, however, may yet be reversed. As one student of the judiciary has noted:

> The past several decades have witnessed a remarkable devolution of judicial power and leadership to the state courts. American constitutionalism no longer may be regarded in monolithic terms, centering almost exclusively on the Supreme Court's work.[75]

But this development, which flows directly from the greater receptivity by the recent Supreme Court to issues of federalism, and which can itself be characterized as a revival of federalism, is ironically symbolic of the distinctly inferior position of federalism in contemporary constitutional theorizing about rights.

This may not seem obvious if one focuses on diversity as the principal advantage of federalism. Surely the enhanced profile of state constitutional law and adjudication means that there will be less national uniformity in constitutional standards pertaining to rights and other matters. Some courts will provide the citizens of their states with wider protections than afforded by the Supreme Court, and others will not. And consequently citizens will be able to exercise their "right of escape" in seeking the jurisdiction most compatible with their preferences. Does Robert Bork, therefore, owe Justice Brennan a measure of gratitude for being the most influential voice in encouraging the diversity associated with a resurgent judicial federalism?

However, if our attention is directed specifically to the nexus between rights and federalism, then the "central virtue of federalism is not heterogeneity but self-government."[76] And here, despite the fact that state courts are much more subject to democratic check and review than federal courts, there is little encouragement to be found in the prospect of judges at the sub-national level determining the substance and scope of our rights. When the engine driving federalism is the judiciary, the notion of rights as entailing a dimension of *public liberty* tends to be submerged in the more immediate agenda of fulfilling this or that set of expectations regarding the specific entitlements we are due as a free people. For the most part, constitutional theorists of aspiration (whether grounded in contemporary moral philosophy or traditional natural rights commitments) and constitutional positivists of various stripes, including latter-day republicans, have relegated the public aspects of rights (of traditional federalism) to a subordinate status in their jurisprudential projects. In the struggle over the contested terrain of rights that marks the present state of constitutional theory, federalism is at best a strategic option and at worst an irrelevancy.

NOTES

1.   While it may be tempting to follow the lead of the realist school (and its latter day critical reincarnation) by explaining all positions on federalism as masking the policy preferences of those who espouse them, in the end we should resist the seductive appeal of this interpretation. If we take the Constitution seriously in the sense that it expresses a coherent vision of philosophical purpose, then there should be no contradiction between a proper understanding of federalism and a particular epistemology of rights. That may not satisfy those who presume such epistemologies to be themselves the masks for other things, but in what follows I will avoid indulging in that presumption, if for no other reason than that it assumes the very ground in dispute, that there exists no genuinely superior constitutional view of the relationship between federalism and rights.

2.   Robert C. Post, "Justice Brennan and Federalism," *Constitutional Commentary*, 7 (1990), p. 236.

3.   William J. Brennan, Jr., "The Bill of Rights and the States: The Revival of State Constitutions as Guardians of Individual Rights," *New York University Law Review*, 61 (1986), p. 536. Justice Brennan's argument in this article may be seen as a post-Warren Court version of the "ratchet theory" he articulated in *Katzenbach v. Morgan*. In that case he argued that Congress could only use its Section 5 power to *strengthen* Fourteenth Amendment protections. Here, in response to the Supreme Court's increasing reluctance to interpret constitutional liberties expansively, he calls upon state courts to fill the void. But this appeal to a "new federalism" was still in the spirit of the old nationalism. "While the Fourteenth Amendment does not permit a state to fall below a common national standard, above this level, our federalism permits diversity" (p. 551). In this regard consider, too, Michael Zuckert's observation: "Madison's completed constitution could never be held to be neutral, never be seen as an association of member states entirely free to define rights for themselves however they chose. ...For Madison, the principle of both the whole and the parts was the same - the natural and inherent rights...as announced in the Declaration of Independence."

4.   The work of E.E. Schattschneider in political science can illuminate the political significance of Brennan's constitutional position. Schattschneider wrote in his most important book of the "long-standing struggle between the conflicting tendencies toward the privatization and socialization of conflict." E.E. Schattschneider, *The Semi-Sovereign People: A Realist's View of Democracy in America* (Hinsdale: The Dryden Press, 1975), p. 7. Socializing conflict means expanding its scope; in terms of federalism, moving it to more centralized level of government. This movement generally benefits the weaker party to a conflict at the expense of

the status quo. Its relevance to rights? "Ideas concerning equality, consistency, equal protection of the laws, justice, liberty, freedom of movement, freedom of speech and association, and civil rights tend to socialize conflict" (p. 7).

5. Soterios A. Barber, *On What the Constitution Means* (Baltimore: The Johns Hopkins University Press, 1984), p. 154.

6. Barber, *On What the Constitution Means*, p. 156. Therefore: "From 1925 to 1972 the Supreme Court helped the nation realize its constitutional aspirations in nationalizing most of the bill of rights" (p. 159).

7. Barber, *On What the Constitution Means*, p. 158. For a very different account, see Robert F. Nagel, "Federalism as a Fundamental Value: National League of Cities in Perspective," in Philip B. Kurland, Gerhard Casper, and Dennis J. Hutchinson, eds., *The Supreme Court Review 1981* (Chicago: University of Chicago Press, 1982). Nagel disputes the notion that the theory of federalism is subordinate to a theory of rights. "The framers' political theory was immediately concerned with organization, not individuals. Their most important contributions had to do with principles of power allocation" (p. 88). The priority attached to rights theory represents a modern bias that distorts the framers' commitment to the structural principles of the separation of powers and federalism. An intermediate position may be found in the work of Charles Black. In his account, it is the *structure* of the Constitution, rather than a theory of rights, that compels, with respect to a right such as free speech, an "inference of some national constitutional protection...against state infringement." Charles L. Black, Jr., *Structure and Relationship in Constitutional Law* (Baton Rouge: Louisiana State University Press, 1969), p. 42.

8. Robert C. Post, "Justice Brennan and Federalism," p. 230.

9. Ronald Dworkin, *Taking Rights Seriously* (Cambridge: Harvard University Press, 1977), p. 185.

10. Ronald Dworkin, *Law's Empire* (Cambridge: Harvard University Press, 1986), p. 404.

11. Dworkin, *Law's Empire*, p. 225.

12. John Kincaid has made the point that "The federal Constitution has come to be understood as the constitution of a national community of individuals." John Kincaid, "Federalism and Community in the American Context," *Publius: The Journal of Federalism*, 20 (1990), p. 75. This turn has undermined traditional notions of community self-government. As we shall see, what is at stake here is not so much two contrasting interpretations of federalism as two competing conceptions of rights.

13. Ronald Dworkin, *Law's Empire*, p. 223. Dworkin is not a specific as Barber in spelling out the exact implications of his theory for federalism's place in the Constitution, although he does indicate that "in a federal system integrity makes demands on the higher-order decisions, taken at the constitutional level, about the division of power between the national and the more local level" (p. 186).

14. Ronald Dworkin, *Taking Rights Seriously*, p. 199.

15. Ronald Dworkin, *Law's Empire*, p. 413.

16. Dworkin, *Law's Empire*, There is one complication in this formulation. What if "what the people we want to be" turns out to be distinguished by its desire to be included in politically meaningful sub-communities? Thus politics in its "broadest sense" may very well come to be defined by territory, power, and process.

17. Dworkin, *Law's Empire*, p. 382.

18. Hadley Arkes, *Beyond the Constitution* (Princeton: Princeton University Press, 1990).

19. Arkes, *Beyond the Constitution*, p. 143.

20. Arkes, *Beyond the Constitution*, p. 138.

21. Arkes, *Beyond the Constitution*, p. 245.

22. Arkes, *Beyond the Constitution*, p. 125. "The federal government could reach any subject that is now addressed through the laws of the states, if the need should arise." p. 139. Unlike most defenders of the remedial power of the federal government, Arkes does not rest his case principally upon the authority of the post-Civil War Amendments. For example, he praises the first Justice Harlan for recognizing that the Congress' authority to reach the wrong of racial segregation was "contained in the original Constitution, in the original logic of a government that was both 'national' and 'republican'" p. 54. For a different view of the relative threats posed by the national and state governments to minority rights and individual liberties see Andrzej Rapaczynski, "From Sovereignty to Process: The Jurisprudence of Federalism After Garcia," in Philip B. Kurland, Gerhard Casper and Dennis J. Hutchinson, eds., *The Supreme Court Review 1985* (Chicago: University of Chicago Press, 1986). Rapaczynski argues that the maintenance of a dominant power elite is much easier at the national level than at the state level, and therefore the possibilities for minority oppression are significantly greater at the higher regions of government. p. 387. It should also be said of Arkes that when he says that the "founders understood" the situation of the national government to the more conducive to the protection of rights than local government, he is not quite accurate. Surely the extended republic argument of Publius makes that claim, but the Constitution should be seen as a compromise between the advocates of that position and the proponents of the more traditional small republic argument. The Founders, in other words, were not in agreement on the advantages associated with the central government.

23. Hadley Arkes, *Beyond the Constitution*, p. 14. Robert Bork has responded directly to Arkes, defending the proposition that a judge, "When he judges, must be...a legal positivist." Robert Bork, "Natural Law and the Constitution," *First Things*, 21 (March 1992), p. 19. "So long as we are unable to convince one another of its content, there will be no agreed-upon moral truths that will give judges definite answers... And no matter how long and cogently he argues, Arkes will never convince Justice Blackmun that abortion is not a natural right." p. 19.

24. Arkes, *Beyond the Constitution*, p. 15.

25. Lino A. Graglia, "Judicial Review, Democracy, and Federalism," *Detroit College of Law Review*, 4 (1991), p. 1362.

26. Graglia, "Judicial Review, Democracy and Federalism," p. 1351.

27. Calvin R. Massey, "The Locus of Sovereignty: Judicial Review, Legislative Supremacy, and Federalism in the Constitutional Traditions of Canada and the United States," *Duke Law Journal*, 1990 (1990), p. 1303.

28. Robert H. Bork. *The Tempting of America: The Political Seduction of the Law* (New York: The Free Press, 1990), p. 53. Bork, however, exaggerates. An equally forceful case can be made, for example, for the neutrality of the extended republic of a multiplicity of interests. Dworkin might say that federalism is taken seriously here because rights are not.

29. Bork, *The Tempting of America*, p. 53

30. The competition of the marketplace is also designed to produce the best product. A familiar theory of federalism, usually identified with Justice Brandeis, views the states as laboratories for experimentation. But this theory was developed for things like welfare policy, rather than for matters directly related to the enforcement of rights. With this in mind, the

difference between Bork and Arkes is nowhere better illustrated than in this comment by the latter: "We would hardly take it as a measure of vitality in the federal system if the different sates were allowed to act as 'laboratories' in trying out different 'moralities' on the question of slavery." Hadley Arkes, *Beyond the Constitution*, p. 154.

31. Richard A. Epstein, "Exit Rights Under Federalism," *Law and Contemporary Problems*, 55 (1992), p. 147. Epstein's argument is made with specific regard to the right of property, which relies on direct protection by the courts as well as the exit right implied in federalism. Bork, it should be noted, is a sympathetic critic of Epstein's activist defense of property rights, particularly as it manifests itself in an expansive interpretation of the takings clause. Bork, *The Tempting of America*, pp. 229-30. See also Andrezej Rapaczynski: "It is precisely because the states are governmental bodies that break the national authorities' monopoly on coercion that they constitute the most fundamental bastion against a successful conversion of the federal government into a vehicle for the worst kind of oppression." Rapaczynski, "From Sovereignty to Process: The Jurisprudence of Federalism Under Garcia," p. 389.

32. John Hart Ely, *Democracy and Distrust: A Theory of Judicial Review* (Cambridge: Harvard University Press, 1980), p. 102.

33. Ely, *Democracy and Distrust*, p. 54. "There simply does not exist a method of moral philosophy" (p. 58). The focus on representation-reinforcement as the guiding constitutional principle in Ely's structural model has been criticized for omitting other elements of the American constitutional scheme. "The representation-reinforcement concept is defective in its failure to take into account a critical aspect of the constitutional system - the concept of federalism." Earl M. Maltz, Federalism and the Fourteenth Amendment: A Comment on *Democracy and Distrust*," *Ohio State Law Journal*, 42 (1981), p. 212. The backdrop for this criticism is Maltz's view that "whatever one's theory of the nature of fundamental rights and protected classes, it should be consistent with the basic concept of dual sovereignty that undergirds the constitutional system." p. 216.

34. Bork, *The Tempting of America*, p. 196.

35. See John Hart Ely, "The Wages of Crying Wolf: A Comment on *Roe v. Wade*," *Yale Law Journal*, 82 (1973).

36. Ely, *Democracy and Distrust*, pp. 73-75. The interventionist decisions of the Warren Court were "fueled not by a desire on the part of the Court to vindicate particular substantive values it had determined were important or fundamental, but rather by a desire to ensure that the political process - which is where such values *are* properly identified, and accommodated - was open to those of all viewpoints on something approaching an equal basis." p. 74.

37. Earl Maltz has shrewdly pointed out that in at least one important area, reapportionment, Ely's advocacy of the one person, one vote standard may undercut the objective of providing special protection to vulnerable minorities. States are prevented from building into their political process special electoral consideration for threatened groups by the judicial imposition of an egalitarian standard of neutrality. Earl M. Maltz, "Federalism and the Fourteenth Amendment," p. 221. One could expand upon this point by examining how Justice Harlan's dissenting opinions in the reapportionment cases establish a subtle but important argument for the protection of rights at the local level.

38. Bruce Ackerman, *We the People: Foundations* (Harvard University Press, 1991), p. 120.

39. Ackerman, *We the People*, p. 44. One of the reviews of Ackerman's book makes the convincing point that his theory "gives movements that support centralized government easier access to constitutional politics than decentralizing movements." Furthermore, "It is no coincidence that each of Ackerman's major constitutional moments...sought to push the system in a nationalistic and rights-oriented direction." Caleb Nelson, "Amending the Constitution," *Commentary*, 94 (1992), p. 62.

40. Jesse H. Choper, "The Scope of national Power Vis-a-Vis the States: the Dispensability of Judicial Review," *Yale Law Journal*, 86 (1977), p. 1611. Choper's history is exceedingly strained, to say the least. He says at one point: "The thrust of the fundamental charter was not to secure rights of individuals against exertions of government power, but rather to distribute power between nation and state. It was the surrender of sovereignty by the states that posed the major barrier to an effective union, and it was that issue rather than personal liberties that was resolved by the great compromise." p. 1613. To suggest that the issue of personal liberties was somehow separable from the debate over sovereignty is simply bad history.

41. Choper, "The Scope of National Power...," p. 1619. The statement appears now oddly dated in light of the new federalism's abandonment of the federal courts for the relatively safe haven of the state judiciaries.

42. Thomas Pangle, "The Achievement of the Constitution, as Viewed by the Leading Federalists, in Robert L. Utley, Jr., ed., *Principles of the Constitutional Order: The Ratification Debates* (Lanham: University Press of America, 1989), p. 58.

43. *West Virginia v. Barnette*, 319 U.S. 624, 655.

44. Jesse H. Choper, "The Scope of National Power...," p. 1556.

45. Michael J. Perry, *The Constitution, the Courts, and Human Rights: An Inquiry into the Legitimacy of Constitutional Policymaking by the Judiciary* (New Haven: Yale University Press, 1982), p. 48. Like Choper, and like the minority in *National League* and the majority in *Garcia*, Perry argues that the political safeguards of federalism militate against judicial intervention (and noninterpretive review) on behalf of the states.

46. Perry, *The Constitution...*, p. 37.

47. Perry, *The Constitution...*, p. 102.

48. Earl M. Maltz, "Federalism and the Fourteenth Amendment," p. 221.

49. David A. J, Richards, *Foundations of American Constitutionalism* (New York: Oxford University Press, 1989), p. 166.

50. Robert Post's comparison of Justices Brennan and Frankfurter supports this argument. He rightly points out that "from Frankfurter's perspective, Brennan's philosophy of individualism systematically undercut the normative basis for federalism." Robert Post, "Justice Brennan and Federalism," p. 234. In the first flag salute case, Frankfurter asserted that "The ultimate foundation for a free society is the binding tie of cohesive sentiment." In effect, this means that the defense of freedom requires the restriction of individual rights in the interest of community. For Frankfurter, the unity of citizens in their local communities is ultimately the most persuasive justification for federalism.

51. William H. Riker, *Federalism: Origin, Operation, Significance* (Boston: Little, Brown and Co., 1964), p. 142.

52. John Kincaid, "Federalism and Community in the American Context," p. 75.

53. For some, as we have seen, the solution is to be found in a "community of principle," which by its very nature is in tension with the local community. Critical legal scholars have not contributed much to the discussion of federalism, but with respect to the decline of the moral

authority of local communities, there is a convergence in liberal and critical legal theory. "The development of an open, dynamic capitalist economy so weakens people's roots in the community, and so homogenizes national culture...that it is hard even to think about the localist structural protection of freedom in a way that parallels the Madisonian vision. Courts, then, are stuck protecting any of its initial political substance." Mark Kelman, *A Guide to Critical Legal Studies* (Cambridge: Harvard University Press, 1987), p. 210.

54. Akhil Reed Amar, "The Bill of Rights and the Fourteenth Amendment," *Yale Law Journal*, 100 (1991), p. 1136.

55. Amar, "The Bill of Rights," pp. 1136-7.

56. Amar, "The Bill of Rights," pp. 1136-7.

57. Needless to say, Tocqueville is essential reading on this subject as well. Consider also Andrezej Rapaczynski's argument: "Freedom to participate in government, rather than freedom from government, is the issue at stake. The meaning of some activity's being 'local' does not lie in its being 'reserved for the states'...but in the fact that, unlike most national issues, it is being handled by a participatory institution." Rapaczynski, "From Sovereignty to Process," p. 408. For another interesting recent account along these lines see Daniel J. Elazar, *The American Constitutional Tradition* (Lincoln: University of Nebraska Press, 1988).

58. Carl J. Friedrich, *The Philosophy of Law in Historical Perspective* (Chicago: University of Chicago Press, 1969), p. 90.

59. The discussion of the jury borrows from my consideration of that institution in Gary J. Jacobsohn, *The Supreme Court and the Decline of Constitutional Aspiration* (Lanham: Rowman & Littlefield, 1986), pp. 29-33.

60. Cass R. Sunstein, "Beyond the Republican Revival," *Yale Law Journal*, 97 (1988), p. 1554.

61. Sunstein, "Beyond the Republican Revival," pp. 1579-80. "The republican conception of political truth...do[es] not depend on a belief in ultimate foundations for political outcomes" (p. 1554).

62. See in this regard Paul W. Kahn, "Community in Contemporary Constitutional Theory," *Yale Law Journal*, 99 (1990), p. 3: "Discourse here does not have the abstract, universal quality of classical, natural-law theories of political science. Rather, the community's discourse is historically specific."

63. Kahn, "Community in Contemporary Constitutional Theory," p. 1563.

64. Kahn, "Community in Contemporary Constitutional Theory," p. 1578.

65. Cass R. Sunstein, "Republicans and the Preference Problem," *Chicago-Kent Law Review*, 66 (1990), p. 200.

66. Sunstein, "Beyond the Republican Revival," p. 1590. Nathan Glazer's observations are quite relevant in this context. "The type of diversity that most concerned the framers of the Constitution was not that of race, religion, and ethnicity, but rather a diversity of political units." Nathan Glazer, "The Constitution and American Diversity," in Robert A. Goldwin, Art Kaufman, and William A. Schambra, eds. *Forging Unity Out of Diversity: The Approaches of Eight Nations* (Washington, D.C.: American Enterprise Institute of Public Policy Research, 1989), pp. 60-61.

67. Sunstein, "Republicans and the Preference Problem," p. 202.

68. Sunstein, "Republicans and the Preference Problem," p. 200; and Sunstein, "Beyond the Republican Revival," p. 1586.

69. Sunstein, "Republicans and the Preference Problem," p. 201.

70. Iris Marion Young, "Polity and Group Difference: A Critique of the Ideal of Universal Citizenship," *Ethics*, 99 (1989), p. 267.

71. Young, "Polity and Group Difference," p. 250. "In a heterogeneous public, differences are publicly recognized and acknowledged as irreducible, by which I mean that persons from one perspective or history can never completely understand and adopt the point of view of those with other group-based perspectives and histories." (p. 258).

72. This essay has addressed issues of contemporary constitutional theory as they apply to the American federal experience and the dominant American understanding of rights. As the question of ascriptive representation suggests, observations made with American constitutionalism in mind should not be assumed to be transferable to polities with different constitutional traditions. What seems appropriate for the United States should not therefore determine one's views about Spain, Nigeria, Malaysia, Belgium, India, or any number of other places.

73. *The Federalist*, Henry Cabot Lodge, ed. (New York: G.P. Putnam's Sons, 1888), p. 99.

74. As the examples in other countries where the federal solution is designed to accommodate the desire for linguistic, cultural, or religious autonomy suggest, federalism and group rights are not strangers to one another. In these places, as Seymour Martin Lipset pointed out many years ago, federalism serves to accentuate and reinforce cleavages that place a stress on democratic institutions. See especially his article, "Some Social Requisites of Democracy: Economic Development and Political Legitimacy," *American Political Science Review*, 53 (1959). While this is by no means fatal for liberal democracy, and indeed may sometimes be necessary to sustain it, in a place such as the United States, where issues concerning diverse identities do not, for the most part, correspond with geographical boundaries, a territorial-based federalism is much to be preferred.

75. Stanley Friedelbaum, "Judicial Federalism: Current Trends and Long-Term Prospects," *Florida State University Law Review*, 19 (1992), p. 1082. See also G. Alan Tarr, "Constitutional Theory and State Constitutional Interpretation," *Rutgers Law Journal*, 22 (1991), p. 841.

76. The thought is borrowed from David Epstein, as quoted in discussion in Goldwin, Kaufman, and Schambra, eds., *Forging Unity Out of Diversity: The Approaches of Eight Nations*, p. 22.

CHAPTER 4

FEDERALISM AND RIGHTS IN THE AMERICAN FOUNDING

Jean Yarbrough[*]

It is a commonplace that Americans today are drowning in a tidal wave of "rights talk."[1] We have lived through a civil rights revolution, and explosions of new rights created in constitutional and administrative law. In area after area of American life, claims that might once have been framed in terms of sound and fair public policy are clothed in the more strident, uncompromising idiom of enforceable legal rights, to be secured and protected by the national government - and often against the states.

Against this background it may be helpful to return to the Founding to understand better how those who gave initial form to our constitutional order understood rights, and how they conceived of the relationship between the protection of rights and the structure of government. The recent Bicentennial of the Bill of Rights only adds impetus to this inquiry.[2]

Late eighteenth century conceptions of rights are not, of course, precisely congruent with contemporary notions of civil liberties and constitutional

[*] I am grateful to my colleague, Richard E. Morgan, for his helpful suggestions in revising an earlier draft of this paper.

rights. Still, included in the Founders' views of liberty were freedom of speech, religion, and the protection of property - rights which find a place on any contemporary list. But the debate about rights also involved questions about the distribution of political power, the meaning of limited government, and how the right to self-government could best be secured, all of which are issues that tend to get short shrift today. Far from rendering the Founders' thoughts obsolete, however, this is the most important reason for returning to both the Federalist and Anti-Federalist conceptions of liberty and the relationship between federalism and rights, first at the Philadelphia Convention and then in the pull and haul of partisan politics in the formative period. In so doing we may come to understand why the emergent federal principle commanded such remarkable adherence from a notoriously liberty-loving people for so much of our history.

THE EMERGENCE OF FEDERALISM

When we return to the debates at the Federal Convention, and then look at the most authoritative defense of the new Constitution, *The Federalist Papers*, what we discover is that many of the leading Framers began as unabashed nationalists, and not federalists at all. And so, it looks at first glance as if they would have approved the steady growth of national power at the expense of the states. To some extent the nationalism of these Framers was a matter of principle: far-sighted men looking to improve the standing of the newly independent country in the eyes of Europe, and to find markets for her growing exports, concluded that only a vigorous national government could accomplish these tasks. But another important reason why men like Madison and Hamilton, Wilson and Morris were nationalists was that federalism as we know it did not exist in 1787. Federalism was the great creation of the Philadelphia Convention, and not surprisingly, when something altogether novel enters the political world, its creators did not immediately recognize its significance for republican government.

Thus, the proper starting place for this investigation must be to explore how the Founders worked their way toward federalism. As the late Martin Diamond persuasively argues, federalism in the eighteenth century meant something quite different from what we mean by federalism today.[3] Prior to the Constitution, the term "federal" was synonymous with "confederal" or "confederacy," and it meant essentially a league of friendship. Federalism referred to a voluntary association of sovereign states for the sake of self-defense. Its chief attributes were three: the equal representation of each member in the central councils; the restriction of the central authority to the members in their collective capacity (that is, to the states but not to the individuals composing them); and finally, the non-interference by the central authority in the internal and domestic affairs of the participating states.[4]

FEDERALISM AND RIGHTS IN THE SMALL REPUBLIC TRADITION

This understanding of federalism was closely related to the larger question of how republican liberty could be maintained. In the eighteenth century many Americans were convinced by Montesquieu's argument that only small republics, which they mistakenly thought to be of the size of the American states, could preserve freedom.[5] But whereas Montesquieu defended a loose confederacy of small republics because he believed that only a small republic could foster civic virtue and unswerving devotion to the common good, the defenders of the small republic-confederacy tradition in America tended to be more concerned with the protection of liberty than with the promotion of virtue, and to understand by liberty minimal government where the citizens willingly obeyed what few laws there were without coercion. The Anti-Federalists were above all committed to minimal government as the key to protecting liberty. They did not wish to remain small so that they could govern themselves directly, for they had no great interest in what today we would call participatory democracy or genuinely classical republican virtue.[6] For them, the question of liberty turned on the men who would represent them in government and the kind of laws they would enact.[7]

According to the Anti-Federalists, "free and mild" government would only work, and liberty be secure, if the people could elect representatives who could be counted upon to represent faithfully their opinions and interests. Much as minorities and women today insist that they need one of their own to be truly represented, the Anti-Federalists argued that elected representatives must be a mirror image of their constituents. As Richard Henry Lee, writing against the Constitution under the pseudonym of the "Federal Farmer" puts it:

> A full and equal representation is, that which possesses the same interests, feelings, opinions, and views as the people themselves would were they all assembled - a fair representation, therefore, should be regulated, that every order of men in the community, according to the common course of elections, can have a share in it - in order to allow professional men, merchants, traders, farmers, mechanics, etc. to bring a just proportion of their best informed men respectively into the legislature.[8]

Indeed, Lee goes even further, insisting that it is "deceiving" a people to give them the right to elect their own representatives if the electoral process tends to put into office men who are not, in their interests, occupations and opinions, just like the people in their district.   Since this kind of interest group representation was possible only in a small territory, opponents of the Constitution insisted that the states be retained as the sovereign units of any future confederation.

But although the Anti-Federalists looked to the states to protect their rights, it is important to note that their conception of rights was not fundamentally different from that of the Federalists. Where they differed was their opinion of where the danger to these liberties lay, and the mode of self-government (loosely speaking) most likely to protect liberty. For the Anti-Federalists, the danger to liberty came from a remote centralized government likely to take a broad view of its powers. By contrast, security for liberty was to be found in a government limited and local. As David N. Mayer writes:

> The libertarian thrust of Anti-Federalist arguments is unmistakable. In referring to the dangers of governmental power, Anti-Federalists continually spoke of the need to "distrust" government, to be "jealous" of one's liberty.[9]

And it was for this reason that Anti-Federalist calls for a Bill of Rights sought principally to limit the power of the federal government which, removed from effective control by the people, would likely overreach its powers and trample on their rights, especially the right of self-government.   For the Anti-Federalists, this was the central "rights issue" of the Founding.

FEDERALISM AND RIGHTS IN THE EXTENDED REPUBLIC

By 1787, a new generation of Americans, having experienced first hand the defects of state sovereignty under the Articles of Confederation, which defects, according to Hamilton, had brought America to "almost the last stage of national humiliation,"[10] challenged the small republic argument on the ground that a large republic could better protect liberty. In the view of James Madison, liberty was most threatened in a small republic where a factious majority could more easily trample on the rights of the minority with impunity.[11] As Madison saw it, the problem with the state governments was precisely that the representatives were all too faithful to their constituents' views. Thus, the legislation they enacted partook of all the evils of democracy: its was unjust, unwise, and unstable.

The Federalists did not diverge seriously from the Anti-Federalists about the primacy of liberty or about its essential elements. Speech, religion, and property remained central, along with self-government. The disagreement, once again, had to do with their view of where the greatest threat to liberty came from, and about the mode of self-government most likely to secure liberty. In the view of the Federalists, the greatest danger to liberty arose from the tyranny of local majorities, and for them, a strong central government was not the problem, but the solution. Hear the words of James Wilson on the floor of the Convention:

> He could not persuade himself the State Govts & sovereignties were so much the idols of the people, nor a natl. Govt so obnoxious to them, as some supposed. Where do the people look at present for relief from the evils of which they complain? Is it from an internal reform of their Govt? No. Sir, it is from the Natl. Councils that relief is expected.[12]

We must not overread Wilson by supposing that all the "evils" vexing the people involved deprivations of liberty or what today we would call rights issues. The early nationalists favored a strong central government for many reasons - commerce, defense, and so on - but an important reason for their nationalism was their view of the states as run by legislatures which were out of control, Rhode Island being the obvious example. Out-of-control local majorities were the most serious threat to liberty, and security lay in self-government, although for the Federalists this was the self-government of the extended republic in which national majorities, operating through more attenuated representative mechanisms, would intervene to protect liberty, especially the rights of property, in the states. For the Federalists, this was the central "rights issue" of the Founding.

Breaking with the entire small republic tradition, Madison, and to a lesser extent Hamilton, defended the entirely novel idea of a large republic composed of states united on a new and more vigorous federal principle. As they developed the argument, first at the Federal Convention and then in *The Federalist Papers*, the large republic would provide greater security for liberty in three ways. First, it would multiply the number of interests, opinions, and religious sects throughout society as a whole, thereby making it more difficult for an overbearing majority to coalesce. Second, it would increase the likelihood that the most talented and virtuous citizens would be elected because only they would be well known in the larger federal electoral districts. And third, it would remove national issues from the immediate reach of the people and their eager state representatives, making it more difficult for a local majority to obstruct the common good. And as a final precaution, should an oppressive majority form in the society at large, it most likely could not prevail under the complex distribution and separation of powers established by the Constitution. Madison could not, of course, guarantee this happy result, but the whole purpose of the new Constitution was to permit majority rule while discouraging majority faction.

THE CONSTITUTION OF THE FEDERAL REPUBLIC

By all accounts, the federalism that emerged from the Federal Convention was a political novelty which not even the most perspicacious Framers fully appreciated at the time. As Tocqueville observed in *Democracy in America*:

This Constitution which at first sight one is tempted to confuse with previous federal constitutions, in fact rests on an entirely new theory, a theory which should be hailed as one of the great discoveries of political science in our age.[13]

And up to the present day, federalism remains the most original invention of American constitutionalism, forming a mean between the older confederacy notion based on state sovereignty and a consolidated central government rooted in undivided national sovereignty. Federalism, by contrast, distributes power between the states and the national government, making each sovereign in its sphere.

How does this work? Or what, precisely, are the federal features of the Constitution? Perhaps the most complete and forthright discussion of this question is to be found in *Federalist* No. 39.[14] In this paper, Madison examines the federal character of the Constitution from five different aspects: its foundation, sources, operation, extent of powers, and amendment procedure. His discussion helps us to appreciate how thoroughly federalism suffuses the American constitutional order.

As Madison explained, the ratification process was a federal act since the Constitution rests on the unanimous consent of the people in the states. No state can be compelled to breach its sovereignty by joining the Union without its express consent.

Considering next the sources from which the ordinary branches of government are derived, Madison concludes that they are "partly national and partly federal." He regards the House of Representatives as national because it represents the people rather than the states. But even then it is not simply national. Representatives are not elected by the people of the nation at large, and congressional districts respect state borders, regardless of larger regional interests. Thus, even in the "national" House of Representatives, federal elements can be discerned. By contrast, the Senate, especially as originally conceived, is the most "federal" branch, since it represents the states equally. But just as Madison exaggerates the national character of the House, so does he overstate the federal character of the Senate. The states possess neither the power of recall nor do their Senators vote as a bloc. Finally, because of the manner of his election, Madison regards the source of executive power as essentially federal. And it is worth keeping in mind that, however much the federal principle has been eroded by national encroachments on traditional state powers, there is still no national office that is elected by a simple majority of the American people without reference to the states. And a deadlocked electoral college, which was a distinct possibility in the summer of 1992, would have magnified the federal character of the election, as each state would have cast its vote as a bloc in the otherwise "national" House of Representatives. The states - or as we shall see, more precisely the people in the states - remain the constituent units of the federal republic.

Turning next to the operation of the new national government, Madison concedes that it is unambiguously national. In contrast to the hobbled national government under the Articles of Confederation, the national government under the Constitution has the power to legislate directly over individuals, but this is a power that is inherent in the very idea of government (*Federalist* No. 15) since laws are bound to be ineffective if there is no way to enforce them.

But the operation of government on the citizens in their individual capacities must be considered in conjunction with the extent of the powers granted to the new government. The national government may enact laws binding on individual citizens, but only on matters within its constitutional jurisdiction, which "extends to certain enumerated objects only." These enumerated powers, it is true, include the vital questions of "war, peace, negotiation and foreign commerce,"[15] but just as important, the Constitution "leaves to the several States a residuary and inviolable sovereignty over all other objects." These, Madison observes, include "all the objects which, in the ordinary course of affairs, concern the lives, liberties, and properties of the people; and the internal order, improvement, and prosperity of the State."[16] Indeed, under the proposed constitutional arrangement, the states are critical to the federal scheme because the national government has no power to act on the myriad issues reserved to the states.[17]

Finally, Madison takes up the amending power, which he regards as partly federal and partly national. Although the states have the power to alter the

Constitution, the amendment process does not, as traditional federal theory would have it, require the unanimous consent of the states. By contrast with the ratification process, the sovereignty of the dissenting states is here breached.

Thus, as Madison describes it, the altogether novel principle of modern federalism which emerged at the Federal Convention contains two distinctive features: it preserves for the states a significant constituent power by involving them in the workings of the national government, principally through the election of federal officials; and it requires that the Constitution recognize and protect the division of powers between the federal government and the states so as to insure individual liberty and self-government. It was on this second issue that the Anti-Federalists voiced their gravest doubts.

ANTI-FEDERALIST MISGIVINGS

Although Madison had spoken of the "residual and inviolable sovereignty" retained by the states over those matters within their rightful jurisdiction, the Anti-Federalists were quick to point out that the Constitution nowhere enumerates those objects or indicates which state powers are "inviolable."[18] Indeed, the Constitution mentions only the limitations on state power. Thus, although the Constitution establishes a federal republic, which distributes power between the nation and the states, the dividing line has always been difficult to draw. The Constitution enumerates only those powers which the national government may exercise and says nothing about those powers which rightly belong to the states. And, short of a constitutional amendment, which itself is only partly federal, since only three-quarters of the states must consent, the final arbiter of these "federal" questions is the Supreme Court. What the Anti-Federalists feared, it turns out not wrongly, is that the Court would act less as an impartial tribunal than as a branch of the national government, upholding the expansion of national powers. As the Anti-Federalist "Brutus" warned:

> Perhaps nothing could have been better conceived to facilitate the abolition of the state governments than the constitution of the judicial. They will be able to extend the limits of the general government gradually, and by insensible degrees, to accommodate themselves to the temper of the people.[19]

To a large extent, these Anti-Federalist fears have been borne out by an activist Supreme Court which has come to regard federalism as an obstacle to civil rights and personal liberty.

Of course, there is little in the debates of the Federal Convention or in *The Federalist* to suggest that even the most national-minded Framers envisioned the Court as the principal agent for the expansion of national powers. Yet in linking the protection of rights with a powerful national government, rather than with the new federal system they helped to create, they may be said indirectly to have encouraged this later reliance upon the courts and thus to have missed the truly novel way in which the federal Constitution secures liberty.[20]

THE NATIONALISM OF THE FEDERALISTS

As we have seen, Madison's hostility to the states was, in an important way, a response to the problem of liberty. Because he believed that the states had failed to protect the rights of the minority and pursue the common good, Madison sought at the Convention to deny them all political representation in the new government and to deprive them of the bulk of their powers. In addition, he proposed that the national government be armed with an absolute veto over all state acts. Had these proposals succeeded, the Federal Convention would have established a basically consolidated national government rather than the genuinely federal system that emerged. For what Madison initially sought was to reduce the states to something like administrative agencies of the national government. As "corporations dependent upon the General Legislature," the states could continue to perform those useful tasks which the national government assigned to them at its discretion, but they would have lost all constitutional power to limit or resist that government,[21] a loss which Madison and Hamilton, and other nationalists such as Wilson, regarded as favorable to liberty.

It is important to be clear about the difference between administrative decentralization and the real federalism which emerged from the Convention. The distinction is subtle, but significant. It rests on opposing views of how liberty and the general good can best be secured. Federalism frankly assumes that a large consolidated government itself threatens republican liberty by dangerously concentrating powers in the executive branch and exposing the government to the corruption and irresponsibility associated with monarchy. Dividing power between the general government and the states lessens this danger, but even then, abuses are possible because power is of an encroaching nature. Federalism does not view the danger to liberty as coming principally from the states; consequently, it seeks to provide constitutional protection to the states as political bodies so that both governments may act as a check upon the undue accumulation and abuse of power by the other. Finally, federalism gives voice to the variety of interests, opinions, and religious views contained within the large republic by allowing these different political communities to govern themselves, within certain important limits, in ways which are most appropriate to their distinctive political cultures. It regards the imposition of one uniform set of laws as dangerous to the right of self-government and to the genuine diversity which is the offspring of liberty.

Administrative decentralization, on the other hand, assumes that the states as political associations are the primary threat to liberty and it looks to the national government for protection against such abuses for much the same reasons Madison outlined in his defense of the extended republic. Because the state legislatures are viewed as the captives of oppressive majorities, advocates of administrative decentralization would reduce them to local corporations, which would administer those objects the general government finds it inconvenient to superintend. So unnecessary are the states as constitutionally protected political bodies to the protection of liberty that, were it possible for the central government to "extend its care to all the minute objects which fall under the cognizance of local jurisdiction,"[22] there would be no need to retain the existing states at all. It is only because the national government can make but "imperfect use" of its power over so large and varied a territory that the states remain necessary; their function is purely administrative.

According to this view, liberty is not secured by the division of power between the federal and state governments, but by a preponderance of power in the national government. The chief mechanisms by which liberty is secured are the proper distribution of power among the three branches of the national government, and by the election of the most qualified citizens as representatives who are all ultimately accountable to the people.[23] Because this was the position of Madison and other early nationalists at the Federal Convention, they opposed the compromises which resulted in the modern federal republic. Their support for the Constitution was given in spite of its federal aspects.

This hostility helps to explain the particular treatment of federalism in *The Federalist Papers*. For although some of the papers appear to be sympathetic to the federal argument that the states are bulwarks of liberty,[24] beneath this apparent praise, there is the constant reminder that one reason why a vigorous national government is necessary is because the states have failed so miserably to protect "public and private rights."

Obviously, these views cannot be openly stated because one of the tasks of *The Federalist* is to persuade citizens that the Constitution establishes a republic which is sufficiently federal in the older (confederal) sense. Accordingly, the authors of *The Federalist* had to defend the Constitution against the charge that it granted the national government too many powers, and the states too few, to preserve the balance essential to liberty. The main tack of *The Federalist* was to emphasize the present power of the states, while at the same time hinting that in the future these powers would accrue to the national government. Thus, "Publius" suggests that as the people become more familiar with the general government and experience firsthand the benefits of its superior and impartial administration, they would welcome its extension to matters of local concern. And as the national government established itself as the center of American life, the proper role of the states would be to administer those objects with which it was inconvenient for the national government to bother.[25] The subtle but unmistakable conclusion is that the two men who played the largest role in framing and explicating the Constitution anticipated and approved the steady expansion of the national government into state and local affairs as essential to the preservation of liberty.[26]

MADISON'S CONVERSION TO THE FEDERAL PRINCIPLE

In view of the steady erosion of state power in the twentieth century, Madison's views on the proper federal-state relations appear prescient. But are they the most authoritative account of what the Framers as a whole intended? After all, Madison's most nationalist proposals were rejected by the Federal Convention in favor of the Connecticut Compromise which laid the foundation for federalism as we have come to know it for so long in America. Madison lost on the national legislative veto over state laws, proportional representation in the Senate, and the manner of electing the Senate. And Hamilton's plan was even wider of the mark, calling as it did for a general legislature armed with the "power to pass all laws whatsoever," an even stronger negative on pending state legislation, and, reversing the federal arrangement, a considerable role for the national government in the operation of state governments.[27] Why then, if we wish to discover the thoughts of the Framers regarding federalism and its relation to rights, do we look to the speeches and writings of the early Madison and other like-minded nationalists? And if we are to look elsewhere, what texts are authoritative?

Interestingly, these are questions which Madison himself explicitly raised in his later life, after he had come to recognize the importance of the federal principle. As is well known, after the Constitution was ratified and the new government installed, Madison began to clash with his old ally Hamilton over the scope of federal powers. Although there were hints of this break in his opposition to certain aspects of Hamilton's economic policies, it was not until the Alien and Sedition Acts in 1798 that Madison came to accept a positive role for the states in preserving republican liberty.

In the Virginia Resolutions, Madison returns to the familiar argument that the Constitution creates a national government of enumerated powers. When the federal government oversteps these bounds, the states must "interpose" to preserve their "authorities, rights and liberties." The failure of the states to resist such encroachments will lead to a "speedy consolidation" of power by the national government. This, in turn, will spell the end of the republic, as power flows to the executive.

Although the Virginia Resolutions have sometimes mistakenly been confused with later extreme states' rights positions - nullification or the state sovereignty theory of the Confederacy - they are actually an endorsement of the federal principle. Because there was considerable ambiguity surrounding the meaning of the Virginia Resolutions - especially when they were paired with the more radical and secessionist Resolutions written by Thomas Jefferson - Madison issued the Clarifying Resolutions of 1800 to show that the Virginia Resolutions belonged within the constitutional tradition. This latter report removed the ambiguity surrounding Madison's use of the word "state" by arguing that it was not the states *qua* states that were parties to the Constitution - and hence "sovereign" - but "the people composing those political societies in their highest sovereign capacity." Thus, when the federal government exceeds its rightful limits, it is the right and duty of the *people* in the states, rather than the state governments, to interpose to restrain these violations. Although the people of the states are the final judges of the constitutionality of government acts, their decisions, as embodied in the declarations of their state legislatures, are only "expressions of opinion." They were not, Madison adds reassuringly, meant to substitute for the judgment of the courts,[28] but rather to arouse the citizens to "promote a remedy according to the rules of the Constitution."[29] This, he noted with considerable satisfaction, was what the election of 1800 had accomplished. With John Adams and the other Federalists out of office, the Alien and Sedition Acts were a dead letter.

The Virginia Resolutions signify Madison's belated recognition that, despite internal checks, the national government was also capable of encroaching upon the rights of the citizens and dangerously consolidating political power. And in a letter written to J. G. Jackson in 1821, Madison suggests that he was mistaken about the permanent dangers facing republican government when he made his proposals at the Federal Convention.

> That most of us carried into the Convention a profound impression produced by the experienced inadequacy of the old Confederation, and by the monitory examples of all similar ones ancient and modern, as to the necessity of binding the States together by a strong Constitution is certain. This view of the crisis made it natural for many in the Convention to lean more than was perhaps in strictness warranted by a proper distinction between causes temporary as some of them doubtless were, and causes permanently inherent in popular frames of government. For myself, having from the first moment of maturing a political opinion, down to the present one, never ceased to be a votary of self Govt, I was among those most anxious to rescue it from the danger which seemed to threaten it; and with that view was willing to give a Govt resting on that foundation, as much energy as would ensure the requisite stability and efficacy. It is possible that in some instances this consideration may have been allowed a weight greater than subsequent reflection within the Convention, or the actual operation of the Govt, would sanction.[30]

It was this revised view of the dangers facing republican liberty that caused Madison to retreat from his earlier nationalism and to embrace, at last, the principle he had so grudgingly defended in 1787.

ON FEDERALISM AND RIGHTS IN OUR TIME

Over any observation about what has happened to federalism in our own time, looms the issue of what kind of actual constitutional change was wrought by Reconstruction and the Fourteenth Amendment. Scholars such as Michael Zuckert, in a paper that appears in this book, and Jack Rakove[31] are surely right in reading the Fourteenth Amendment as a renewed expression of the early Madison-nationalist concern that the central government be empowered to protect liberty against encroachments by the state governments. This said, it must also be noted that the *extent* to which the Amendment was intended to alter traditional understandings of federalism is a matter of (to say the least) lively contention.[32] Certainly, as Zuckert argues, the national Congress (and, by implication, the Supreme Court) was given some "corrective power" over rights violations by the states. But whether this corrective commission was as general as Zuckert suggests is open to doubt. Without judging this issue, which lies well beyond the scope of this paper, it is the case that the extent of the erosion of federalism in our own time can neither be fully explained nor justified by any reasonable interpretation of the scope of the Fourteenth Amendment. Something more is at work here. When Philip Kurland declared that "federalism is dead and the Supreme Court killed it," he was guilty of only slight hyperbole.

It is now clear that the abandonment of federalism resulted, in large part, from an enthusiasm for using the powers of the national government to protect rights and liberties. But there is an irony here, since modern federalism came into being precisely to protect rights and liberties. Since both sides claim the protection of rights as their goal, it is worth reflecting on what is gained, as well as what is lost, in an ever more centralized governmental arrangement.

Although it would appear that Madison's about-face on the role of federalism in protecting rights against an over-active national government would have immediate and obvious implications for present-day politics, none but hard core conservatives seem to have much use for the principle. Even the conservatives are not so consistent, calling, as they do, for the expansion of the national government to protect the right to life and other areas traditionally the preserve of the states. Despite calls for a "new federalism" by both Richard Nixon and Ronald Reagan, it is the early nationalism of Madison which today seems almost irresistible, especially when the message is driven home daily by the thoroughly national media. Although there are probably many non-political reasons for this, having to do with the centralizing tendencies of commerce, communications and technology, I shall briefly mention two more broadly political issues which have operated to undermine federalism in our time.

The first involves the problem of race, and the securing of rights to African Americans. Because the states for so long proved recalcitrant in this area, and because civil rights for blacks in the South only began to be secure when the national government became involved, many Americans assume that the national government must expand its role in protecting rights, not only for blacks, but for all minorities and women, against obstructive state legislatures. I do not deny that the national government played a vital role in helping to achieve some kind of racial justice during the early years of the civil rights struggle precisely by removing the issue from oppressive local majorities, but I question whether this means that the states should no longer be entrusted with securing any of our rights. The tendency to look to the federal government for national policies on every question of rights strikes me as ominous. Might it not be wiser to view the issues of racial justice as presenting Americans with a moral and political challenge in a class by itself, with solutions appropriate only to it, and even then, not always successful? If this is the case, then resort to national power does not become the model for every rights issue. After all, the one absolutely uncontroversial change in traditional federalism wrought by the Fourteenth Amendment lies in its concern that national power be created to protect Freedmen in the South from the apartheid system imposed by the Black Codes. While this probably did not imply that the national government was empowered to act against all racial discrimination by the states, the centrality of concern with race is clear where so much else about the reach of the Amendment is murky.

The resort to the black civil rights paradigm by any and all who claim to be oppressed is neither constitutionally nor morally justified. The situation of Americans of African descent is unique. No other case approaches it in moral seriousness; consequently, extensions of national power that were justified in the context of racial discrimination may be serious constitutional mistakes in other contexts. In this connection, it is worth noting the depth of feeling with which blacks reject what they perceive as the hijacking of the civil rights paradigm, first by women, and now by homosexuals and others.[33] The hard truth, of which we so rarely speak, is that the extraordinary difficulties in achieving racial justice must not be allowed to distort the entire constitutional order.

My second point regarding the decline of federalism has to do with the political psychology of democratic societies. Here again, Tocqueville helps us to appreciate one of the greatest paradoxes of democracy. To rule wisely and well, democracies need complex institutions which will restrain them from their first unthoughtful, if not dangerous, impulses. Yet democratic peoples are unlikely to understand the reasons why these institutions are necessary, and so strive to simplify them. In the name of democracy, they destroy the very institutions which preserve democracy. As Tocqueville put it: "The federal system rests on a complicated theory which, in application, demands that the governed should use the lights of their reason every day." And although he was impressed with how well this worked in the early years of the republic, he anticipates the inevitable dilemma: "It is only simple conceptions which take hold of a people's mind. A false but clear and precise idea always has more power in the world than one which is true but complex."[34] This, as we have seen, was true to some extent even for the Framers, as they came up against the difficulty of apportioning power between the states and the federal government, and it is even more true today. For, as Tocqueville also recognized, freedom no longer emerges naturally from our institutions, but must be carefully cultivated by art. With Tocqueville's insight in mind, I invite my readers to reflect on whether the proliferation of national legal rights and remedies over the past four decades or so has left Americans with more liberty or less, and whether more is being lost with the passing of the federal principle than is popularly supposed.

NOTES

1.   See Mary Ann Glendon, *Rights Talk* (Cambridge: Harvard University Press, 1990). For an earlier and less communitarian assessment of the problem, see Richard E. Morgan, *Disabling America: The Rights Industry in Our Time* (New York: Basic Books, 1984).

2.   Recent examples include the symposium on "The Bill of Rights: An Historical Perspective," *Southern Illinois Law Journal*, 16 (Winter 1992); Michael J. Lacy and Knud Haakonssen, eds., *A Culture of Rights* (New York: Cambridge University Press, 1991); John Phillip Reid, *Constitutional History of the American Revolution*, esp. vol. 1, *The Authority of Rights* (Madison: University of Wisconsin Press, 1986); Gordon S. Wood, *The Radicalism of the American Revolution* (New York: Alfred A. Knopf, 1992).

3.   Martin Diamond, "The *Federalist's* View of Federalism," in George C. S. Benson, ed., *Essays in Federalism* (Claremont: Institute for Studies in Federalism, 1962), pp. 21-64.

4.   Alexander Hamilton, James Madison and John Jay, *The Federalist Papers*, ed. Jacob E. Cooke (Middletown: Wesleyan University Press, 1961), no. 9, p. 55.

5.   Montesquieu, *The Spirit of the Laws*, trans. and ed. Anne M. Cohler, Basia C. Miller and Harold S. Stone (Cambridge: Cambridge University Press, 1989), book 8, chap. 16. For the persistence of this argument, see Alexis de Tocqueville, *Democracy in America*, ed. J. P. Mayer (New York: Anchor Press, 1969), vol. 1, pp. 158-163.

6.   The emphasis upon genuine classical republican virtue is crucial, for while some of the most important historical studies of the Founding stress the concern with republican virtue or civic humanism, they tend to misunderstand what classical republican virtue entailed. See, for example, J. G. A. Pocock, *The Machiavellian Moment: Florintine Political Thought and the Atlantic Republican Tradition* (Princeton: Princeton University Press, 1975); Gordon Wood, *The Creation of the American Republic, 1776-1787* (Chapel Hill: University of North Carolina Press, 1969); and Paul Rahe, *Republics: Ancient and Modern* (Chapel Hill: University of North Carolina Press, 1992).

7.   Herbert Storing, *What the Anti-Federalists Were For* (Chicago: University of Chicago Press, 1985).

8.   "Federal Farmer," in *The Anti-Federalists*, ed. Herbert Storing (Chicago: University of Chicago Press, 1985), p. 35.

9.   David N. Mayer, "The Natural Rights Bias of the Ninth Amendment: A Reply to Professor McAffee," *Southern Illinois Law Journal*, 16 (Winter 1992), p. 321.

10.   *The Federalist Papers* No. 15, p. 91.

11.   *The Federalist Papers* No. 10, p. 57.

12.   *The Records of the Federal Convention*, ed. Max Farrand, 4 vols. (New York and London: Yale University Press, 1937).

13.   Tocqueville, *Democracy in America*, p. 156.

14. Compare with Hamilton's treatment of this question in *Federalist* No. 9; see also Diamond, *"The Federalist's* View." and Jean Yarbrough, "Rethinking the *Federalist's* View of Federalism," *Publius: The Journal of Federalism*, 15 (Winter 1985): 31-53.

15. *Federalist* No. 45, p. 313.

16. *Federalist* No. 45, p. 313.

17. *Federalist* No. 14, p. 86.

18. Not even the Tenth Amendment, the last refuge of states' rights theory, does this. For a discussion of the Bill of Rights, and of Madison's role in making sure that the Anti-Federalists did not eviscerate the constitutional distribution of powers, see Herbert Storing, "The Constitution and the Bill of Rights," in *The American Founding*, eds. Ralph Rossum and Gary McDowell (Fort Washington: Kennikat Press, 1981), pp. 29-45. For a different view, which sees the Bill of Rights as a set of limitations on the national government intended to insure the continued viability and governmental integrity of the states, see Akhil Reed Amar, "The Creation and Reconstruction of the Bill of Rights," *Southern Illinois Law Journal*, 16 (Winter 1992).

19. "Brutus," in Storing, *The Anti-Federalists*, "The Constitution and the Bill of Rights," p. 186.

20. For a somewhat different interpretation, which stresses the variety of federal options at the Convention, see Michael P. Zuckert, "Federalism and the Founding: Toward a Reinterpretation of the Constitutional Convention," *The Review of Politics*, 48 (Spring 1986): 166-210. I agree with Zuckert that the federalism which emerged from the Convention was far less national than Madison or Hamilton wanted. But that Madison and Hamilton were unabashed nationalists is also undeniable.

21. Farrand, *The Records*, vol. 1, pp. 357-358; also Hamilton I, pp. 287.

22. Madison, in Farrand, *The Records*, vol. 1 pp. 357-358. In this same speech, Madison expressly rules out any danger from "the probable abuse of the general power."

23. *Federalist* No. 31, p. 197; No. 28, p. 178.

24. See especially *Federalist* Nos. 45 and 46.

25. See especially *Federalist* Nos. 27 and 46.

26. See especially Diamond, "The *Federalist's* View."

27. See Hamilton in Farrand, *The Records.*, vol. 1, pp. 283-287; and the discussion in Zuckert, "Federalism and the Founding."

28. An interesting point since judicial review of legislation passed by coordinate branches - rather than by state governments - would not be established until *Marbury v. Madison* in 1803.

29. James Madison, *The Writings of James Madison*, ed. Gaillard Hunt, 9 vols. (New York and London: G. P. Putnam's Sons, 1906), vol. 6, pp. 348, 402.

30. Farrand, *The Records.*, vol. 3, pp. 449.

31. Jack N. Rakove, "Parchment Barriers and the Politics of Rights," in Lacy and Haakonssen, eds., *A Culture of Rights*, pp. 142-143.

32. See, for example, Earl Maltz, *Civil Rights, the Constitution, and Congress* (Lawrence: University of Kansas Press, 1991).

33. *New York Times* (June 28, 1993), p. 1.

34. Tocqueville, *Democracy in America*, p. 164.

CHAPTER 5

TOWARD A THEORY OF CORRECTIVE FEDERALISM: THE UNITED STATES CONSTITUTION, FEDERALISM, AND RIGHTS

Michael P. Zuckert

Thirty years ago, the received wisdom about federalism and rights was simple and straightforward: federalism is an enemy of rights and for that reason, not a very good thing. This judgment was easy enough to understand. It was the era of the civil rights movement when appeals to federalism or states rights appeared to be nothing but thinly veiled attempts to maintain segregation and other morally suspect social practices. It was also not too long after the New Deal acceptance in America of the positive state, in the way of which federalism also appeared to stand.

Political scientists of both liberal and conservative leanings shared the hostility toward federalism of the early sixties. Grant McConnell, for example, in his *Private Power and American Democracy* appealed to Madisonian principles to justify a yet more complete shift toward centralized authority, partly in the name of better rights-securing from Washington than from Little Rock or Springfield. The conservative Martin Diamond sounded y like the liberal McConnell in justifying the overcoming of federalism for the sake of more justly securing rights. Diamond went so far as to suggest that federalism, once taken to be the pride of American government, had been a mistake, an irrational compromise forced upon a reluctant Madison and doomed from the start.[1]

Federalism is no longer in such uniform ill-repute. Nonetheless, even among those who now favor federalism, service to rights is rarely mentioned as one of its chief virtues. Current interest in federalism seems to focus instead on themes like democratic participation and self-government on the one hand, and the possibilities for political integration through the accommodation of diversity on the other.[2] Both of these are, of course, time-honored themes in federalist theory and practice, but I plan to focus here more directly on issues surrounding rights.

I want to argue that rights and federalism, far from being inherently hostile to each other, are deeply - although not inevitably - compatible with each other. I intend to pursue this theme of compatibility from both sides: (1) what rights do for federalism, or how acceptance of natural rights philosophy was the prerequisite for the emergence of modern federalism; and (2) what federalism does for rights, or how federalism can serve as a uniquely effective means of rights-securing within the context of a healthy democratic political order. In order to make this last point I wish to propose a conceptualization of American federalism, which I shall call corrective federalism, as an alternative to the more standard theory of dual federalism. Corrective federalism better reveals the relation between federalism and rights and provides us better guidance in thinking about this important topic. Along the way, I wish to suggest that the 1960s suspicion of federalism was not entirely misguided either. Partly because of the sway of the theory of dual federalism, the system of corrective federalism has never been able to take full effect, or did so in such severely distorted form that federalism has played an ambiguous role relative to rights over the course of American history.

RIGHTS AS PREREQUISITE OF MODERN FEDERALISM

Modern federalism, Daniel Elazar concludes, begins with the American federal experiment.[3] James Madison, the inventor of American federalism, insisted that the new American federalism was wholly new - a break with all federal systems of the past. It was, he said, "a system without a precedent ancient or modern." Past federalism had served only as "beacons...giving warning of the course to be shunned, without pointing out that which ought to be pursued."[4] Montesquieu captured the character of the old (pre-Madison) federalism when he wrote of it as "an agreement by which several states agree to become members of a larger one." A federal state is thus "a kind of society of societies."[5] The members of the federal state, in other words, are not individual human beings, but states, organized political communities as such. The understanding of federalism prevailing prior to Madison's reformulations took its bearing from this description of a federal state as "a society of societies." To paraphrase Lincoln, federalism was conceived of as government of the states, by the states, and for the states.[6] A federal union was for the states in that the purposes it was established to serve were purposes of the member states rather than of the states' human members. These purposes always included mutual defense, and occasionally a few other matters, such as common care for religious shrines or arrangements regarding commerce among the members or with outsiders.[7]

Pre-Madisonian federalism was government *by the states* in that the agents of government were selected by and responsible to the governments of the member states, or were often merely existing bodies within the member states' governments. Thus the "legislative power," so far as it made sense to speak of one, was normally contained in an assembly or congress of delegates from the member states. This assembly was thus quite different from whatever internal legislative body the member states might have possessed for their own governance. Moreover, since other governing functions were carried out by the member states, typically federal states had quite undeveloped separate organs of execution or adjudication of their own.

Finally, federal unions were governments *of the states*. So far as the federation governed, it applied itself to its member states and not to the individual human beings who made up those states. Thus, the "government" under the Articles of Confederation lacked power to reach into the pockets of the human citizens of the states, but only could apply to its members, the states, for funds. The Articles of Confederation was an extremely clear version of the old federalism, for it operated exclusively in terms of the federal principle, the relating of one level of government to the other level of government, rather than in terms of the national principle, the operation of government in relation to human citizens.

Madison's great invention was to deploy national elements within a system that was to remain federal, but in an entirely new sense. His new federalism innovated in all three of Lincoln's dimensions of governance. The new federalism was no longer to be "government of the states," for the new union was to operate directly on the human individuals who were now understood to be its citizens as well as citizens of the member states. The reasoning in favor of this modification of traditional federalism is well known through the famous exposition of it in *Federalist* 15-17, and requires no re-statement here.[8]

It is no longer "government by the states" either, for the agents of governance for the union were not to be agents of the member states, but were to be genuine agents of the government of the union itself. The legislature under the new form of federalism is to be parallel in character to that of the member legislatures, and the government of the union is to have its own executive and judiciary.

The new federalism departed most daringly from the old in no longer being strictly "for the states." In an analysis since made overly famous in *Federalist* 10, Madison challenged the then prevailing wisdom about republics, that firmly placing control of government in the hands of (qualified) majorities would guarantee safe and just government. To the contrary, Madison demonstrated the possibility of majority tyranny and mismanagement, equally serious, and almost equally likely threats as royal tyranny and mismanagement. The "small republic" member states had fallen prey to these evils, and successful reform of the "vices of the political system of the U.S." would require correction of these evils as much as correction of the defects more particularly centered in the general government.

Because of *Federalist* 10, Madison's analysis of the defects of small republics is well-known, but the role federalism was to play in their solution is much less clearly understood. Madison never thought that transfer of all or most governing authority from the small republics of the states to the large republic of the union was the solution to the problem of injustice in the states. He rather sought to use the general government as a way to correct or check unjust or unwise measures in the states, not to replace them as the chief locus of governance in the United States. Madison was unable to extract from the Convention all that he wished for in this matter, but he did accomplish some significant concessions in the form of explicit prohibitions against some of the most egregious state injustices, prohibitions to be enforced by the new government of the union. Article I, section 10, for example, prohibits the states from passing *ex post facto* laws, or from impairing the obligation of contracts. By including such provisions, the new federalism in these specific matters goes beyond being "government for the states" exclusively. The federal system is here used to serve ends that are not the ends of the member states themselves, but are rather the ends of the individual citizens themselves. These provisions serve individual rights directly.

The Americans' commitment to rights, as expressed in the Declaration of Independence, contributed to the emergence of this new federalism in three different ways. The new federalism differed from the old in projecting significant elements of national action into the member states. Such innovations were radical in that they constituted a degree of intrusion into the member units theretofore unprecedented in the history of federations, and thus a compromise of the integrity and autonomy of the member units far beyond what traditional federations required. The agreement prevailing in the new American states on the natural rights philosophy was the precondition for this new intrusiveness.[9] It was important both as an agreement as such, and as the particular agreement it was. Different as the colonies (now states) had originally been, an agreement on political fundamentals was necessary for producing the level of trust and common effort required by the new level of federal intrusiveness.

It was not only the fact of agreement that was important, however. The rights philosophy, developed in the crucible of the seventeenth century's intense theological-political conflict, was tailored by nature and design to suit a society (or a federal society of societies) driven by disagreements over various fundamentals. It placed political life on universally secular grounds, made room for, but relegated to a pluralistic private sphere, all the matters of fundamental moral and religious disagreement upon which so many political communities had run aground in the past. In place of any comprehensive ordering of political life to any particular vision of virtue, the good life, or the pious life, the rights philosophy affirmed a much narrower set of goals and criteria of political legitimacy. Government exists to "secure" the rights to "life, liberty, and pursuit of happiness." Since these rights were universally understood as what are now called negative rights, this commitment was important but relatively limited and plausibly universal. The legitimate business and end of politics is, in other words, tremendously contracted within the rights philosophy, and partnership in securing the new end is conceived to be entirely voluntary. The very narrowness and universality of the political task makes possible the kind of new arrangement the new federalism mandated. Although there was much greater intrusion into the lives of the specific member communities, the narrowed understanding of the political sphere as a whole insured that the intrusion meant much less than it otherwise might have. Given, for example, Aristotle's understanding of the comprehensive ends of polity, it is hard to imagine him endorsing an agreement so compromising the autonomy of the primary political unit. Given the intense theological commitments of various forms of earlier Christian

~~political~~ theory, it is just as difficult to imagine, say, a Massachusetts and a Pennsylvania in the seventeenth century coming together into anything like the new federalism.

Secondly, the rights philosophy served as prerequisite to the new federalism by pointing toward a solution to the thorny problem of sovereignty. Ever since the doctrine of sovereignty burst on the world, it had stood as an apparently insurmountable barrier to the kind of federalism the Americans developed. The new federalism stood or fell with the possibility of the co-presence of two governments operating equally and without subordination within one territory and with respect to one population. It was precisely the possibility of such a division of authority that the doctrine of sovereignty denied. Somewhere in every community there must exist a truly supreme and indivisible authority. The Articles of Confederation loudly proclaimed that in America that place was the member states. So long as sovereignty was thought to inhere in the member states, a system of government of the states by the states, and for the states, was nearly inevitable.

The solution, as is well known, came with the reconceptualization of the locus of sovereignty.[10] The people, not the states are sovereign; they possess the absolute, unlimited, indivisible power proclaimed within the theory of sovereignty, but they allocate or delegate portions of that power to government, which is no longer seen as sovereign, but as a mere trustee of popular power. This conceptual breakthrough allowed the Americans to find a theoretical account for a variety of practices that seemed inconsistent with the logic of sovereignty - separation of powers, limited government, reserved rights, and finally, federalism.[11] The people can divide and allocate authority to different levels of government, which can remain equal to each other "in their respective spheres" while being subordinate to and derivative from the sovereign people.

The Lockean theory of rights was in turn the conceptual foundation for the new doctrine of popular sovereignty which made the new federalism conceptually intelligible. It is no accident that only in the natural rights era did a firm theory of sovereignty in federal systems arise. The Lockean theory made possible a response to both the older notions of sovereignty necessarily residing in the member units and not in the union, and to the newer notion of indivisible centralized sovereignty as developed by Thomas Hobbes.

Because each individual is conceived within liberal rights theory as having rights prior to and independent of political society and positive law, the sovereignty of the people was necessarily thought individualistically within it -

popular sovereignty meant the collective or additive sovereign power of individuals, not the sovereign power of the community as such.

Popular sovereignty as communal sovereignty was the pre-natural rights era idea, and figured in earlier forms of contractarian political philosophy. The conceptualization of communal sovereignty, when applied to the problem of federalism, led to the old federalism - government of, by, and for the member states. The new individualistic or desegregated notion of popular sovereignty allowed the parcelling out of powers, authorities, and rights which made federalism possible. Among other things, it allowed one to circumvent entirely the question of which community - the union or the member states - is sovereign. The same conception of political power as primordially located in individual rights bearers in its Lockean version allowed the Americans to escape the inexorable Hobbesian logic of sovereignty. As possessors of inalienable rights, the original contractors in the Lockean scheme were logically incapable of creating the sovereign leviathan-state of Hobbes' imaginings; not merely need they not, but they could not surrender all their rights to a sovereign entity; they surrendered only what in their judgment is rational and prudent. The primordial political power of the people is not, then, one and indivisible. Rights and powers can (and must) be reserved; by the same token they can be divided among different political authorities, thus making possible not only federalism, but separation of powers and bills of rights.

Finally, the commitment to rights was a prerequisite for the new federalism in that the tasks of the new federalism were very much defined in terms of contributing to the rights securing affirmed in the rights philosophy. This last point requires separate treatment, however, for it is nothing but the doctrine of corrective federalism itself.

FEDERALISM AS PREREQUISITE TO RIGHTS-SECURING

Three or perhaps four important versions of corrective federalism have been developed in the course of American political and constitutional history: (1) *Madison Federalism*, as embodied in his plan for a new constitution, a pale version of which was adopted in the Constitution itself; (2) *Bingham Federalism*, as embodied in the post-Civil War Constitution, especially the Fourteenth Amendment, of which Bingham was the chief craftsman; (3) *Field Federalism*, as developed in the substantive due-process-oriented Constitution of the late nineteenth and early twentieth centuries, the theoretical foundations of which were laid by Justice Field; and (4) *Hamilton "Federalism,"* the version of corrective federalism, if it is correctly labeled as such, prevalent today, but best understood conceptually in terms of Alexander Hamilton's plan for a union.

Madison's Corrective Federalism

Prior to Madison it was believed in America that the one thing needful for just, rights-securing government was keeping government safely in check - mostly through empowering the people to control it. This pre-Madisonian republican theory cohered very well with pre-Madisonian federal theory, for both converged on government of the states, by the states, and for the states as the ideal. The states were smaller, closer to the people, and thus more readily subject to popular control, *i.e.*, they were better all around.

On the basis of the kind of analysis he presented in *Federalist* 10, Madison came to see that the requirements of a rights-securing republicanism were far more complex than merely assuring community control of government, however. "The great desideratum in government," he said, "is such a modification of the sovereignty as will render it sufficiently neutral between the different interests and factions, to control one part of the society from invading the rights of another, and at the same time sufficiently controlled itself, from setting up an interest adverse to the whole society." Madison's identification of the political task was not only more complex than the prevailing theory; it was also extremely difficult to achieve, for the two elements of his "great desideratum" seem to point in opposite directions. On the one hand, government must be neutral *vis-a-vis* the interests in society, so that it can act "disinterestedly," and control them rather than be controlled by some of them. This requires a certain distance or independence of the political authorities from the forces in society. On the other hand, the government must remain dependent on and controlled by society, so that it does not impose a separate interest of its own on society as a whole.[12]

Each requirement can be met tolerably well in a form of government well known to history. The kind of republic his compatriots favored could respond to the second problem. Keeping government on a very "short leash," as they would do, could prevent it from developing or pursuing an interest separate from that of the whole community. Hereditary monarchy, on the other hand, can supply the other requirement. The prince, not dependent on the forces in society for his position or for the exercise of his powers, is free to be neutral or disinterested *vis-a-vis* those interests. But, as he is free to disregard the particular claims of any faction, so he is free to disregard the interests of the whole as well. Neither republic nor monarchy satisfies both requirements, however.

Madison saw the possibility of a solution in a combination of the two regimes: "A limited monarchy tempers the evils of an absolute one." A limited monarchy, like Britain's, combines the two pure forms - a hereditary prince and an elected republican legislature. The one supplies neutrality, the other supplies safety. Madison saw that the British constitution could be the model for a new departure on the problem of rights-securing in America: "As a limited monarchy tempers the evils of an absolute one; so an extensive Republic meliorates the administration of a small Republic." Madison saw the solution not in the replacement of the small republic by the large, as many contemporary scholars believe, but rather in the combination of the two, in the new kind of federal system he invented. It was a "system without a precedent" which "so combines the federal form with the form of individual republics, as may enable each to supply the defects of the other and obtain the advantages of both."[13]

In the new kind of combination he projected, the "large republic" was formed to supply the disinterest, neutrality, and distance from society characteristic of the monarchic element in the British limited monarchy. Madison counted on the mechanisms outlined in *The Federalist* to achieve this goal; the majorities that typically can form in a large republic will be different from those existing in a small republic. Majorities in a large republic are more likely to serve the common good and to respect the rights of all; they are more likely to mimic the neutrality and disinterest of a hereditary monarch. In the limited monarchy, the monarchic element exercises its role through the possession of a negative power on legislation. The king is not given a positive legislative power, but makes his contribution of neutrality through a veto power. The republican legislature, Parliament, possesses the positive legislative power. The balance between the institutions and the powers they possess secure that combination of the two requirements which seemed so difficult to achieve.

In the American federal system, Madison envisaged the same combination of structures and powers, in this case with the government of the extended republic in place of the prince possessing a negative power, and the small republics of the states possessing positive legislative powers. Just as the limited monarchy does not arm the prince with positive legislative powers, so the large-small republic combination of the new federalism does not arm the large republic with positive legislative power. Madison wanted to grant the Congress of the general government a power analogous to the king's - the power to negate all laws made by the states. Through the exercise of this veto power, the large republic, in concert with the small republics of the states, could achieve the two desiderata much as the limited monarchy did.

In the face of much opposition Madison adhered firmly to his idea for a Congressional negative over state legislation because it allowed him to solve the problem of rights without adopting either a non-republican system or a fully unitary or centralized system.[14] He found both very objectionable.

Madison's opposition to a unitary or wholly national system requires some comment because many scholars believe that his famous argument in favor of the extended republic would seem to support such a unified system. That argument led Madison not to a unified system, however, but to corrective federalism via the Congressional negative. The negative could secure the "great desideratum of government" at least as well as the simple extended republic. Indeed, Madison identified three reasons why the small-extended republic combination would be even more effective at securing the "great desideratum" than the extended republic alone. More than once at the Convention, Madison emphasized that the United States were too extensive and too various to be subjected to one uniform legislative power. Responding to some of the small-state delegates, for example, he argued:

> The expedient proposed by them was that all the States should be thrown into one mass and a new partition be made into 13 equal parts. Would such a scheme be practicable? The dissimilarities existing in the rules of property, as well as in the manners, habits, and prejudices of the different states amounted to a prohibition of the attempt.

Madison was quite emphatic in his support for the states: "I mean...to preserve the State rights with the same care, as I would trials by jury." And why was Madison so strong on "State rights"?

> The great objection made against an abolition of the State Government was that the General Government could not extend its care to all the minute objects which fall under the cognizance of the local jurisdictions. The objection as stated lay not against the probable abuse of the general power, but against the imperfect use that could be made of it throughout so great a variety of objects.[15]

Moreover, even though the extended republic is republican and through its electoral controls supplies some of that dependence on society that is needed to provide safety against government oppression, Madison had serious reservations about the efficacy of republican safeguards in a very large republic.

It must be observed, however, [he wrote to Jefferson] that this doctrine can only hold within a sphere of a mean extent. As in too small a sphere oppressive combinations may be too easily formed against the weaker part; so into extensive a one, a defensive concert may be rendered too difficult against the oppression of those entrusted with the administration.[16]

A federal rather than a unitary extended republic is Madison's hedge against the uncertain safety devices in the very large area.

In Madison's original plan of federalism, the numerous inconveniences of a unitary system and of small republicanism are avoided by reliance on the Congressional negative. As Madison wrote to George Washington before the Convention: "Might not the national prerogative here suggested [*i.e.*, the negative] be found sufficiently disinterested for the decision of local questions of policy, whilst it would itself be sufficiently restrained from the pursuit of interests adverse to those of the whole society."[17]   Madison emphasized it is the prerogative, that is, the nature of the power itself, that is restrained so as to secure the requisite safety.

A negative power also secures the desired neutrality more effectively than a positive legislative power would.   Would not the negative, he asked Washington, "be found sufficiently disinterested for the decision of local questions of policy?"   The general government's disinterest is grounded largely on the localism of those local questions of policy, on the absence of a direct stake of the general government in the issues or their outcome.   That distance, and therefore that disinterest, would be overcome if the general government had a positive legislative authority, which would transform a series of unconnected local issues of policy into questions of national policy. So long as the legislature of the general government exercises a negative, and does so in the context of a review of decisions essentially taken elsewhere, the questions retain their distinctly local character.

In a word, Madison saw federalism as the solution to the problems of rights-securing that could not be solved in any other manner.   The Constitutional Convention, of course, did not follow Madison's advice on this matter, and produced a Constitution that was a mere shadow of his hopes. Madison could not win the convention to his proposal, but he did not fail altogether.   Some of the more obvious evils in the states - paper money, impairments of contract, bills of attainder - were directly forbidden in the Constitution.   These were then to be enforced by the courts.   Madison considered this an unsatisfactory and pale version of his negative, but it went at least part way toward serving the ends peculiar to his vision of union, and stands as a key part of American federalism.   The Convention's Constitution embodied corrective federalism to a much smaller degree than Madison had hoped, but it did indeed embody it: dual federalism was never an adequate theory of the Constitution.

Madison's scheme is so interesting because in an unparalleled way he attempted to bring federalism into service as a means to protect rights. For the sake of rights he propounded a corrective federalism - the line between congressional and state power is to be taken seriously and maintained, but in the interest of rights protection the general government via the congressional negative is to have power to correct missteps by the states. But the general government is not to supplant the states from their chief business of governing the nation.

Bingham's Corrective Federalism

Madison failed to embody his version of corrective federalism in the Constitution, but after the Civil War the Republicans who controlled Congress, faced with massive evidence of the failure of the original Constitution to secure rights, rediscovered corrective federalism and proceeded to plant a very robust version of it into the Constitution in the form of the reconstruction amendments. One of the great advantages of the theory of corrective federalism is that it allows us to identify the nature of the post-war constitution reform and to make good sense of the confusing and controversial Reconstruction amendments.

Confusing these amendments have been - especially that protean piece of text, the Fourteenth Amendment, a text framed in large and grandiose but apparently ill-defined and vague terms like privileges and immunities, due process of law, and equal protection of the law. The history of the adoption of the amendment has been as confusing as the text - confusing enough to spawn two plausible but very different interpretations of what the founders were attempting to do.

One group of scholars notes the deep and undeniable concern the drafters had for rights, and notes their appreciation of the fact that the traditional federal system had allowed the systematic violation of rights in the states. Some scholars hold that the framers sought to provide for rights at the expense of the federal system. They conclude, in other words, that the Reconstruction amendments wrought a thoroughgoing constitutional revolution, overturning federalism in favor of a far more nationalist or even unitary constitutional order.

Another group of scholars notices that the drafters of the amendments show no general hostility to federalism and indeed endorse it strongly. John Bingham, the author of the Fourteenth Amendment, for example, was so committed to federalism that he insisted that "no right reserved by the constitution to the states should be impaired."[18] This is not what we would expect from someone sponsoring a constitutional revolution to overturn federalism. This group of scholars thus concludes that the Reconstruction amendments were, on the whole, pretty conservative, reaffirming traditional federalism and supplying additional protection to rights only within boundaries defined by their commitment to constitutional federalism.

Both theories of the amendments are plausible, but only the theory of corrective federalism makes sense of all the facts that each theory one-sidedly emphasizes, both the continued commitment to a healthy federalism and the commitment to substantially expanded rights-protection against the states. The drafters of the Reconstruction amendments recaptured Madison's basic idea, but only at the level of general conception and not at the level of detail. The particular means adopted in the amendment were rather different from Madison's negative. Madison's solution was political in that he attempted to institute a process that would produce rights-protecting results according to the dynamics of majority formation in an extended republic. The framers of the post-war amendments for the most part opted for a more directly constitutional and legal solution: the rights to be protected, as well as appropriate legal limits and empowerments, were specified directly in the constitutional text.

States are to continue to act in all the areas in which they acted within the traditional federal system, but they must not intrude on the set of rights defined in the amendments. The rights serve as what Robert Nozick called "side-constraints."[19] They do not so much tell the states what they can or should do, but set boundaries around them in doing whatever they do. Both the definition of side-constraint rights so protected and the enforcement mechanisms require further brief discussion.

The rights protected in the three amendments are in fact quite diverse, and the language in which they are expressed has defied simple analysis. The best way to understand the sweep of rights in the three amendments is in terms of a distinction among types of rights extremely prevalent at the time - natural rights, civil rights, political rights. These rights are progressively less universal; all human beings possess the same natural rights; civil rights may vary from political community to political community and frequently are unequally distributed within a community; political rights are least widely distributed, for frequently a person may be a full citizen, enjoying full civil rights, and yet not possess the right to participate in the governance of the community, and thus lack some or all political rights. The Thirteenth and part of the Fourteenth Amendments deal with natural rights; other aspects of the Fourteenth provide for civil rights, and the Fifteenth deals with a political right of great importance, the right to vote.

The Fifteenth Amendment raises many very interesting issues but I will limit myself here to one only. So far as it mandates the incorporation of racial minorities into the electorate it attempts to supply rights-protection through requiring the states to structure their political processes so that oppression of racial minorities is less likely than it otherwise might be. Being process oriented, the Fifteenth Amendment is closer to Madison's own approach, and thus stands somewhat farther away from the chief devices of corrective federalism in the other two amendments.

The Thirteenth Amendment prohibits slavery; it therefore secures the natural right to liberty as a side-constraint on the states, as least so far as to protect against outright seizure of one's liberty. What more it does, however, is most unclear. Shortly after the Amendment was adopted the southern states enacted the very restrictive Black Codes, which Congress attempted to negate in the Civil Rights Act of 1866. That Act was ostensibly passed under authority of the Thirteenth Amendment, and in many ways operated like Madison's proposed negative. The states passed laws, and Congress in effect declared them null and void. Congress was acting in terms of the principles of action appropriate to corrective federalism. Nonetheless, much reasonable uncertainty persisted over whether the Civil Rights Act was valid, and if so, on what theory of the Thirteenth Amendment.[20] Although Congress was proceeding in a manner consistent with corrective federalism, the truth is the drafters of the Thirteenth Amendment and the Civil Rights Act had not sufficiently thought through the inter-relations between rights and federalism that they were aspiring to incorporate into the reconstruction legislation.

The task remained to be worked out during he consideration of the Fourteenth Amendment, and seems largely to have been the work of the Amendment's chief author, John Bingham of Ohio. The Fourteenth Amendment attempted to redo more adequately what the Thirteenth Amendment had attempted to do, to reorder the original constitutional ordering of rights and federalism. In the Fourteenth Amendment, we find a clear delineation of corrective federalism.

We can best discern the Amendment's corrective federalist scheme through a comparison of an important rough draft of the amendment with the final text as adopted. Both drafts were written by the same man, John Bingham. The rough draft provides:

> The congress shall have power to make all laws which shall be necessary and proper to secure to all persons in the several states equal protection in the rights of life, liberty and property.

The final wording, of course, reads:

> All persons born or naturalized in the United States and subject to the jurisdiction thereof, are citizens of the United States and of the State wherein they reside. No state shall make or enforce any law which shall abridge the privileges or immunities of citizens of the Unites States; nor shall any state deprive any person of life, liberty, or property, without due process of law; nor deny any person within its jurisdiction the equal protection of the laws.

The most striking difference between the two versions of the Amendment lies in the fact that the final version is cast in terms of prohibitions against the states, while the draft contains congressional empowerment. But for the moment let us focus attention on another important difference. Where the final version contains three sets of protections - privileges and immunities, due process, and equal protection - the draft contains two sets of protections - privileges and immunities and "equal protection in the rights of life, liberty, and property." The second of those two clauses provides protection for the familiar triad of rights: life, liberty, and property, *i.e.*, the triad of natural rights.

The second clause of the draft then would appear to grant Congress power to see to it that "all persons" receive equal protection of their natural rights. This is a helpful insight for it sheds much light on what might otherwise appear to be opaque language in the final text of the Amendment. In the final version the language of this draft clause has been split into two clauses: "Nor shall any state deprive any person of life, liberty, or property without due process of law; nor deny to any person within its jurisdiction the equal protection of the laws." Judging by language and punctuation, the due process and equal protection clauses of the final amendment are directly descended from the equal protection clause of the earlier draft. The principle responsible for the bifurcation of the one clause into two is quite easy to discern. The earlier version empowered Congress to see to the provision of equal protection of the natural rights, but the final version instead made this into a prohibition against the states' failing to secure persons in their natural rights. Now there are two ways, and only two ways, in which states may fail to secure natural rights. First, a state may itself threaten rights by depriving persons of those objects to which they have rights—their lives, their liberties, and their properties. Since it is the business of states to apply coercion against persons who violate legitimate laws, states threaten rights only where they deprive persons of these objects of rights outside the law, *i.e.*, without due process of law, *i.e.*, without a proper legal authorization and without proper legal process. The due process clause thus provides a part of the protection to natural rights originally contemplated in the second clause of the earlier draft, protection against unwarranted deprivation of rights by the state itself.

States are not the only agents capable of depriving a person of natural rights, however. According to natural rights-social contract philosophy, the primary threats to rights arise from other individuals. These threats form the basis and purpose for the creation of the state as such. The business of the state is to supply protection for rights, that is, to establish laws and legal processes which will secure the rights of individuals against the actions of other individuals. If the state fails to supply protection for rights (that is, to establish laws and legal processes which will secure the rights of individuals against the actions of other individuals), or supplies some persons quite inferior protection, it is failing in its primary duty of rights-protection. Thus the equal protection clause of the final amendment forbids states from denying rights by failing to provide protection.

Tracing the modification in the texts through the two drafts of the Fourteenth Amendment thus leads to the conclusion that the two clauses, the due process and equal protection clauses, are devoted to protection of natural rights of persons against the states. Prior to the Thirteenth and the Fourteenth Amendments, these rights had no constitutional status *vis-a-vis* the states. The original Constitution took for granted that the states bore chief responsibility for supplying protection to natural rights, but, with a few exceptions, the United States Constitution placed no restrictions or duties on the states in their dealing with these rights. The Fourteenth Amendment works a major shift; under its terms, all persons within the United States now have a federal constitutional right to their natural rights - a right to protection by and from the states. The Fourteenth Amendment does not transfer custody of these rights to the general government, however. The states remain the agents involved with rights, but parameters are now defined which they must respect, on pain of being corrected by agents of the general government.

In addition to its clause about natural rights, the early draft had a clause empowering Congress to see to protection of "privileges and immunities." With two exceptions, this language is carried directly into the final version of the Amendment. As with the other clause, it is recast into the form of a prohibition against state actions. The second change is for the moment, even more significant: "privileges and immunities of citizens in the several states" became "privileges or immunities of citizens of the United States." This change can best be understood in terms of John Bingham's special theory about the privileges and immunities clause of Article IV, Section 2 of the Constitution. He believed that this clause actually was meant to read, "privileges and immunities of citizens *of the United States* in the several states." Bingham believed that Article IV, Section 2 was always intended to protect a certain class of rights, "privileges, and immunities of citizens of the United States." The language he wrote into the final version of the Amendment clearly emphasizes this view of what should be protected, even if the dominant line of constitutional interpretation up to his time did not support his reading of Article IV, Section 2.

This, too, is an extremely helpful insight, for it provides solid pointers towards the meaning of one of the more elusive phrases in the entire Constitution. In the first place, the privileges and immunities clause of the Amendment (in either draft) must protect some set of rights different from the natural rights protected by the due process and equal protection clauses. The very language of the clauses suggests a significant difference, for natural rights are claims due to all persons by virtue of their humanity and therefore imply universality. Privileges and immunities suggest something less than universality, however, A "privilege" is not shared by all; nor is an "immunity." Accordingly, the text of the Amendment identifies privileges and immunities as belonging to "citizens," and rights as belonging to "all persons."

Privileges and immunities belong to citizens and thus depend for their existence on positive law and the existence of government. Privileges and immunities are thus civil rights, not natural rights. Since their content depends on the particular political community which grants them, there can be no question of a universal table of privileges and immunities. They depend upon the actual civil society in which they are enjoyed. The Fourteenth Amendment singles out the privileges and immunities of "citizens of the United States" and prohibits states from abridging these. In the American federal system, individuals are simultaneously citizens both of their state and of the United States, a situation which the Fourteenth Amendment obtrusively reaffirms in its very opening sentence. Being citizens of two different political entities, individuals possess two sets of privileges and immunities. The Amendment protects only those attached to citizenship in the United States. These privileges and immunities must either be defined in the constituting law of the United States (the Constitution) or be implicit in the very existence of such an entity as the United States. The Constitution does indeed identify in several places special rights which belong to its citizens. Article I, Section 9 is one such place; the Bill of Rights is another. Analysis of the text of the draft of the Amendment thus leads to the conclusion that the privileges and immunities clause means to protect (at least) the rights identified in the Bill of Rights against "abridgement" by the states.

Prior to the Fourteenth Amendment, the privileges and immunities of United States citizens as so understood were not protected against abridgement by the states. As Chief Justice John Marshall pronounced in *Barron v. Baltimore*, the Bill of Rights bound only the general government and not the states.[21] The Fourteenth Amendment would change that situation, in a way again consistent with the model of corrective federalism, for now the Bill of Rights would set limits on what the states could do (or even more, on how they could do what they did), but would not supplant the states. The consistency of applying the Bill of Rights against the states with Madison's model of corrective federalism is indicated well enough by the fact that, after failing to incorporate the negative in the Constitution, he attempted to write into the Bill of Rights some of the same limitations on state action as were adopted against action by the general government.

The corrective federalist conception behind the Reconstruction amendments also provided mechanisms by which agents of the general government could act to correct actions by the states violative of the rights protected against the states. Since the limitations were placed into the Constitution as explicit legal provisions, the Supreme Court is to enforce these limitations as it does other such constitutional provisions. The Court's role here is clearly consistent with the corrective federalist model. In addition to the Court's role, Congress also has power to act as corrector under Section 2 of the Thirteenth and Fifteenth Amendments and Section 5 of the Fourteenth. In the first instance, Congress has power to enforce the Amendment, to correct state violations of the rights protected under the amendments. The Civil Rights Act of 1866 serves as model for the kind of corrective action anticipated under the amendments, for in it penalties are set against officials of states who, "under color of law," engage in the kinds of rights violations prohibited by the amendments.

Congressional power under the Fourteenth Amendment goes beyond this power to act on, or correct states and their officials, however. Among other things, states are prohibited from denying equal protection of the laws. A state violation of this prohibition typically takes the form of a certain kind of inaction, *i.e.*, a failure to supply the required protection. Under the logic of the amendment, which is once again consistent with the logic of corrective federalism, Congress has the power to step in and supply the required protection if the states show a pattern of failure in supplying the protection themselves. Thus, under its power to enforce the equal protection clause, Congress would have power, under certain circumstances, to supply direct protection to individuals in their natural rights, not only against action by states and state officials, but against private individuals as well.[22] Such congressional action moves toward the very outer edge of any permissible power under a theory of corrective federalism, but it remains within corrective federalism by virtue of the requirement of prior state failure.

Field's Corrective Federalism

The Reconstruction amendments embodied a coherent plan for reordering American federalism in order to make it more unequivocally consistent with rights-protection. The originally intended model hardly lasted a day, however, before the Supreme Court and then Congress itself abandoned it. The sequence of cases from *Slaughterhouse* to *Plessy* was a carefully designed demolition of corrective federalism. Nonetheless, what the Supreme Court taketh away, the Supreme Court can give back. So powerful is the basic idea of corrective federalism that, despite the abandonment of it after the Civil War, the Court soon restored it - only to abandon it once again, and then to reinstate it in drastically modified form at yet another time.

Constitutional history since 1877 is almost nothing but the history of the rise and fall of these two new versions of corrective federalism, so that our account of them here must be brief and rather schematic. Not too long after the Court had its way with the post-war amendments, it restored a version of corrective federalism via its doctrine of substantive due process. Having failed to find much rights-protecting power in the Fourteenth Amendment in its early cases, the Court reversed itself and found in the Amendment's due process clause a potent source of rights, chiefly, although not exclusively of an economic sort. Under the aegis of the due process clause the Court intervened numerous times to counteract state legislative efforts allegedly incompatible with rights.[23]

The Constitution as read through the lens supplied by the doctrine of substantive due process qualifies as a form of corrective federalism, although much transformed from the earlier Madison and Bingham versions. It belongs

within the broad confines of corrective federalism because it includes the two
chief elements which all corrective federalisms share. First, it is a federalism
in that the states are the chief locus of governance, possessing their powers by
constitutional right and not by congressional sufferance. The Court in the era
of substantive due process was in fact quite protective of state power. Indeed,
this was probably the high point in constitutional history of limitations
imposed on the general government for the sake of federalism. The
constitutionalism of the substantive due process era was, secondly, a corrective
federalism. The Court, an agency of the general government, intervened to
protect rights in the states at the same time that it left most governance to the
states.

The rights-protection function was to be filled by the federal judiciary
because Field Federalism was based on an analysis that identified the problem
of rights in a democracy as more pervasive and intractable than either Madison
or Bingham had. Democratic majorities, it appeared in the late nineteenth
century, were naturally prone to violate property rights, and therefore, it was
not sufficient to look to better national majorities to correct worse state
majorities, as Madison Federalism would entirely and Bingham Federalism
partly would do. Only an agency distant from majorities could be sufficiently
independent to secure rights against the depredation of majorities. The federal
system helped provide such an agency, for the judiciary of the general
government stands farther from, and more independent of all majorities, and
especially of majorities in the states where most governance occurs, than any
other agency of governance in America.

Despite being as unquestionably a form of corrective federalism as the two
earlier versions, the Constitution of substantive due process differed in
significant ways from these earlier versions, differences which ultimately
contributed to the dissolution of this form of corrective federalism and to the
discrediting of federalism itself. Despite being an outgrowth of the earlier
Bingham form of corrective federalism, the new substantive due process
version differs from its predecessor in three important respects. Just as
Bingham's corrective federalism was far more legalistic than Madison's
political federalism in that Bingham attempted to establish a legal rule of
action (the Fourteenth Amendment itself) and a legal agency (courts) in place
of a prudential rule (do justice, secure rights) based on a universal power (the
negative) vested in a political body (the Congress), so due process corrective
federalism is far more legalistic than Bingham's. This can be seen by the
entire dropping out of political agency. On the one hand, the post-Civil War
amendments had provided certain requirements for the political processes

within the states themselves, via the Fifteenth Amendment. Although the Court never repudiated the Fifteenth Amendment to the extent it repudiated the Fourteenth, the Court in its due process phase never sought the means to make the Fifteenth Amendment an effective force in the structuring of state political processes. On the other hand, Bingham's corrective federalism looked to Congress as at least a supplementary agent of correction, and perhaps even as the primary enforcer, on the model of the Civil Rights Act of 1866, and the Civil Rights Act of 1871 (aimed at preventing Ku Klux Klan violence by providing direct federal protection from the Klan). Congressional power under the Fourteenth Amendment was one of the main targets of the Court in its initial reaction against Bingham Federalism, and when the Court moved later to institute its due process federalism, it carefully refrained from restoring the congressional role as envisaged in the earlier version.

A second major difference between Bingham Federalism and Field Federalism lay in the substantiation of the due process clause. Within Field Federalism the due process clause is clearly taken in a substantive sense - it sets substantive limits to what states may do, rather than merely mandating processes that must be followed by states. It is far too large a topic to here explore the legitimacy of this innovation or even whether it was completely novel.[24] It is clear that Field Federalism developed the substantive possibilities of the due process clause far more full-bloodedly than the architects of Bingham Federalism ever contemplated.

The substantiation of due process is closely related to the third important shift: whereas in Bingham Federalism the equal protection clause was parallel in importance and meaning to the due process clause, and had a substantive meaning, in Field Federalism the equal protection clause has little role, and what role it has is formal. The equal protection clause becomes merely a formal test of categorization in the law, rather than a substantive right to legal protection of one's natural rights by the states. The due process vein of corrective federalism, in other words, only responded to one-half of the problem of rights protection as originally conceived within the natural rights philosophy and as embodied in Bingham's corrective federalism. It protected against government as a threat to rights, but lost sight of the need for government to supply protection to rights. Substantive due process corrective federalism took a one-sided and essentially negative stance towards the problem of rights in a federal system. Although popular mythology overestimates the number of times courts intervened to overturn state laws on behalf of rights, nonetheless, the one-sided interpretation of the task of rights-protection lent a sharp edge to the review of state laws.

Courts not only intervened more frequently, but their interventions were heavily concentrated on one class of rights, economic rights, such as liberty of contract, and tended to ignore whole classes of rights which Bingham's version of corrective federalism had been crafted to protect. Despite the fact that substantive due process constitutionalism saw the beginnings of incorporation, the Court under the sway of Field Federalism showed no particular care for the rights of blacks in the states, nor for the rights enumerated in the Bill of Rights, both of which had been central to Bingham Federalism.

Field Federalism came to a resounding, crashing demise with the New Deal Court crisis. In that moment both elements of corrective federalism came under suspicion, in large part because of the three modifications Field Federalism worked in the earlier Madison and Bingham versions. From Madison's point of view Bingham Federalism had already taken a dangerous turn by relying so heavily on courts. Madison sought a "wholly republican solution to the problem of republicanism," and for him this meant reliance on institutions which operate according to the principle of majority rule and responsibility to the public. It was not a mere accident that had Madison rely on Congress as the agent of his corrective federalism. He meant to control bad or unjust majorities in one arena with better and more just majorities in another. He did not consider it legitimate or advisable to rely instead on a "will independent of society," as he put it in *Federalist* 51. But the reliance on courts was precisely that, and so it was perceived when the Court more and more came to be seen as a counter-majoritarian institution. The role of courts in the corrective federalism of the original Constitution and even in Bingham Federalism was not so much a problem because corrective federalism was relatively limited and narrow in those two versions. With the expansion of rights protection under Field Federalism and the focus on economic rights at the very moment when the political branches were attempting to get the economy more in hand, the court as a "will independent of society" came to be far more intolerable within the democratic polity.

"The switch in time" and the subsequent dissolution of the old jurisprudence left little of corrective federalism standing: the Court was an undemocratic institution illegitimately attempting to resist the will of the people and the common good; and both rights and federalism were held to be masks for economic interests and barriers to needed public policies. With the triumph of the Roosevelt Court, corrective federalism once again went into eclipse.

Hamilton's Corrective Federalism

Like a Cartesian doll, corrective federalism has amazing powers to bounce back, for within a very short period of time the Supreme Court once again began to restore a version of corrective federalism. This kind of federalism reached maturity with the Warren Court, and remains the constitutional dispensation under which we live. This version is quite different from all the others, however, so different that it is no longer clear it deserves the name of federalism, corrective or otherwise.

Although the three earlier types of corrective federalism we have considered differed considerably from each other, all remain within the general domain of Madison's original scheme for using federalism as a means to secure rights. That can no longer be said of our current "federalism," for the theory of it is best captured not by Madison but by his sometime collaborator and sometime nemesis, Alexander Hamilton. At the Constitutional Convention, Hamilton broke his long silence with a daylong speech outlining an alternative plan for a constitution to that developed by Madison. Despite his later collaboration with Madison in explaining and defending the new Constitution in *The Federalist*, Hamilton announced himself "unfriendly" to Madison's original plan from which the Constitution was developed. He was "unfriendly" to Madison's scheme, because, novel as it was, it remained a form of federalism. He was "fully convinced, that no amendment of the Confederation, leaving the states in possession of their sovereignty could possibly answer the purpose." Instead of federalism of any sort, Hamilton preferred a system that would vest "a complete sovereignty in the general government."[25]

Nonetheless, in order not "to shock public opinion" too much, Hamilton proposed a scheme embodying some degree of federalism, but it was a far cry from the federalism of the Constitution, or, arguably, from a genuine federalism of any sort. It was clearly an adaptation of Madison's scheme, but it moved Madison's scheme decidedly in the direction of a simply nationalist or unified system. With regard to the theories of corrective federalism, two Hamiltonian modifications are especially worthy of note. Hamilton's plan remains arguably federalist, because it retains the states as quasi-independent entities engaging in governance not undertaken by the general government. It is, Hamilton insisted, still a version of a "society of societies." Madison's proposal and the final Constitution both divide powers between the two levels of government, therefore making the general government a body possessing specifically delegated powers, but Hamilton would instead vest "the legislature of the United States with power to pass all laws whatsoever."[26]   Hamilton Federalism, then, would have no room for anything like constitutionally reserved powers of the states. Whatever powers the states exercise are those the general government leaves to them. Conversely, federalism would imply no limitation on the power of the general government, unlike all the forms of corrective federalism we have thus far noted. Hamilton Federalism is thus barely a form of federalism at all.

The difference from Madison Federalism also stands forth in regard to the corrective aspects of corrective federalism. Hamilton borrowed from Madison the idea of a negative on the laws of the states, but he would place that power not in Congress, but in the governors of each state, themselves appointed by the life tenured executive head of the general government.[27]   Hamilton's modification of Madison's idea would help overcome one of the great objections to Madison's version of corrective federalism; it appeared hopelessly complex and time-consuming to have Congress review all the laws of all the states. Each governor could surely do this better for his own state than Congress could for all the states. The negative power so vested would undoubtedly be used more frequently and more effectively.

Although some of the details are different, Hamilton's model of corrective federalism describes quite well the late twentieth century Constitution. In effect Congress exercises and the Court accepts the sort of legislative power Hamilton wished to give it. This is the operational truth, if not the explicit doctrine of the modern Constitution. Limitations on the powers of Congress deriving from the Bill of Rights and the separation of powers are still recognized, but limitations deriving from federalism or from a theory of non-delegated powers are not. To support such a claim one need merely recite the names of some of the most important cases of the past half-century: *NLRB v. Jones and Laughlin, Steward Machine Co. v. Davis, Heart of Atlanta Motel v. U.S., Jones v. Mayer, Garcia v. San Antonio Metropolitan Transit Authority, South Dakota v. Dole* to name just a few.[28]

The corrective part of the contemporary Constitution again differs in details but bears a striking resemblance to Hamilton Federalism. Not appointed governors of the states, but the federal judiciary exercises the corrective power. As we have already noticed, the judiciary shares with Hamilton's appointive governors the quality of being "a will independent of society." Our Hamilton Federalism thus shares this important feature with Field Federalism, but the courts today are not nearly so limited in the array of rights on behalf of which they intervene as the corrective agencies within either Bingham or Field Federalism. Like Hamilton's governors who have a discretionary negative, the judiciary acts on behalf of an expansive and rather indefinite table of rights. It is the combination of effectively plenary congressional power, corrective supervision via a will independent of society, and an indefinite authorization of the corrective agency that makes our present arrangement so like Hamilton's and so unlike the other three versions of corrective federalism. It is the combination of these three features that produces doubts both about the federal character of the system and about whether it continues to satisfy Madison's criterion of a wholly "republican remedy for the diseases most incident to republican government."

In closing, let us contrast briefly the model of authentic corrective federalism with the more standard model of federalism, dual federalism. The latter theory of federalism takes its bearings from the division of objects and powers between the state and general governments and from the separateness and equality of the two strata of government thereafter. The theory of dual federalism surely captures part of historic American federalism, but it fails to seize on those aspects of the federal system that the corrective federalism model highlights. In particular, the dual federalist model fails to see how federalism has been conceived as a contribution to the solution of the problem of rights-protection in the American order. So far as dual federalism dominated thinking about federalism, the latter's potential with regard to rights has been unrealized. So far as dual federalism has given way in America to something much closer to the unitary or consolidated system Madison, Bingham, and the others tried to avoid, we fail to realize the goods that federalism could bring - and, under corrective federalism, could bring without sacrifice of rights.

NOTES

1.   Grant McConnell, *Private Power and American Democracy*, Martin Diamond, *"The Federalist*'s View of Federalism" in George Benson, *et. al.*, eds. *Essays in Federalism* (1961); "What the Framers Meant by Federalism," in Robert Golden, ed., *A Nation of States: Essays in the Federal System* (Chicago, 1974); "The Federalist on Federalism: Neither a National nor a Federal Constitution, but a Composite of Both," *Yale Law Journal*, (1977).

2.   Elazar, *Exploring Federalism*, pp. 143-144.

3.   Elazar, *Exploring Federalism*.

4.   James Madison, "Preface to Delegates in the Convention of 1787" in *The Records of the Federal Convention of 1787*, Max Farrand ed, (New Haven, 1966) vol. 3, p. 539; *Federalist* 37.

5.   Montesquieu, *Spirit of the Laws*,vol. 9, pp. 1-3.

6.   For additional discussion, see Michael P. Zuckert, "A System without Precedent: Federalism in the American Constitution," in Leonard Levy and Dennis Mahoney, eds. *The Framing and Ratification of the Constitution* (New York, 1987), pp. 133-137.

7.   A good presentation of the ends of American federalism in terms of traditional federal purposes is Randolph's speech introducing the Virginia Plan at the Constitutional Convention. For discussion, see Michael P. Zuckert, "Federalism and the Founding," *Review of Politics*, 48 (Spring 1986), pp. 174-177.

8.   See Zuckert, "Federalism," pp. 180-182; Vincent Ostrom, *The Meaning of Federalism* (San Francisco, 1991), p. 23.

9.   Testimony to the widespread agreement on the natural rights philosophy at the time of the emergence of the new federalism can be garnered from the appeal made by both Federalists and Anti-Federalists to it, see Brutus II, Storing, *The Anti-Federalist*, p. 117; *Federalist* Nos. 39, 40.

10.   Cf. Elazar, *Exploring Federalism*; Michael Zuckert, "System without Precedent," pp. 149-50.

11.   Cf. Hobbes, *Leviathan*, chaps. 18, 26; Jean Hampton, "Democracy and the Rule of Law;" and Michael Zuckert, "Hobbes, Locke, and the Problem of the Rule of Law," forthcoming in Ian Shapiro, ed., *Nomos*, (1993).

12.   Madison to Jefferson, Oct. 24, 1787, *Papers*, vol. 9, p. 208.

13.   *Papers*, Madison, "Preface," p. 539.

14.   For a discussion of the reasons behind this commitment to a wholly republican solution, see Michael Zuckert, "The Virtuous Polity, the Responsible Polity: Freedom and Responsibility in *The Federalist*," *Publius: The Journal of Federalism*, 22 (Winter 1992).

15.   Speeches of June 21 and June 30 in Madison, *Notes*, pp. 356-7; 499-500.

16.   Madison to Jefferson, Oct. 24, 1787, p. 208.

17.   Madison to Washington, April 16, 1787, *Papers*, vol. 9, p. 83.

18.   *Congressional Globe*, 42nd Congress, 1st session H.R., pp. 84-85.

19.   Robert Nozick, *Anarchy, State, and Utopia* (New York, 1974).

20.   For fuller discussion, see Michael P. Zuckert, "Completing the Constitution: The Fourteenth Amendment," *Publius: The Journal of Federalism*, 22 (Spring 1992): 69-92.

21.   *Barron v. Baltimore*, 32 U.S. 243 (1838).

22.   For fuller discussion, see Michael P. Zuckert, "Congressional Power under the Fourteenth Amendment," *Constitutional Commentary*, (Winter 1986): 123-56.

23.   See John P. Semonche, *Charting the Future: The Supreme Court Responds to a Changing Society, 1890-1920* (Westport: Greenwood Press, 1975).

24.   See Samuel Krislov, "Property as a Constitutional Right in the Nineteenth Century" *Publius: The Journal of Federalism*, 22 (Spring 1992): 47-68.

25.   Speech of June 18, 1787, Madison, *Notes*.

26.   Madison, *Notes*.

27.   Madison, *Notes*.

28.   *NLRB v. Jones and Laughlin Steel Corp*, 301 U.S. 1 (1937); *Steward Machine Co. v. Davis*, 301 U.S. 548 (1937); *U.S. v. Darby*, 312 U.S. 100 (1941); *Heart of Atlanta Motel v. U.S.*, 379 U.S. 241 (1964); *Jones v. Mayer*, 392 U.S. 409 (1968); *Garcia v. San Antonio Metropolitan Transit Authority*, 469 U.S. 528 (1985); *South Dakota v. Dole*, 483 U.S. 107 (1987).

CHAPTER 6

FEDERALISM AND THE PROTECTION OF INDIVIDUAL RIGHTS: THE AMERICAN STATE CONSTITUTIONAL PERSPECTIVE

Dorothy Toth Beasley[*]

In the American constitutional system, who decides about individual rights? The immediate response for many would be the United States Supreme Court, interpreting the federal Bill of Rights. Yet this answer is inadequate. It ignores the fact that for most of the nation's history, the federal Bill of Rights did not apply to actions by the state governments.[1] Indeed, only in the latter half of this century, by and large, has the Supreme Court "selectively incorporated" the provisions of the Bill of Rights and applied them to the actions of state governments.[2] It also ignores the fact that the United States is a federal system, with both state and federal constitutions and with state as well as federal bills of rights.

I wish to acknowledge the generous assistance of Professor Robert F. Williams and others in the preparation of this paper and of Anne Peters and Dorothy Coffey in the word processing of it.

This chapter analyzes the important role that state bills of rights have played and continue to play in safeguarding individual rights. It also explores the complexities of a system of dual constitutional protections, documenting the shifting division of responsibility between state and federal courts and explaining the rationale for this dual system. Finally, looking in particular at state guarantees of privacy, it demonstrates the contributions that state bills of rights have made to the protection of individual rights.

STATE CONSTITUTIONAL PROTECTIONS

Express constitutional protections of rights made their first appearance in the bills or declarations of rights found in the constitutions adopted by the various states following independence. These first state constitutions often placed the bills or declarations of rights at the *beginning* of the constitution. This indicated that rights protections were foremost in the minds of the Revolutionary state constitution drafters and were seen as necessary to establish before a government was constituted.[3] Actually, though, the main controversies surrounding the first state constitutions did not have to do as much with written *rights* protections as with questions about the *structure* of government, and who would *participate* in the exercise of governmental power through office holding, voting, and other matters.[4] It was, however, the state constitutional rights protections that received the most attention in Europe during the period prior to the adoption of the federal Bill of Rights.[5]

These declarations of rights also were important in the creation of the federal Bill of Rights. When people in the states were considering the new proposed federal Constitution in the 1787-1789 ratification conventions, one of the most important criticisms made by the Anti-Federalists was that the federal Constitution did not contain a bill of rights. Because of their experience with the state constitutions during the "founding decade" prior to the adoption of the federal Constitution, it simply stood to reason that any "real" constitution would have a bill of rights.[6] The Federalists, on the other hand, argued that a bill of rights was not necessary because the new federal government was restricted to certain narrow, enumerated powers and the state constitutions were in place to protect citizens' rights. Ultimately a compromise was reached, and James Madison and others agreed to prepare a bill of rights during the first meeting of Congress under the new federal Constitution. Madison relied on the rights that were already provided for in the state constitutions, together with amendments that had been suggested by the state ratifying conventions.[7]

This historical account might suggest a basic uniformity of constitutional guarantees. While there are certainly similarities between federal and state bills of rights, state bills of rights differ significantly from their federal counterpart -and from each other. For one thing, not all states immediately adopted bills of rights. For another, the contents of state bills of rights have changed over time. The experience of my own state of Georgia illustrates how the independent development of state bills of rights is governed by the perception of the people of the state, and particularly the drafters at each stage at which change is made towards their own state government.

Georgia's first constitution preceded the U. S. Constitution by more than a decade, the state had a temporary constitution in 1776 and new constitutions in 1777, 1789, and 1798. Yet none of these constitutions included a bill of rights. The constitution of 1789 was amended in 1795 to state that "all powers not delegated by the constitution as amended, are retained by the people." That constitution also secured, in the body of the constitution, the right to vote; the right to civil trial in the defendant's county and criminal trial where the crime was committed; freedom of press and the right to trial by jury; the right to the writ of *habeas corpus*; free exercise of religion and prohibition of forced support of other religions; prohibition of entail of estates; and distribution of an intestate's estate so as to protect wife and children.

This "retained powers" provision was omitted in the constitution of 1798, but when the bill of rights was added in 1861, it concluded with a broad substitute which remains today: "The enumeration of rights herein contained shall not be construed to deny to the people any inherent rights which they have hitherto enjoyed." That first bill of rights in 1861 was denominated a "declaration of fundamental principles" and included rights existing in the federal Constitution, which was thought to no longer govern in the states which, like Georgia, had seceded from the union. So it has freedom of religion, of speech, of the press, of the right to assemble, of the right to bear arms, of the right to be secure against unreasonable searches and seizures, of the right to a speedy jury trial in criminal cases, and others which are in the U. S. Bill of Rights.

Georgia's present bill of rights, which forms Article I of the constitution of 1983, includes twenty-eight paragraphs devoted to the rights of persons, nine to the origin and structure of government, and three to "general provisions." Illustrative of the broader protection than is given in the U. S. Bill of Rights is provision not only for freedom of religion but also for freedom of conscience. The Georgia bill of rights protects not only against cruel and unusual punishment but also against abuse "in being arrested, while under arrest, or in prison." Government is given an affirmative duty with a specific standard: "Protection to person and property is the paramount duty of government and shall be impartial and complete." For the first time in 1983, equal protection was expressly incorporated: "No person shall be denied the equal protection of the laws."

LEGAL COMPLEXITIES OF DUAL CONSTITUTIONALISM

The American system of dual constitutionalism and dual guarantees of rights requires that a balance be struck regarding "who decides." The basic legal principles governing this jurisdictional balance are clear, but their application is both complex and controversial.

Legal Principles

The fifty-one supreme courts in the United States are the authoritative exponents of the constitutions under which they were established, reversible only by constitutional amendment. Thus the United States Supreme Court has the final say on what the United States Bill of Rights means in a given context. Similarly, the supreme courts of the fifty states have the final say on what their respective bills of rights mean. This means that if a state court rules that the state constitution protects an individual, then it is moot whether the federal constitution does so or not.[8] If a state court does not recognize a state constitutional claim, then the U. S. Constitution represents the last hope for the litigant.

Although the U. S. Supreme Court need not concern itself with construing state constitutions, state supreme courts frequently address federal constitutional questions when litigants challenge governmental actions under both federal and state constitutions. When the U. S. Supreme Court has already ruled on the issue, the responsibility of the state court is to follow the authoritative precedents. When the Supreme Court has not ruled on the issue, however, state courts must give their best interpretation of the federal provision.[9] Conceivably, the Supreme Court may be influenced by the state court's interpretation when it ultimately addresses the issue.

The more controversial legal issue involves the influence that U. S. Supreme Court rulings should have on state court interpretation of state constitutions. Because state provisions may resemble those in the federal Constitution, there may be some assumption that they should be similarly construed, that state courts should follow the Supreme Court's interpretation.[10]

This, however, conflicts with the notion that state courts are the authoritative interpreters of their state constitutions. A state may see its constitution's protection of rights as overlapping; or identical to; or independent, separate, and distinct from; or greater than; or lesser than the protections enshrined in the federal Constitution. Of course, if the state's protection is lesser, the state court must still enforce the greater federal protection.

The U. S. Supreme Court has repeatedly held that nothing in the federal Constitution precludes a state from adopting in its own constitution individual liberties more expansive than those conferred by the U. S. Constitution, or state courts from interpreting even identical language more expansively. In *City of Mesquite v. Aladdin's Castle*,[11] for example, the Court stated that "a state court is entirely free to read its own State's constitution more broadly than this Court reads the Federal Constitution, or to reject the mode of analysis used by this Court in favor of a different analysis of its corresponding constitutional guarantee."[12] In *Pruneyard Shopping Center v. Robbins*,[13] the Court held that the California Supreme Court's decision recognizing a right of solicitors for signatures on a petition, to exercise their state constitution-protected rights of expression (speech) on the shopping center premises did not violate Fifth or Fourteenth Amendment property rights of the center's owners nor their First Amendment free speech rights. Here is an example of state constitutional rights, broadly construed by the state Court, being held by the federal Court not to offend others' federal constitutional rights. Even earlier, in *Oregon v. Hass*,[14] the Court held: "A state is free as a matter of its own law to impose greater restrictions on police activity than those this [the supreme] court hold to be necessary upon federal constitutional standards." And earlier still, in *Cooper v. California*:[15] "The state has power to impose higher standards on searches and seizures than required by the federal constitution if it chooses to do so."

Applying the Principles

Though these principles may be clear in theory, they are difficult to apply, and their application has produced tensions between state supreme courts and the U. S. Supreme Court. *Michigan v. Long*,[16] a state case involving search and seizure, illustrates these difficulties, as well as the changing orientation of the Supreme Court toward state judicial rulings.

When *Michigan v. Long* came before the U. S. Supreme Court on appeal, the first question confronting the justices was jurisdictional, *i.e.*, was there a federal question? The justices examined the state supreme court opinion, which was somewhat unclear as to whether it was based on state or federal constitutional law, to ascertain if the state court decided a federal question which should be reviewed. They concluded that the only way to be sure that the issue was *not* decided on a state constitutional basis, over which the U. S. Supreme Court would have no jurisdiction, was to see if it indicated "clearly and expressly that it is alternatively based on bona fide separate, adequate, and independent grounds."[17] The Court decided that it *had* jurisdiction to decide the case, on Fourth Amendment grounds, because of "the absence of a plain statement [by the state supreme court] that the decision below rested on an adequate and independent state ground."[18]

The Court acknowledged that previously it had not been consistent. Sometimes it dismissed a case if it was not clear whether the ground for the state court decision was state or federal. Sometimes it vacated or continued a case to get clarification about the state court decision. Sometimes it examined state law to determine the decision's basis. Thus, *Long's* new rule requiring clear exposition of the basis for decisions, seemed likely to help intercourt relationships operate more smoothly.

Not everyone agreed with this new approach, however. Justice John Paul Stevens published a lengthy dissent in *Long*, contending that the relationship between state and federal courts was more important than the search and seizure question. He argued that the "need for uniformity in federal law" referred to by the majority in finding jurisdiction, "is truly an ungovernable engine. That same need is no less present when it is perfectly clear that a state ground is both independent and adequate."[19] He urged the Court to be more charitable in construing state decisions as resting on state grounds.

Justice Stevens repeated his concerns a year later, in his concurring opinion in *Massachusetts v. Upton*,[20] another search and seizure case. He chastised the Supreme Judicial Court of Massachusetts for resting its decision on the federal Fourth Amendment without saying whether the warrant was valid under Massachusetts law. This, he wrote, was "an error of a more fundamental character than the one this court corrects today."[21] He pointed out the results of error were to increase the burdens of the Massachusetts high court as well as that of the U. S. Supreme Court. The state high court's burdens were increased because, following the U. S. Supreme Court's ruling that the search and seizure did not violate the federal constitution, the state high court would have to again decide the issue, albeit under the state constitution, on remand. If the search and seizure *did* violate the state constitution, "much of that court's first opinion and all of this court's opinion are for naught."[22] If there was not a state constitutional violation, then the second proceeding, on remand, would have been unnecessary. He quoted the Oregon Supreme Court for what *should* have happened:

> The proper sequence is to analyze the state's law, including its constitutional law, before reaching a federal constitutional claim. This is required, not for the sake either of parochialism or of style, but because the state does not deny any right claimed under the federal Constitution when the claim before the court in fact is fully met by state law. *Sterling v. Cupp*, 290 Ore. 611, 614, 625 P2d 123, 126 (1981).[23]

Sure enough, upon remand of *Upton*, the Supreme Judicial Court of Massachusetts, considering its statute on search warrant affidavits and its state constitutional Declaration of Rights (Article 14), rejected the "totality of the circumstances" rule of the Fourth Amendment, as fashioned by the U. S. Supreme Court in *Illinois v. Gates*.[24] Instead, it adopted for its state constitution an earlier standard which had been created by the U. S. Supreme Court for the Fourth Amendment and subsequently abandoned: The more restrictive *Aguilar-Spinelli* standard (the two-prong "basis of knowledge" and "veracity" tests).[25]

In examining its own state constitutional provision and its origin and case law history, the Massachusetts court noted that "the Constitution of the Commonwealth preceded and is independent of the Constitution of the United States. In fact, portions of the Constitution of the United States are based on provisions in the Constitution of the Commonwealth, and this has been thought to be particularly true of the relationship between the Fourth Amendment and Article 14."[26] It concluded that Article 14 was more protective of criminal defendants than was the Fourth Amendment.[27] Applying the stricter test to the search warrant affidavit in this case, it concluded that it did not demonstrate probable cause, and further, that under the state constitution the mobile home did not fit within the automobile exception to the warrant requirement. It reversed Upton's conviction and sent the case back for a new trial because there was other evidence to support a conviction.

The Massachusetts experience is not unique. A similar problem occurred in Oregon's *Kennedy* case, referred to earlier, which preceded by a year *Sterling v. Cupp*'s determination that the Oregon Court should turn to the federal Constitution only after having resolved state law issues. The Oregon Court of Appeals had not followed this procedure in deciding *Kennedy*,[28] and that error is what led to the U. S. Supreme Court case of *Oregon v. Kennedy*.

The trial court in *Kennedy* had declared a mistrial after the prosecutor asked a witness whether he had ever done business with the Kennedys, and when the witness replied that he had not, the prosecutor asked, "Is that because he is a crook?" On retrial, Kennedy's double jeopardy plea was rejected and he was convicted. The Court of Appeals of Oregon agreed with Kennedy. Applying the federal constitutional test of prosecutorial overreaching developed by the Supreme Court in *United States v. Jorn*,[29] it concluded that the prosecutor's question was "flagrant overreaching."

After the Supreme Court of Oregon refused to review the case, the State of Oregon asked the U. S. Supreme Court to review the federal constitutional question. That court rejected Kennedy's contention that the decision was based on the *state* constitution, examined federal constitutional law, concluded that the Court of Appeals of Oregon had misinterpreted the breadth of the federal double jeopardy clause, and remanded the case for further proceedings.

The state constitutional ground, which had been there all along, was finally ruled on by the Court of Appeals, which concluded that "with respect to the precise and narrow issue under consideration, both constitutions embody the same standard."[30] Thus it held that a second trial of Kennedy did not violate the state's prohibition against double jeopardy.

On appeal, the Supreme Court of Oregon found that its own constitution was not violated, *not* for the reason the Court of Appeals erroneously used but because an independent review of the state constitution led to that conclusion.[31] The Court of Appeals had based its interpretation of the state constitution on the U. S. Supreme Court's interpretation of the Fifth Amendment.[32]

The delay, expense, extended lack of finality of a simple theft case, the involvement of the chronically overburdened U. S. Supreme Court, and the unnecessary articulation of a federal constitutional standard could all have been avoided if the state appellate court had followed a fundamental principle of federalism. Had the Oregon courts decided the question on the basis of state constitutional law to begin with, as Justice Stevens pointed out in *Upton*, the U. S. Supreme Court would in all likelihood not have taken the case *even if* the federal ground was *also* ruled on by the Oregon courts, because it has a policy of avoiding the unnecessary adjudication of federal constitutional questions.[33]

THE ADVANTAGES OF DUAL PROTECTIONS OF RIGHTS

One might well wonder what value there is in struggling with these complexities. Why retain the cumbersome and confusing distinctions between the two constitutions and clear lines of constitutional authority in a federal system? Why not just have one bill of rights or co-extensive bills of rights? Studies of dual guarantees of rights suggest that there are benefits that make the costs worth bearing.

1. The states are comprised of differing populations and ethnic groupings, which bring a diversity of views and different cultures into the fabric of each. The states have differing styles of government and are able to offer different qualities of life. A dual system of constitutional protections allows flexibility for states to accommodate these distinctions, which are related to the size of the country and heterogeneity of its population and environments.

2. The states and their individual constitutions have differing histories, as illustrated by the Massachusetts Supreme Judicial Court when it finally decided the state constitutional question in Upton's case. Georgia's volatile constitutional history, through ten constitutions and an evolution of express rights arising from different concerns, also is illustrative. Eighteen states have ratified new constitutions during the twentieth century, ten since 1960.[34] Another aspect of history is that the original states created the union and the federal Bill of Rights; state constitutional bills of rights did not arise from a national constituency.

3. Dual bills of rights allow for experiment and creativity on the state level, where they can be laboratories for weaving common law and case law with constitutional law, advancing by trial and error, subject to easier amendment. As Justice Brandeis succinctly approved, in a dissent in *New State Ice Co. v. Liebmann*:[35] "It is one of the happy incidents of the federal system that a single courageous state may, if its citizens choose, serve as a laboratory; and try novel social and economic experiments without risk to the rest of the country."

This aspect of federalism was recognized more recently by Justice O'Connor in a concurring opinion in the right-to-die case of *Cruzan v. Missouri*.[36] At issue was the constitutionality of the state's procedures for exercising a desire not to maintain life in certain circumstances. The Court held, five-to-four, that the state requirement that the incompetent's wishes as to withdrawal of life-sustaining treatment be proved by clear and convincing evidence was not violative of Fourteenth Amendment due process. Justice O'Connor wrote:

> As is evident from the court's survey of state court decisions,....no national consensus has yet emerged on the best solution for this difficult and sensitive problem. Today we decide only that one State's practice does not violate the Constitution; the more challenging task of crafting appropriate procedures for safeguarding incompetents' liberty interests [in appropriate handling of the life versus death question for incompetents] is entrusted to the "laboratory" of the states,[37]

citing Brandeis' famous dissent.

The men who met in Philadelphia to adopt a new constitution in 1787 made the job of amending the U. S. Constitution very difficult, and deliberately so. On the other hand, Georgia, for example, passed thirty-two amendments to its 1983 Constitution, as of the 1990 election; amendments allowing a state lottery and the appointment rather than election of the state school superintendent were passed in 1992. The people of Georgia can amend their constitution by a majority of voters favoring of a proposal which originates in either the General Assembly or by constitutional convention and passes that body by a two-thirds vote of its members.[38]

4. A system of dual constitutions allows a "wider wisdom" to be brought to bear on the development of individual rights. With respect to construing the United States Constitution, the U. S. Supreme Court can call upon not only the written views of state courts as to its meaning but also as to the meaning of similar provisions in their respective state constitutions. In a two-way vertical dialogue, the state supreme courts can likewise learn from the written views of the U. S. Supreme Court on the federal Constitution, when considering their own constitutions, although they are not *bound* to. The "wider wisdom" is enhanced by the fifty-by-fifty-way dialogue horizontally as well. States can look to other states for persuasive reasoning when construing their own constitutions.[39]

5. State bills of rights impose a more immediate local responsibility and local authority on courts which are closer to the people. They contribute to the shared responsibility of governing the huge nation. They impose separate responsibilities on government, at a lower level. They provide for a greater degree of democracy and at the same time greater manageability. The people have a more direct influence on the content and meaning of their state constitutions than on their U. S. Constitution: content can be changed more easily and quickly on a state level. Meaning is given to the state constitutions by judges often elected by the people for specified terms or at least appointed by a more local official than the President of the United States, whereas ultimate meaning is given to the U. S. Constitution by judges who are appointed for life by a President, with the advice and consent of the Senate.[40] Thus, rather than leave the ultimate protection of individual rights to nine elite jurists appointed by a national political process for life, the ultimate protection is dispersed and shared with several hundred jurists who are selected in more local, diverse political processes for state supreme courts.

6. Dual bills of rights constitute a check and balance on the protection of individual rights. They keep each government from infringing too much on

individual rights. Two sets of judges operate independently of each other except for the U. S. Supreme Court, and *it* does not have to be involved if the *state* set of judges provide relief on state grounds. The federal standard will always be a country-wide minimum, a national constitutional standard,[41] crafted to affect diverse and far-flung peoples. A state constitution can provide more; yet, where it provides a lesser degree of protection, the federal Bill of Rights can rescue the individual.

7. Dual bills of rights serve the goals of expediency and finality in the dispute resolution process, without requiring resort to the U. S. Constitution and the federal judiciary.[42] A proper approach to the hierarchy of laws will achieve finality more quickly and at less cost.

8. Developing state constitutional law is a *principled* practice of federalism, necessary to maintain the integrity of a dual system of government.

STATE CONSTITUTIONAL INTERPRETATION: THE RIGHT TO PRIVACY

Despite the advantages of a system of dual protections for rights, the incorporation of most provisions of the federal Bill of Rights during the twentieth century turned the attention of lawyers, scholars, and judges away from state bills of rights. When state bills of rights were rediscovered in the early 1970s, concern was expressed that there was no basis for the development of a distinctive body of state civil liberties law. Indeed, this objection is heard even today.[43] To see whether this objection has validity, let us examine the personal right to privacy, as developed in state constitutional law.

First, how can this right be described? The Georgia Supreme Court first defined this right in *Pavesich v. New England Life Ins. Co.*,[44] where it was recognized as the basis for a common law tort claim involving an invasion of privacy by another person, rather than an incursion by government. Pavesich sued the insurance company and a photographer, claiming that they had violated his right to privacy by publishing in a newspaper his picture and his "testimony" for the life insurance. In fact, Pavesich had never consented to the picture or the testimony, never had said such words, and had no such life insurance.

The Georgia court first established that the law recognized, within proper limits, a legal right to privacy. It then concluded that publication of one's picture by another, without one's consent, for the purpose of increasing the profits of the advertiser, invaded that right. It said:

> The right of privacy, or the right of the individual to be let alone, is a personal right,
> which is not without judicial recognition. It is the complement of the right to the
> immunity of one's person. The individual has always been entitled to be protected
> in the exclusive use and enjoyment of that which is his own. The common law
> regarded his person and property as inviolate, and he has the absolute right to be let
> alone. Cooley, *Torts*, p. 29.[45]

In saying this, the court was quoting from a dissenting opinion in *Roberson v. Rochester Folding Box Co*,[46] a New York supreme court case in which a plaintiff had unsuccessfully advanced a privacy claim. The Georgia Supreme Court endorsed the theory of the dissenting justice, making it the first state supreme court to recognize such a common law right.

Second, where is the right to privacy articulated in the U. S. Constitution and state constitutions? The right to privacy is not expressly stated in the U. S. Constitution. In *Griswold v. Connecticut*,[47] Justice Douglas, speaking for the Court, found a concern for privacy underlying various provisions of the Bill of Rights. As he put it, "specific guarantees in the bill of rights have penumbras, formed by emanations from those guarantees that help give them life and substance."[48] Other justices, however, had different bases for the right to privacy, and some have denied that a federal constitutional right to privacy exists. In *Griswold*, for example, three justices found a right to privacy in the Ninth Amendment, and two justices rejected claims of a right to privacy. The controversy over the source and scope of the federal constitutional right to privacy, initiated in *Griswold*, has continued to the present day.

Many state constitutions, in contrast, offer more explicit constitutional protection. Between 1968 and 1990, seven states - Hawaii (twice), Illinois, South Carolina, Louisiana, California, Montana, and Alaska (for a second time) - amended their constitutions to include a right to privacy.[49] In doing so, they joined Florida, Washington, and Arizona, which had already included privacy protections in their constitutions. Courts in other states have also found constitutional language supporting a right to privacy. For example, although the Georgia Supreme Court in *Pavesich* relied on the due process clauses of the state and federal constitutions,[50] it could also have looked to the last provision of the Georgia Bill of Rights: "The enumeration of rights herein contained as a part of this constitution shall not be construed to deny to the people any inherent rights which they may have hitherto enjoyed."[51]

Interpretation of the Right to Privacy: Florida

The experience in Florida reveals how states can develop their own body of constitutional law. In 1980 the Florida constitution was amended to provide:

> Right to privacy - Every natural person has the right to be let alone and free from governmental intrusion into his private life except as otherwise provided herein. This section shall not be construed to limit the public's right of access to public records and meetings as provided by law.[52]

In 1989 the Florida Supreme Court had occasion to apply this provision in the case of *In re T. W.*[53] The plurality applied the strict scrutiny standard to the state statute, as a *state* standard. The challenged state statute required pregnant minors to obtain parental consent or judicial approval for an abortion. The court found that the state's interest in preserving fetal life did not become "compelling" until the fetus developed to viability. It further held that the state had not chosen the least restrictive means for achieving its objectives of protecting minors and preserving the unity of families.

In reaching its decision, the court stated: "The [Florida privacy] amendment embraces more privacy interests, and extends more protection to the individual in those interests, than does the federal constitution."[54] The court resolved the case and precluded a federal question by stating, in compliance with *Michigan v. Long*, that since it held that the state statute conflicted with the state constitution, "no further analysis under the federal law is required. We expressly decide this case on state law grounds and cite federal precedent only to the extent that it illuminates Florida law."[55] (This case is a model of how to do state constitutional law when confronted with claims under both state and federal constitutions.)[56]

Planned Parenthood of Southeastern Pennsylvania v. Casey[57] highlights the differences between privacy rights under state and federal constitutions. In *Casey* the U. S. Supreme Court let stand a parental consent requirement very similar to that invalidated in *In re T. W.* Moreover, whereas the Florida Court required a compelling state interest for restrictions on privacy rights, three justices in *Casey* chose an "undue burden" standard, four justices chose the "rational relation" standard enunciated in *Webster v. Reproductive Health Services*,[58] and two justices adhered to the "strict scrutiny" standard announced in *Roe v. Wade*.[59] Independent state constitutional law analysis and application led to a quite different understanding of privacy rights.

Contrast this development with the Florida case of *State v. Jimeno*.[60] In that case the Florida privacy provision had to yield to an express 1982 amendment to the Florida constitution, which required the Florida Court to construe search and seizure issues in conformity with rulings of the U. S. Supreme Court.[61] The state issue was thereby merged with the federal and was no longer open to independent analysis.

The Florida Court had *first* held that Jimeno's consent to a search of his vehicle did not extend to a closed brown paper bag. The U. S. Supreme Court said it did, as a general consent, thus disagreeing with the Supreme Court of Florida about the extent of the Fourth Amendment right against unreasonable search and seizure. The U. S. Supreme Court held that the police did not have to ask separate permission to search the container.

"Reasonableness" is the touchstone of the constitutional interpretation by the courts, and here in *Florida v. Jimeno* we find that reasonable men and women will differ as to what is reasonable.[62] The two dissenters on the U. S. Supreme Court focused on "an individual['s]...heightened expectation of privacy in the contents of a closed container."[63]

When the case was remanded to the Florida Supreme Court for further proceedings, it ruled as did the U. S. Supreme Court with respect to its state constitution.[64] It had to, because when the people of Florida amended their state constitution in 1982 to incorporate the federal exclusionary rule of *Weeks v. United States*[65] into their state constitution, they abdicated state responsibility for individually protecting the privacy rights against unreasonable searches and seizures.[66] As the Florida Court noted in *Bernie v. State*,[67] the amendment brought "the state's search and seizure laws into conformity with all decisions of the U. S. Supreme Court rendered before and subsequent to the adoption of that amendment." Even the explicit constitutional right to privacy did not modify the later-adopted search and seizure requirement of deference to federal construction.

Nevertheless, "privacy" is a generic right, and its inclusion in the Florida constitution has spawned claims in areas perhaps not contemplated by those who adopted the amendment. *In re Guardianship of Estelle M. Browning, State of Fla. v. Herbert*[68] is a case in point. The Florida Supreme Court held in that case that the right to privacy embraced a proxy or surrogate's decision, without prior judicial approval, to remove feeding tubes and life support systems from an incompetent person if, while competent, the person had expressed these wishes orally or in writing.[69]

The Florida Court also recognized the right to privacy, as well as to the free exercise of religion, in *Public Health Trust of Dade County v. Wons*.[70]

In that case it upheld that the right of a mother of two children to refuse a blood transfusion was superior to the interests of the state in maintaining life and protecting the children's right to a two-parent home. The Court further held that if a hospital wishes to contest a patient's refusal of treatment, it must convince a court that the state has a compelling interest which outweighs the patient's constitutional rights.[71] A concurring opinion reiterated that the state constitution's express privacy provision showed that the people intended to establish a broader right to privacy than was available under the U. S. Constitution.

Implicit Rights to Privacy

The absence of an express provision in the state constitution protecting the right to privacy has not prevented certain state courts from finding and enforcing one. In *State Emp. Union v. Dept. of Mental Health*,[72] the Supreme Court of Texas held that the State Department of Mental Health and Mental Retardation's policy of mandatory polygraph examinations for its employees violated their personal rights of privacy. It was persuaded by U. S. Supreme Court decisions recognizing implicit "zones of privacy" in the U. S. Bill of Rights and found the same in similar Texas provisions.[73] It concluded that such a right "is implicit among those 'general, great, and essential principles of liberty and free government' established by the Texas Bill of Rights," taking the words from the *introduction* to the bill of rights.

The test it imposed on the government was the two-pronged "compelling interest/less restrictive" test: "This right to privacy should yield only when the government can demonstrate that an intrusion is reasonably warranted for the achievement of a compelling governmental objective that can be achieved by no less intrusive, more reasonable means."[74] It is interesting to note that, having selected this test to be applied when the right to privacy is claimed, Texas may measure state restrictions on abortion under the same test despite the U. S. Supreme Court's subsequent shift to an "undue burden" test.

So, as is always true in these cases, the court looked at the competing interests and balanced them. This is how the *substance* of a constitutional claim is measured. What will differ among courts is, first, the degree of importance which the court attaches to the right (is it "fundamental," for example?) as compared with the degree of importance of the competing right or interest. Second, the source of the right and the source of the competition will differ (is it constitutional, or statutory, for example?). Third, the standard chosen by which to measure the restriction on the liberty will differ among various courts (does the restriction serve a "compelling interest" of the public, or is it an "undue burden" on the liberty, or need the restriction only have a "rational relation" to a particular public interest?).

Another privacy case arose in Massachusetts, which had been chastised by Justice Stevens in *Massachusetts v. Upton* for failing to decide the state constitutional issue. A Boston Police Department rule permitted urinalysis drug testing of police officers both on reasonable suspicion and on a random basis. A Boston police officer challenged the rule, relying solely on Article 14 of the Massachusetts Declaration of Rights, which governs search and seizure, because he believed that a federal constitutional challenge was precluded by a previous ruling of the U. S. Supreme Court. In *Guiney v. Police Commissioner of Boston*,[75] the Massachusetts Court held in a four-to-three decision that *random* testing was a violation of the right to privacy established by Article 14. It concluded that the government did not make "a strong factual showing that a substantial public need exists for the imposition of such a process a...sufficiently compelling reason to justify the highly invasive monitored urine specimen collection,"[76] "a concrete, substantial governmental interest that will be well served by imposing random urinalysis on unconsenting citizens."[77]

What is of particular interest is that the court expressly rejected the view of the majority of U. S. Supreme Court justices expressed in *National Treasury Employees Union v. Von Raab*.[78] The U. S. Supreme Court had decided that such particularized proof was not required because "it is sufficient that the government have a compelling interest in preventing an otherwise pervasive societal problem from spreading to the particular context."[79]

Earlier, the Supreme Court of Georgia, in deciding a case similar to the Massachusetts case, had agreed with some of the rationale of the federal Court of Appeals in *Von Raab*; the U. S. Supreme Court had not yet ruled. In *City of East Point v. Smith*,[80] Fire Inspector Smith had been discharged from employment after urinalysis showed the use of marijuana. The police department had required all employees of the city having police power to be tested after it received reports that some officers were smoking marijuana in public and the department could not find the offenders "through conventional investigative means."[81] Smith pursued only his state constitutional claim on appeal, so the case was decided solely on the state constitution's prohibition against unreasonable searches and seizures.[82]

In analyzing reasonableness, the Court wrote: "We first examine the invasion of the employee's personal rights." It cited the federal Court of Appeals' version of *Von Raab* in support of its own statement that "it is clear that the employees have a legitimate expectation of privacy in the wealth of personal information which examination of their urine can disclose."[83] But in the Court's view, again cued by *Von Raab*, the urinalysis procedure was not as intrusive as an invasion of bodily integrity or of the home, or as imposing such indignity as body cavity or strip searches. Obviously, as noted earlier, there could be a difference of opinion about that, especially since Smith, a twenty-one-year employee and captain in the fire department, had to submit a urine sample in the presence of the assistant police chief.

In examining what was on the other side of the scales, *i.e.*, the government's *justification* for the urinalysis, the Court concluded that the unchallenged reports of marijuana use, the city's interest in preventing use, and its attempt first to resolve identity by conventional means showed a "compelling need" for the urinalysis. It again cited *Von Raab*, but it *did* find a fairly particularized need although it did not categorize the justification as that.

It then looked at the other prong of the federally developed test, which it adopted as its own test, *i.e.*, whether the government used the least restrictive means to achieve its legitimate goal. The Georgia Supreme Court referred to this as the "protective aspect" of the urinalysis program, and concluded that this contributed to its reasonableness: There was no discretion in who had to submit to the test, so there was no danger of it its being used for harassment; the test was *only* for marijuana, so it was no broader than the city needed.

What is of particular note is that in deciding this state constitutional issue, the only cases which the Court looked to for precedent or analogue were federal appellate cases and one federal district court case. Here is not only horizontal, but also cross-system sharing of constitutional thinking. The Court rejected the views of the writer of the Georgia Court of Appeals opinion[84] and one of its own brethren, that the test violated the state constitution as an unreasonable search and seizure because the government had no reasonable, individualized suspicion that Smith was using marijuana. These judges would have demanded a greater degree of particularization.

Dual Constitutionalism and the Right to Privacy

The legal development of the right to privacy exemplifies the interplay of federal and state constitutions and courts in the enunciation of rights. The idea of a legal right to privacy originated in a law review article in 1890, as a personal right of one person against the property rights of another, and was seized upon by a state court in deciding a common-law tort case.[85] Now it is recognized as a constitutionally protected right, no longer limited to the impetus which gave it birth, under both the U. S. Constitution and many state constitutions. Indeed, in recent decades some states have amended their constitutions to add express protections for privacy rights.

The right to privacy now reaches beyond the relationships among private citizens and extends to the relationship between a private citizen and the government at all levels. This personal right is expressed in a multitude of ways and often relates to current societal activity which may wax and wane. It is affected by the practice and advances of medicine and science, the proliferation of drugs, the change in places for public intercourse, the collection and dissemination of personal information, and so on. The scope of the right to privacy is decided on a case-by-case basis, in a dialogue between and among state and federal courts. These two systems of government are given the opportunity to identify and draw an inner zone of privacy which is guaranteed to every person in the United States. It is a national common denominator. But there being two sides to every coin; the *state* side of the dual system is given the added opportunity to identify and draw outer zones of privacy which are guaranteed to every person in their respective states.

It is on the edges, which are drawn by the states, that the action is, even though we pay by far the greatest attention to the drawing of the inner zone. Saying *it* counts most is only short-sighted, for once a broader circle is drawn in one state, it may influence the expansion of the circle in other states. And on the other hand, the U. S. Constitution may itself exceed them, if the nine justices so decide. As a recent observer noted:

> Federalism was designed to promote, not to impede, the growth of this nation's understanding of liberty...even if federal judicial activism often offends federalism, state judicial activism does not. Some of the forgotten history of constitutional federalism suggests that recent generations have underestimated or overlooked the capacity of the states to contribute to individual freedom.[86]

NOTES

1. *Barron v. Baltimore*, 32 U. S. 243 (1833).

2. Richard C. Cortner, *The Supreme Court and the Second Bill of Rights: The Fourteenth Amendment and the Nationalization of Civil Liberties* (Madison: University of Wisconsin Press, 1981).

3. Daniel Elazar, "The Principles and Traditions Underling State Constitutions," *Publius: The Journal of Federalism*, 12 (1982): 15.

4. Robert F. Williams, "The State Constitutions of the Founding Decade: Pennsylvania's Radical 1776 Constitution and Its Influences on American Constitutionalism," *Temple Law Review*, 62 (1989): 544-545.

5. George Athan Billias, "American Constitutionalism and Europe, 1776-1848," *American Constitutionalism Abroad* (1990), pp. 13-23; Bourne, "American Constitutional Precedents in the French National Assembly," *American Historical Review*, 8 (1903): 466.

6. Bernard Schwartz, *The Great Rights of Mankind*, pp. 119-159.

7. Schwartz, *The Great Rights of Mankind*, pp. 160-191.

8. Hans A. Linde, "First Things First: Rediscovering the States' Bills of Rights" *University of Baltimore Law Review*, 9 (1980): 379; Harold R. Clarke, "Independent State Grounds: How to Win Through the First Door Out," *Georgia State Bar Journal*, 23 (May 1987): 183.

9. *E.g.*, *Regents of the University of California v. Bakke*, 438 U. S. 265 (1978).

10. See Robert F. Williams, "In the Supreme Court's Shadow: Legitimacy of State Rejection of Supreme Court Reasoning and Result," *South Carolina Law Review*, 35 (1984): 353, and literature cited therein.

11. 455 U. S. 283 (1982).

12. 455 U. S. at 293.

13. 447 U. S. 74 (1980).

14. 420 U. S. 714, 719 (1975).

15. 386 U. S. 58, 62 (1966).

16. 463 U. S. 1032 (1983).

17. *Id.* at 1041.

18. *Id.* at 1044.

19. *Id.* at 1070-1071.

20. 466 U. S. 727, 735 (1984).

21. *Id.* at 735.

22. *Id.* at 735.

23. *Id.* at 736.

24. 462 U. S. 213 (1983); reh. den., 463 U. S. 1237 (1983).

25. *Commonwealth v. Upton*, 394 Mass. 363 (476 NE2d 548) (1985).

26. *Id.* at 555.

27. *Id.* at 556.

28. 49 Or. App. 415 (619 P2d 948) (1980).

29. 400 U. S. 470, 485 (1971).

30. *State v. Kennedy*, 61 Or. App. 469 (657 P2d 717, 719) (1983).

31. *State v. Kennedy*, 295 Or. 260 (666 P2d 1316) (1983).

32. This opinion, by Justice Hans A. Linde, shows how to properly raise and brief and analyze a state constitutional question. See also Hans A. Linde, "E Pluribus: Constitutional Theory and State Courts," *Georgia Law Review*, 18 (1984): 165.

33. *City of Mesquite v. Aladdin's Castle, Inc., supra.*

34. Sturm, "The Development of American State Constitutions," *Publius: The Journal of Federalism*, 12 (1982): 57, 75, table 3 (figures updated to 1990).

35. 285 U. S. 262, 311 (1932).

36. 497 U. S. 261 (1990).

37. 497 U. S. at 292.

38. 1983 Constitution of Georgia, Article X. See generally Michael G. Colantuono, "The Revision of American State Constitutions: Legislative Power, Popular Sovereignty, and Constitutional Change," *California Law Review*, 75 (1987): 1473.

39. See discussion of horizontal federalism in Mary Cornelia Porter and G. Alan Tarr, "Introduction," *State Supreme Courts: Policymakers in the Federal System* (Westport: Greenwood Press, 1982), pp. xxi-xxii.

40. "Horizontal federalism" is a term attributed to Mary Cornelia Porter and G. Alan Tarr. See Robert F. Williams, "Methodology Problems in Enforcing State Constitutional Rights," *Georgia State University Law Review*, 3 (1986-87): 143, 152 n.34. See also Burt Neuborne, Foreword, "State Constitutions and the Evolution of Positive Rights," *Rutgers Law Journal*, 20 (1989): 881.

41. Justice Robert Utter, for one, refers to it as the "lowest common denominator," in *Alderwood Assoc. v. Washington Environmental Council*, 96 Wash.2d 230, 242 (635 P2d 108, 115) (1981).

42. Clarke, "Independent State Grounds."

43. But see James A. Gardner, "The Failed Discourse of State Constitutionalism," *Michigan Law Review*, 90 (1992): 761.

44. 122 Ga. 190, 213-214 (50 SE 68) (1905).

45. 122 Ga. at 213-214.

46. 171 N.Y. 532, 540 (64 NE 442, 449, 89 Am. St. Rep. 828) (1902). See "Comment" on *Roberson*, *Yale Law Journal*, 12 (1902-1903), p. 35; W. Prosser and W. Keeton, *The Law of Torts* (5th ed. 1984), pp. 849-51. The dissenter in *Roberson* cited Cooley, *Torts*, p. 29.

47. 381 U. S. 479, 484 (1965).

48. *Id.* at 484.

49. John M. Devlin, "State Constitutional Autonomy Rights in an Age of Federal Retrenchment: Some Thoughts on the Interpretation of State Rights Derived from Federal Sources," *Emerging Issues in State Constitutional Law*, 3 (1990): 195.

50. *Id.* at 197.

51. See generally Louis Karl Bonham, "Note, Unenumerated Rights Clauses in State Constitutions," *Texas Law Review*, 63 (1985): 1321.

52. Florida Constitution, Art. I, Sec. I, Par. 23.

53. 551 So2d 1186 (Fla. 1989).

54. *Id.* at 1192.

55. *Id.* at 1196.

56. See Daniel R. Gordon, "One Privacy Provision, Two Privacy Protections: The Right to Privacy in Florida after *Roe v. Wade*," *Wisconsin Women's Law Journal*, 5 (1990): 81; "Developments in State Constitutional Law: 1989," *Rutgers Law Journal*, 21 (1990): 903, 905-911.

57. 112 SC 2791, 120 LE2d 674 (1992).

58. 492 U. S. 490 (1989).

59. 410 U. S. 113 (1973).

60. 588 So2d 233 (Fla. 1991).

61. See Slobogin, "State Adoption of Federal Law: Exploring the Limits of Florida's 'Forced Linkage' Amendment," *University of Florida Law Review*, 39 (1987): 653.

62. 111 SC 1801, 114 LE2d 297 (1991).

63. *Id.* III SC at 1805.

64. *State v. Jimeno*, 588 So2d 233 (Fla. 1991).

65. 232 U. S. 383 (1914).

66. *Week* had been made applicable to the states in *Mapp v. Ohio*, 367 U. S. 643, 655 (1961), but was narrowed by a "good faith" exception in *United States v. Leon*, 468 U. S. 897 (1984). The good faith exception of *Leon* was rejected in *State v. Garcia*, 547 So2d 628 (Fla. 1989), on a state *statutory* analysis.

67. 524 So2d 988, 992 (Fla. 1988).

68. 568 So2d 4 (Fla. 1990).

69. See also *In re L.H.R.*, 253 Ga. 439 (321 SE2d 716) (1984) (exercise of right to refuse medical treatment or terminate treatment, as part of right to privacy, does not need judicial approval.) Also *State of Georgia v. McAfee*, 259 Ga. 579 (385 SE2d 651) (1989); *Zant v. Prevatte*, 248 Ga. 832 (286 SE2d 715) (1982).

70. 541 So2d 96 (Fla. 1989).

71. See Daniel R. Gordon, "The Right to Die: *Public Health Trust v. Wons*: Florida Moves Away from Massachusetts and New Jersey toward California and Mississippi despite *Cruzan v. Harmon*," *New York Law School Journal of Human Rights*, 7 (1990): 40.

72. 746 SW2d 203 (Tex. 1987).

73. It found zones of privacy in the right against arbitrary deprivation of life and liberty, freedom of speech, freedom from compelled self-incrimination, guarantee of sanctity of home and person against unreasonable intrusion, and rights of conscience in matters of religion. *Id.* at 205.

74. *Id.* at 205.

75. 411 Mass. 328 (582 NE2d 523) (1991).

76. 582 NE2d at 525.

77. *Id.* at 526.

78. 489 U. S. 656, 675 n.4 (1989).

79. 489 U. S. at 675 n.4.

80. 258 Ga. 111 (365 SE2d 432) (1988).

81. *Id.* at 111.

82. Georgia Constitution 1983, Art. I, Sec. I, Par. XIII.

83. *Id.* at 112.

84. One judge concurred in judgment only, and one judge concurred with the reversal of the trial court but on the ground that a procedural impediment precluded reaching the question.

85. Louis D. Brandeis and Samuel D. Warren, "Rights of a Citizen to His Reputation," *Harvard Law Review*, 4 (1890): 193.

86. Harry F. Tepker, Jr., "Abortion, Privacy and State Constitutional Law: A Speculation If (or When) *Roe v. Wade* is Overturned," *Emerging Issues in State Constitutional Law*, 2 (1989): 173.

CHAPTER 7

RIGHTS AND FEDERALISM: AN AGENDA TO ADVANCE THE VISION OF JUSTICE BRENNAN

Talbot D'Alemberte

The idea that federalism serves to protect the rights of Americans is an important one. Madison's *Federalist* No. 51 assured us that dividing power between two distinct governments and then subdividing it into separate departments would give our rights greater protection. Until the United States Constitution was adopted, this idea had never been applied on such a grand scale and now, two centuries later, we are still working out the details.

One of the great modern visions of federalism was that of Justice William Brennan who, in 1977, wrote his seminal article for the *Harvard Law Review* encouraging the development of state constitutional principles for the protection of individual rights.[1] Justice Brennan's thesis was that state courts need not defer to federal decisions which narrowly interpret the federal Constitution where the state constitution has language supporting a parallel right. That article was published almost twenty years ago, and much has happened which vindicates Justice Brennan's view. Professor Robert F. Williams, a leading scholar on state constitutional law, has stated, "We have...experienced a constitutional revolution in the judicial interpretation of individual rights provisions of state constitutions since the early 1970s."[2]

The period in which the article by Justice Brennan was written was the heyday of the Burger Court, and a time when Professor Lawrence Tribe wrote, "no great acumen is required to detect in recent decisions of the United States Supreme Court a retreat from the rigorous defense of liberty and equality." Professor Tribe observed: "The primary victims of this shift in judicial attitude have been our society's oppressed; its clearest beneficiaries have not been among those in special need of judicial assistance."[3]

Yet Professor Tribe, writing in the same volume of *Harvard Law Review* as Justice Brennan, saw the principles of federalism in a very different way from Justice Brennan. Tribe was concerned that "the extravagant claims of state sovereignty" were encouraged by the "Court's talismatic invocations of federalism."[4] His article urged the Congress to correct the decision in *National League of Cities v. Usery*,[5] which had held that the minimum wage laws did not apply to the states in those areas of service for which the states have traditionally afforded service.

I linger over Professor Tribe's statement which sets up the idea that claims of federalism are invoked to defeat the claims of rights. What Professor Tribe saw in the way principles of federalism were being applied was a threat to the further development of rights for the oppressed. Justice Brennan saw in revived state court activism new opportunities to vindicate those very rights. We see that the principles of federalism and rights are used at the same time to advance individual rights and to resist individual rights. Justice Brennan and Professor Tribe may both be right and we may have to concede that a discussion of federalism and rights will not lead to bright line principles. We can at least struggle with these ideas so that we can better understand what is at play when principles of federalism and comity are injected into the debate about individual rights.

Justice Brennan reminded us that the state courts and the state constitutions can be the basis for vindicating claims of rights and he encouraged state courts to use state constitutions to expand individual rights. Justice Brennan, writing at the time he turned seventy, both applauded the reach of federal constitutional law applied to the states under the Fourteenth Amendment and admonished us:

> The legal revolution which has brought federal law to the fore must not be allowed to inhibit the independent protective force of state law - for without it, the full realization of our liberties cannot be guaranteed.[6]

He urged that decisions of the United States Supreme Court "are not, and should not be, dispositive of questions regarding rights guaranteed by counterpart provisions of state law."[7]

Brennan declared himself to be a "devout believer" in federalism, but noted in words which reflect Professor Tribe's view: "Unfortunately, federalism has taken on a new meaning of late. In its name, many of the door-closing decisions...have been rendered."[8] Justice Brennan's article listed a long series of cases where he felt that the Burger Court had not provided sufficient recognition to significant rights.

One of the cases Justice Brennan Brennan mentioned dealt with the question of whether, in First Amendment jurisprudence, the public forum doctrine (which protects the rights of citizens to speak in places which are traditionally the sites for public discussion) applies to privately owned suburban shopping centers.[9] Justice Brennan referred to "essential public forums" and he argued that Supreme Court decisions in this area (among many others) were too restrictive of citizens' rights.

Not long after Justice Brennan's article, the Supreme Court handed down a decision which I believe is one of the most important cases on the public forum doctrine in recent times - Justice Rehnquist's 1980 opinion in *Pruneyard Shopping Center v. Robins.*[10] This case dealt with the subject that Justice Brennan wrote about which had been addressed several times by the U.S. Supreme Court with contradictory results: whether the modern shopping center is a public forum for purposes of free speech, entitling speakers entry onto private property. At issue in these cases is a conflict between the right to speak, picket or pass out literature in a shopping center versus the shopping center owner's property rights to prohibit such activity. By the time *Pruneyard* reached the U.S. Supreme Court, that Court had vacillated - first holding that shopping centers, like company towns, were places where the public had the same rights of free speech as in a public right-of-way, and then retreating to favor property rights. Ultimately, the Supreme Court found that the federal Constitution provided no basis for protecting the pamphleteers in a shopping center. The California Supreme Court, construing the California constitution and its free speech guarantee, reached the opposite result when it decided *Pruneyard*, favoring free speech over property rights. Justice Rehnquist and the Court majority held that this decision of the California courts would stand, however, because a state court that clearly relied on its own state constitution should be given deference by the federal courts.

The *Pruneyard* decision came just as Justice Brennan's words were being understood and, with the election of President Reagan in that same year, many advocates and organizations who sought to advance the agenda of civil rights saw that the federal courts were not likely to be hospitable to claims of expanded rights. In this environment, many civil rights lawyers began to rethink the issues of federalism and to look to the state courts and state constitutions. In some areas, the results have been notable, but no coherent principles have emerged to allow us to say that the Brennan vision has prevailed over the Tribe assessment.

In many cases, all we can say about the play between the effort to expand individual rights and the concepts of federalism is that people who identify with the movements to expand rights and those who resist these movements are willing to use principles of federalism when those principles suit their argument.

THE UPCOMING BATTLES

The Center for the Study of Federalism's conference on federalism and rights was held only a few days after the 1992 presidential election, and because of the timing, it was interesting to think about how federalism and rights are likely to be addressed in some of the major battles likely to take place in the upcoming political battles and use those subjects to illustrate how conveniently we deal with the questions of federalism and rights. I address only two of these, each challenging and controversial.

Federal Tort Legislation

The first area I would like to address is federal tort legislation. The long-ranging battle over this subject is being fought out in the old-fashioned way, through heavy campaign contributions and constituent pressure, and the result is more likely to be dictated by PAC promises than by large principle, but there are some principles involved. The issue is whether the rights of people who claim injury, particularly injury from defective products, should be left to state law or defined through federal legislation.

The proponents of federal tort legislation (including the National Association of Manufacturing) urge that products are produced for national distribution, and that the rules governing these products should be national rules. In opposition, most consumer groups and all personal injury lawyer groups assert that the legislation is not only an attempt to limit the rights of injured persons but an intrusion on principles of federalism. We may wonder whether these lawyer groups care as much about defending the principle of federalism as in protecting the rights to sue. (I associate myself with their view, but this does not place that view above ridicule.) We hear some of these same groups bemoan the failure of federal regulatory agencies to provide strict regulation in various areas, the failure to tighten up on safety standards or auto emission standards, and surely there are principles of federalism involved in those disputes for increased federal regulation displaces the state regulatory role.

Moreover, the lawyers' groups who defend the states' rights to define tort liability and to shape the remedies are perfectly willing to support expanded civil rights legislation, and never with more enthusiasm than when it is coupled with a provision for attorneys' fees to be awarded to the successful civil rights plaintiff. Recent news articles report a series of cases in which the lawyer is compensated for bringing a civil rights case despite a nominal judgment for the plaintiff. In one such case, a prison inmate sued and won a nominal damage award of one dollar, and the lawyer received a fee of $40,000. This application of federal law to determine rights and to set the standard of recovery has never bothered those of us in lawyer organizations as much of a problem with principles of federalism.

Before leaving this area of tort liability and the question of whether the rights of the injured should be determined by state or federal principles, I would like to pause on one special area of tort law, the law of defamation, and observe that this is an area of tort law which has been thoroughly federalized largely through court decisions. When I was in law school, defamation was taught as a torts subject, but law students today are far more likely to study defamation in a course on United States constitutional law. The rules governing defamation since the decision in *New York Times v. Sullivan*[11] all are tied ultimately to First Amendment principles, and the rich collection of common law principles has been cut off, thereby destroying quaint, ancient principles, a few which even had some utility in protecting rights of free speech in libel and slander cases.

As we all recognize, the principles of *New York Times v. Sullivan* were developed in large part because state defamation law was being used by public officials and others to repress the civil rights movement, and to punish criticism of state and local officials in the South. As Anthony Lewis' recent book, *Make No Law*, reminds us, the *Sullivan* case was brought not only against the *New York Times*, but against the civil rights leaders who signed the advertisement.

I refer to this history only to say that those people who, like me, urge that there not be a federal products liability law or federal medical malpractice law, thus leaving the development of these rights to state law, are many times the same people who believe that Justice Brennan's decision in *New York Times v. Sullivan* is one of the most important decisions ever rendered by the Court, and I do not object, on principles of federalism, to having the state tort law of libel and slander subjected to federal principles.

In short, there has been no clear principle of federalism to guide discussion in the tort area, and federalism is usually discussed as just another argument, one not taken too seriously.

Federal Habeas Corpus Proceedings

The second area of upcoming interest that I would like to examine may be the one which has proven the most intractable in the attempt to rationalize federalism and rights, and it is the area of federal *habeas corpus*.

If principles of federalism demand a measure of respect for the determinations by state courts, the process of *habeas corpus* post-conviction litigation strains those principles. I look particularly at *habeas* in capital cases, for this is precisely the category of case which is most likely to be highly publicized and where considerable passion is most likely to be present. Pressure for tough and swift punishment is very high when a brutal crime has been committed, and it is understandable that prosecutors and elected state judges feel this pressure.

But it is in this very category of case where a rational justice system will take the most care. Death is different, and the risk of executing an innocent person is a risk which is not lightly borne.[12]

The facts that the death penalty is imposed in a number of states which have serious inadequacies in their public defender or appointed counsel arrangement, and that far too often capital cases are tried by incompetent counsel or without adequate investigation, mean that there will be a number of cases where the state system fails to accord capital defendants their right to effective assistance of counsel, their right to due process, and other federally protected rights.

Where elected state appellate judges fail to correct these errors, the task of correcting them falls to federal judges, and this activity is understandably seen as a departure from the principles of comity. Moreover, this departure takes place in a context which is very easily politicized. The public passion for speedy action is easily stirred by political figures and usually cruel facts of the crime are much easier to convey to the public than the technical failures of the defense.

If the public is outraged over a violent crime, it is not likely that the niceties of protecting a defendant's rights will have much sway. Moreover, there are not many political figures who are even making the argument for protection of these rights. Therefore, the task of assuring that rights of criminal defendants are protected often falls on the federal courts, and the courts have struggled with the problems of comity.

In recent years, the United States Supreme Court has announced judicial doctrine which eliminates federal *habeas* claims where successor writs are involved and in circumstances where the writ has been abused. The Court has also developed rules relating to retroactivity. Taken together, these rules have substantially reduced the alleged abuses in *habeas* and have demonstrated the Supreme Court's proper concern with principles of federalism, but the application of these principles in this area has undoubtedly lessened individual rights in the area of capital crime post-conviction proceedings.

This area of federal *habeas* is also of concern to Congress, and crime legislation offers congressmen rich opportunities to vote for measures touted as "tough on crime." The temptation to further intrude into the area of *habeas*, reducing the rights of defendants, may be too great to resist, particularly when there is the attractive banner of federalism under which to rally on this issue. After all, federal courts use *habeas* authority to question settled state cases which have been tried, appealed and become final adjudications.

There have been several major studies of this problem, one conducted by a federal commission chaired by retired Justice Powell, and one a task force organized by the American Bar Association. There were technical differences but they agreed on one important fact - the tensions in *habeas* litigation were caused in very large measure by a failure of the state justice system to provide adequately trained, adequately compensated defense counsel for criminal defendants. This failure, I believe, is especially contemptible in capital cases. Flowing from this failure, the rate of success in federal *habeas* challenges to state capital convictions remains quite high, probably around 35 to 40 percent.

A number of people look at the large number of federal *habeas* cases which grant relief and bemoan the result, citing principles of federalism and comity. This conflict between the ideals of rights and the principles of federalism is all the more severe because it deals with such a politically sensitive area, yet it is unthinkable that we will continue to respect judicial systems which have operated in a way which is so neglectful of rights.

It is not necessary to recount the episodes of neglect and incompetence. We can merely say that there are states where there is no public defender system and a cap on fees for appointed counsel is in place. These caps have been as low as the $1,000 range and we should not be surprised that lawyers for capital defendants have done inadequate jobs of defending their clients, that lawyers have failed to do proper investigation, that they have failed to raise essential defenses, that they have tried lawsuits in a careless and superficial manner, even where the very highest stakes are involved for the defendant. States which operate a criminal justice system of the type which disregards rights is a system which is not entitled to comity, and one approach to the *habeas* question is to defer to state court final adjudication only where the state court systems have provided adequate counsel, investigative services and access to litigation support such as expert witnesses. Rights of criminal defendants should trump the claim of comity in these cases and, when we know that defendants' rights are being neglected by state justice systems, comity should not apply.

Where states do meet minimum standards of criminal defense, the tensions between the state and the federal role can be reduced. Where the state provides qualified defense counsel, the resources for investigation and expert witnesses and competent appellate counsel and, further, has in place a system which assures the independence of judges and an adequate safety valve to protect true claims of innocence, we could - in those circumstances - apply the judicial principles which bar successor writs and the principles which require dismissal of cases where the writ is abused.

Now, I do admit that this is comity with a price and I do not have the details worked out, but some such system would serve as an incentive for states to recognize their duty to protect the rights of criminal defendants in the first instance and thereby eliminate the great expense and great tension involved in post-conviction proceedings. It is state neglect which is causing the problem and only the states which are fair should be respected.

The rich catalog of federal *habeas* cases convinces me that, though I can join Justice Brennan's call for federalism to be a "double source of protection for the rights of our citizens,"[13] I cannot embrace state courts as the reliable venue for the protection of rights.

This now leads me from a discussion of examples about the ways in which the federalism and rights debate is likely to be played out in several specific areas to an assessment of the fundamental weakness in the Brennan thesis.

THE RISKS OF ADJUDICATING INDIVIDUAL RIGHTS AT THE STATE LEVEL

The difficulty with looking to state courts and state constitutions for the protection of individual rights is in large part the fact that the state judiciary and the state constitution are much more subject to majoritarian forces than are federal judges and the United States Constitution. If we remind ourselves of the unsuccessful efforts to impeach Earl Warren, a goal proclaimed by billboards throughout the South in the wake of school integration, and of the many unsuccessful efforts to amend the Constitution, we will frame the largest problem with Justice Brennan's proposal.

I would like to use Florida examples for both the problem of judicial vulnerability at the state level and the play of forces which may lead to modification of the state constitution.

Campaigns Directed at Judges Who Follow the Brennan Philosophy

The Florida Constitution has a section explicitly recognizing the right of privacy:

> Every natural person has the right to be let alone and free from governmental intrusion into his private life except as otherwise provided herein.[14]

This amendment to the Florida Constitution was originally proposed by the Constitution Revision Commission in 1978 and rejected as a part of a larger package. In 1980, it was offered again and placed on the ballot as a discrete amendment. The history of its adoption is interesting for, in the area of state constitutional amendments, history in Florida is that newspaper endorsements have a very strong influence on the outcome, and this amendment was opposed by all but a few of the state's leading newspapers. Ironically, the amendment was on the ballot at the same election in which Ronald Reagan sounded the theme that we should get government off the back of the American people and the Florida Privacy Amendment carried by a solid majority despite the opposition of most of Florida's newspapers and other powerful groups such as law enforcement officials who warned that the adoption of the amendment might provide the basis for court challenge to search and seizure activities as well as present a barrier to laws attempting to reach such activities as private sexual conduct and possession of pornography.

That amendment has been the basis for a number of rights decisions in Florida, including the right of a person to refuse medical treatment,[15] but the privacy decision which has drawn the most attention is the decision which held that the "right to be let alone" protected a woman's right to chose an abortion at the early stages of a pregnancy.[16] Justice Brennan would no doubt applaud this development.

He might not applaud the campaign which was conducted in 1990 against Leander Shaw, the first African-American Chief Justice in Florida, or the campaign in 1992 against Rosemary Barkett, the first woman Chief Justice in Florida, for both of those merit retention campaigns were based largely on the fact that these justices had applied the state privacy provision in a way which most lawyers thought entirely correct. These campaigns conjured up memories of the California merit retention campaign against then Chief Justice Rose Bird and two of her colleagues based largely on their opinions which expanded individual rights - particularly in the area of the rights of criminal defendants charged with capital crimes.

The Florida campaigns were filled with distortions, and reeked of racism and sexism. Happily, both justices prevailed. When we look at the Florida merit retention campaigns and net the results of those two campaigns against the California campaign against Rose Bird, it is hard to make the case that state judges have the kind of independence which equips them for the role Justice Brennan proposed. Even in Florida, where at least the justices prevailed, there was some sense that their rulings in favor of cases of individual rights exposed them to significant political risks. After all, in 1992, there were three justices up for retention but only one, Chief Justice Barkett, was challenged, undoubtedly because the others were not considered to be as receptive to claims of individual rights.

Campaigns to Amend the State Constitution

In analyzing Justice Brennan's vision of expanded individual rights secured by the states through adjudication based on state constitutional grounds there is a second interesting area relating to the play of political forces at the state level and I will again use a series of events in Florida to make my point. After Justice Brennan's article, the strategy of invoking the Florida Constitution proved to be very successful in the area of search and seizure. Indeed, as the United States Supreme Court demonstrated an increasingly crabbed attitude toward claims that defendants' rights had been infringed under search and seizure principles, the Florida Supreme Court took a separate path, adhering to earlier federal court principles and basing its decisions squarely on the state constitution, thereby insulating the case from review by the United States Supreme Court under the principle that the state court decision rested on independent state grounds.[17] This departure from federal case law was particularly appropriate in certain cases because the Florida Constitution as revised in 1968 carried a specific reference to the right to be protected against "the unreasonable interception of private communications by any means," and the history of that section demonstrated some very real concern with electronic surveillance.

There was such success in this strategy of maintaining and even expanding rights of defendants that the state Attorney General and prosecutors went to the state legislature and succeeded in getting it to adopt a provision which was approved by the voters in 1982. The language added to the search and seizure provision of the Florida Constitution is surely one of the most curious examples of federalism at work. The amendment states, in part:

> This right shall be construed in conformity with the 4th Amendment to the United States Constitution, as interpreted by the United States Supreme Court.[18]

This 1982 amendment has been construed to displace the independent state basis for decision and, in a recent four-to-three decision, the Court held that the amendment did not merely adopt the interpretations of the United States Supreme Court as of its effective date but, rather, the amendment requires that the state courts follow the decisions of the United States Supreme Court in current cases.[19]

The 1982 addition to Florida's constitutional language on search and seizure is interesting because the law enforcement community achieved this amendment not by arguing from any principles of federalism, but rather from the conviction that the federal courts were likely to be more restrictive on the rights of defendants than state courts.

This amendment runs counter to the idea of federalism and the development of rights by the states which was the thesis of Justice Brennan's 1977 law review article and which was embraced by then-Justice Rehnquist's 1980 opinion in *Pruneyard*, but both Justice Brennan and, in this instance, law enforcement officials in Florida seemed to agree that the state courts might be more hospitable to defendants' claims of rights.

The two types of political campaigns illustrated by events in Florida - one, the campaign against a judge who is accused of being too friendly to individual rights, and the other, the direct campaign to render state adjudication slave to the federal decisions - are important obstacles to achieving Justice Brennan's vision. Without a great measure of judicial independence, it is doubtful that state judges will embark on the road that Justice Brennan maps for them.

In the case of the right of privacy, the state court justices who heeded Justice Brennan's words were rewarded with vicious negative campaigns. Where a state route for search and seizure was developed, the reward was a constitutional amendment which cut off this route.

The two examples I have used of Florida constitutional development since 1977 and of the reaction are both examples where the advocates of civil rights and the rights of criminal defendants have been served by renewed state court interest in state constitution-based rights, but these examples do not lead me to endorse any general principles of rights and federalism which rely on state courts.

AN AGENDA TO ADVANCE THE BRENNAN VISION

Where, then, can those of us who profess belief in both individual rights and federalism turn for an agenda, a program? How can those who agreed with Justice Brennan help achieve his vision? In addressing that question, I find myself looking backward wistfully at the developments which occurred in legislative apportionment about the time I entered law practice thirty years ago.

In purely practical terms, state power substantially diminished with the vast growth of federal power during the period of the Great Depression and World War II, which one scholar has called "the nadir of state vigor and prestige."[20]   In 1939, Harold Laski wrote an article entitled   "The Obsolescence of Federalism,"[21] and, if there were real questions about the utility of state governments, there was not much question about the relative power of state and federal governments.

The revitalization of state governments, an objective of scholars and civil activists, was greatly aided in the 1960s and 1970s by court-ordered reapportionment following *Baker v. Carr* in 1962. Indeed, *Baker v. Carr* is an excellent departure point for discussion of federalism and rights.

After *Baker v. Carr* was decided, state legislatures were suddenly transformed, and new members tackled long-neglected programs of education, transportation, government reorganization and constitutional reform.

Baker v. Carr's recognition of federally protected *rights* was an essential step in revitalizing federalism because it allowed the processes of state government to function. This case is our best example of how rights, even rights recognized by federal courts, can advance the interests of federalism. What can rights advocates do to advance the cause of federalism without abandoning the rights agenda?

I do not have any novel proposals, nor any idea about a grand principle of federally based rights which serves to advance the state interest in the way that *Baker v. Carr* worked. There is, however, a political strategy which will serve the rights agenda without harm to principles of federalism and that is the strategy of court reform.

The problem with partisan elected state judges is that they are (in urban areas, at least) less competent and more corrupt, and that they are also less reliable protectors of individual rights because they have no real independence. If Justice Brennan's thesis is to be successful, we must have state courts which are genuinely independent and free of political pressure.

There is an agenda for state court reform and there was a time when the energies of lawyers and political scientists and civic groups were dedicated to judicial reform, but the sad truth is that the movement has lagged. The great energy of the citizens' movement for court reform organized so effectively by the American Judicature Society during the late 1950s and into the early 1970s brought into existence the institutions of judicial discipline, the consolidation of trial courts, and, in many places, a greater measure of judicial independence through merit selection and merit retention of judges.

Court reform of state court systems is urgent quite apart from any agenda to further the Brennan vision. I have recently completed a year as President of the American Bar Association and, although I do not have time to recount all the stories of court corruption and incompetence where there are elected systems in urban areas, I do know that the problems of Chicago exposed in the prosecution known as "Operation Greylord" are not unique to Chicago. Recent news stories in Miami, Philadelphia, and other places attest to the widespread difficulties with the elected judiciary in urban areas. The problem, however, is greater than that of corruption, although this problem undoubtedly drains public confidence from the courts. The larger problem, which most trial lawyers will concede in private conversations, is that there is a severe question of competence where there is an elected state judiciary in urban areas. The simple truth is that the people who know the system best are frequently the most in despair about it.

The agenda I propose to achieve the Brennan vision is one of a renewed program to improve the state court system, particularly the methods of selecting judges and tenuring them.

This is not the place to spell out a full agenda for court reform; improvements in judicial ethics, judicial education, judicial compensation, and citizen participation may all play a part in improving the court system. My principal interest here is in judicial independence, which will equip the state judiciary to serve the role Justice Brennan envisioned.

The difficulty of achieving judicial independence through laws and constitutional amendments is obvious: it is necessary to convince majorities of state legislatures and majorities of the electorate that there is a value to an independent judiciary, capable of overruling the majority. The case for judicial reform can usually be made best at a time of crisis, particularly at a time when there is broad public knowledge of the failings of the existing system. The reform movement then gets bound up with the effort to turn the "rascals" out and is most likely to be successful. It is my thesis that the popular dissatisfaction with the administration of justice (to borrow Dean Roscoe Pound's phrase) is at a level which will support broad efforts to improve the system and that it is in that context that change is most likely to happen.

I believe that the agenda for change should be led by efforts to improve the independence of the judiciary, but I recognize that there are skeptics about the efficacy of change, particularly if change means going from an elected judiciary to a merit selection/merit retention process (or "Missouri Plan"). There are several studies critical of the claims of judicial improvement made by reformers.[22]

Whether the studies so critical of the claims made in support of the Missouri Plan are valid where there has been a process of education for the nominating commission members, some better thinking about the criteria for judicial selection, a greater diversity in the backgrounds of commission members, and a better developed culture embracing more idealistic principles is not certain, but the studies published in 1969 (Watson and Downing) and 1978 (Glick) do not, in any event, undermine the two principal objectives of the reform movement proposed here.

Those objectives - increased independence and increased competence - derive at least some support from the two studies. The Watson and Downing study found that the Missouri Plan "has tended to eliminate highly incompetent persons from the state judiciary."[23] Moreover, the Missouri Plan does foster judicial independence[24] and it is this characteristic which should most appeal to those who seek to advance an agenda of individual rights in the state courts.

This is not to say that the Missouri Plan is the ideal device to provide independence nor to attract more competent judges, but it is a device which has found acceptability to the majorities which are required to support any change from the existing system.

One of the curious aspects of recent movements to establish a more independent judiciary through such mechanisms as the Missouri Plan for merit selection and retention is the resistance of the very groups which we would think should benefit from judicial independence, and these are minority groups. The reason for this resistance is undoubtedly the new-found political power which has been achieved in many areas and the prospect that the application of the federal Voting Rights Act will result in single member, minority controlled districts for electing judges. This prospect is itself challenging to the ideal of an independent judiciary but, at present, the power of this idea over minority legislators hampers the movement to establish mechanisms to establish greater independence.

If the people who believe in Justice Brennan's vision are to succeed in a movement to improve judicial independence, this vision must be communicated to the legislators and people who will have the most stake in such a movement.

In 1977, Justice Brennan gave us an important way to think about rights and federalism. That idea can now be achieved only by returning to the movement to improve the judicial system and to strengthen judicial independence.

NOTES

1.   William Brennan, "State Constitutions and the Protection of Individual Rights," *Harvard Law Review*, 489 (1977).

2.   Professor Robert F. Williams, *State Constitutional Law: Cases and Materials* (Washington, D.C.: U. S. Advisory Commission on Intergovernmental Relations, 1990), p. 1.

3.   Lawrence H. Tribe, "Unraveling *National League of Cities*: The New Federalism and Affirmative Rights to Essential Government Services," *Harvard Law Review*, 90 (April 1977): 1065.

4.   Tribe, "Unraveling *National League of Cities*," p. 1104.

5.   426 U. S. 833 (1976).

6.   Brennan, "State Constitutions," p. 490.

7.   Brennan, "State Constitutions," p. 502.

8.   Brennan, "State Constitutions," p. 502.

9.   Brennan, "State Constitutions," p. 496. He cites *Hudgens v. NLRB*, 424 U.S. 507 (1976), which overruled *Food Employees Union Local 590 v. Logan Valley Plaza, Inc.*, 391 U.S. 308 (1968), and *Lloyd v. Tanner*, 407 U.S. 551 (1972).

10.   447 U.S. 74 (1980).

11.   376 U.S. 254 (1964).

12. The United States Supreme Court has dealt with this issue recently and rendered a very ambiguous result. *Herrera v. Collins* (1993) held that the petitioner had not demonstrated a proper claim to invoke federal jurisdiction but at least three members of the Court's six-person majority indicated that they would be willing to consider federal jurisdiction in a proper case.

13. Brennan, "State Constitutions," p. 503.

14. Article 1, Section 23.

15. *Public Health Trust v. Wins*, 541 So.2d 96 (Fla. 1989).

16. *In re T.W.*, 543 So.2d 837 (Fla. 1989).

17. See the principles set out in *Michigan v. Long*, 463 U.S. 1032 (1982), which announced the "plain statement" rule.

18. Article 1, Section 12.

19. *Perez v. State*, 18 Fla. Law Weekly S361 (1993).

20. Stanley Friedelbaum, "Judicial Federalism: Current Trends and Long Term Projects," *Florida State Law Review*, 19 (1992): 1053, 1054.

21. *The New Republic*, (May 3, 1939): 367-369.

22. See Henry R. Glick, "The Promise and the Performance of the Missouri Plan: Judicial Section in the Fifty States," *University of Miami Law Review*, 32 (June 1978): 509; Richard A. Watson and Randal G. Downing, *The Politics of the Bench and the Bar* (New York: John Wiley and Sons, Inc., 1969).

23. Watson and Downing, *The Politics of the Bench and the Bar*, p. 345.

24. Watson and Downing, *The Politics of the Bench and the Bar*, p. 346.

CHAPTER 8

FEDERALISM AND RIGHTS IN THE EUROPEAN COMMUNITY

Koen Lenaerts

The relationship between federalism and rights in the European Community is both problematic and intriguing. It is problematic because there is still a lot to be said about the "federal," "confederal," "supranational," or *sui generis* nature of the system of divided powers operating inside the legal order of the European Community,[1] so that the examination of the relationship between federalism and rights should logically concentrate first on the "federalism" aspect to see if, and if so, how much, it is present in the European Community. However, the relationship between federalism and rights in the European Community is also intriguing because it appears to be precisely the concept of rights - which from the beginning was introduced by the European Court of Justice to characterize a whole range of entitlements held by private parties on the basis of Community law - that suggests that the constitutional structure of the European Community is a federal arrangement.

The argument of this chapter is that federalism and rights have had a mutually reinforcing impact on each other. The European Community became more federal because it developed the tools of protecting the rights which private parties can claim under Community law. The development of such tools was largely legitimated by reference to what were essentially federal intentions of the Founding Fathers (*i.e.*, the Member States' representatives). Even though these representatives did not use the term "federal" anywhere in the text of the treaties,[2] they included a whole range of provisions indicating that the treaties were about to establish a novel kind of international organization, *i.e.*, one with lawmaking powers, that would create rights and enforce them at the request of private parties. It is this reality which the Treaty on European Union, signed at Maastricht on February 7, 1992, and entered into force on November 1, 1993, takes as the starting point for any further development of the system of divided powers between Europe and its component entities (the Member States and their subdivisions), when it calls for "respecting and building upon the *acquis communautaire*,"[3] and marking "a new stage in the process of creating an ever closer union among the peoples of Europe, in which decisions are taken as closely as possible to the citizen."[4] The first part of this chapter examines how the concept of rights became over time the principal catalyst in the judicial shaping of the federal features of the European Community. The second part analyzes the principal rights conferred to private parties by Community law and shows how the determination of the scope of these rights (by the political and the judicial processes) is influenced by the federal features of the European Community.

THE EUROPEAN COURT OF JUSTICE, FEDERALISM, AND RIGHTS

In the formative first decade of the European Community, the issue arose whether private parties could rely on provisions of Community law before national courts, in order to see these provisions enforced over inconsistent legislation of the Member States. This in turn raised the related questions of the "direct effect" and the "supremacy" of Community law in the legal orders of the Member States. The Court of Justice confronted these questions when a Dutch court submitted a request for a preliminary ruling on "whether Article 12 of the Treaty has direct application in national law in the sense that nationals of Member States may on the basis of this Article lay claim to rights which the national court must protect."[5] Article 12 of the EEC Treaty provides that "Member States shall refrain from introducing between themselves any new customs duties on imports or exports or any charges having equivalent effect, and from increasing those which they already apply in their trade with each other." A Dutch company, Van Gend & Loos, relied on this provision in an action brought before a Dutch court against the Netherlands Inland Revenue Administration aiming at the recovery of taxes which it said were unduly paid on the import of goods from Germany. The Netherlands - so it was argued - had levied the taxes at a higher rate than that which previously applied and thus infringed the stand-still obligation contained in Article 12. The Dutch Government, supported by the Belgian Government, argued in the Court of Justice that private parties could not claim rights under Article 12, because this provision was part of a treaty which creates rights and obligations only for the subjects of international law involved, *i.e.* the Member States and the Community. In case of infringement by a Member State of such rights and obligations, the Commission (representing the Community) and the other Member States could seek declaratory relief from the Court of Justice pursuant to the procedure laid down to that effect in Articles 169 and 170 of the EEC Treaty.[6] Private parties, not being subjects of international law, would thus be precluded from drawing rights from a treaty provision and from seeking to enforce them in the national courts (interacting in turn with the Court of Justice through the preliminary rulings procedure). If the Court had followed that argument, it would have closed the door for Community law rules to operate fully in the legal orders of the Member States as federal law does within the legal orders of the several states in the United States. Community law would thus have become a kind of interstate law which does not directly affect the legal situation of private parties. It would have precluded viewing the European Community as a system of divided powers to be exercised by two lawmaking authorities, *i.e.*, the Community and the Member States, each of which may address its legal rules - enacted within its proper sphere of powers - to the same private parties (*i.e.*, all natural and legal persons coming under the jurisdiction of the Member States of the European Community).

The Court rejected the Dutch/Belgian argument, emphasizing "the objective of the EEC Treaty, which is to establish a Common Market, the functioning of which is of direct concern to interested parties in the Community," and found "that this Treaty is more than an agreement which merely creates mutual obligations between the contracting States." It based its finding on "the preamble to the Treaty which refers not only to governments but to peoples," as well as on "the establishment of institutions endowed with sovereign rights, the exercise of which affects Member States and also their citizens." The Court further justified its finding by noting the presence of a kind of representative democracy inside the constitutional structure of the European Community, which seemed to indicate an intention to create an international organization different from all previous international organizations. The difference in question was then rephrased in legal terms, when the Court stressed its own task under Article 177, "the object of which is to secure uniform interpretation of the Treaty by national courts and tribunals" and drew the conclusion that "the States have acknowledged that Community law has an authority which can be invoked by their nationals before those courts and tribunals."[7]

The Court concluded its landmark ruling in a way that linked "federalism" to "rights":

> [The] Community constitutes a new legal order of international law for the benefit of which the States have limited their sovereign rights, albeit within limited fields, and *the subjects of which comprise not only Member States but also their nationals.* Independently of the legislation of Member States, *Community law* therefore not only imposes obligations on individuals but *is also intended to confer upon them rights* which become part of their legal heritage. *These rights arise not only where they are expressly granted by the Treaty, but also by reason of obligations which the Treaty imposes in a clearly defined way upon individuals as well as upon the Member States and upon the institutions of the Community* (emphases added).[8]

What is important for the sake of our analysis is that the Court summed up first all the features inherent in the constitutional structure of the European Community which enabled it to conclude that "a new legal order of international law" had been established, and then took leverage on this conclusion to state a principle unseen before in the landscape of international law, *i.e.*, that individuals could derive *rights* from the rules governing this "new legal order," rights which correspond to the obligations imposed by these rules upon other individuals, the Member States (or any public authority within them) or the institutions of the Community (*i.e.*, the "federal government").

The Community government's power to enact rules which may reach out directly to the citizens, the Member States, or the Community institutions themselves, and to impose upon them obligations and create for them rights parallels what the federal government can do in the United States. But what makes things so different is that in the United States this lawmaking power is clearly defined in the Constitution itself, whereas the treaties establishing the European Communities - the Community "constitution" - are ambiguous at best in this respect. It therefore took an intensive work of judicial construction, approaching the matter through the angle of the rights to be drawn by individuals from Community law, to arrive at the conclusion that a similar lawmaking power must lie with the European Community. It follows that this work of judicial construction contained all by itself the cornerstone of the "federalization" of the constitutional structure of the European Community.

This process only began with the statement that private parties could claim rights under the Community constitution. The Court of Justice had still to construct the tools which were to enable it to guarantee the effectiveness, the supremacy, and the uniform enforcement of Community law rights throughout the several Member States. The provisions of the treaties were, of course, not entirely unhelpful for the construction of these tools, but their international-law origin, which had largely determined their precise wording, had to be discounted considerably before the Court could rely on them having regard to the overall object and purpose of the treaties.[9]

The central provision in this connection proves to be Article 5 of the EC Treaty, the so-called "fidelity clause." It reads as follows:

> Member States shall take all appropriate measures, whether general or particular, to ensure fulfillment of the obligations arising out of this Treaty or resulting from action taken by the institutions of the Community. They shall abstain from any measure which could jeopardize the attainment of the objectives of this Treaty.[10]

Although the obligation for the authorities of the Member States (including their judges, as the Court would later hold[11]) to be loyal to the Community is certainly important for the coherence of Community "federalism," it must be admitted that it falls far short of the explicitness of the Supremacy Clause of the U.S. Constitution (Article VI, Section 2), which contains a judicially enforceable rule - binding upon all federal and state judges - in case of conflict between federal and state law. The equivalent of such a clause is absent from the treaties. Its substance was constructed by the Court of Justice, mainly by interesting private parties in the correct application of Community law by the national courts before which they can bring the appropriate actions to enforce their "rights" flowing from this law against the Member States' authorities and other private parties. In its *Van Gend & Loos* ruling, the Court found that "the vigilance of individuals concerned to protect their rights amounts to an effective supervision [of a Member State's compliance with Community law] in addition to the supervision entrusted by Articles 169 and 170 to the diligence of the Commission and of the Member States."[12]

The Court could hardly have been more explicit that enforcement by the Court of the "rights" of private parties was to be a (judicially constructed) parallel mechanism for ensuring that the Member States fulfilled their Community law obligations and in particular recognized the supremacy of Community law over any inconsistent rule of national law. In *Van Gend & Loos*, the Court concluded "that, according to the spirit, the general scheme and the wording of the Treaty, Article 12 must be interpreted as producing direct effects and creating individual rights which national courts must protect."[13]   Thus, for the first time in the Community's history, a *Dutch* company could recover unduly paid taxes from the *Dutch* authorities on the basis of the rights which it held under Community law with which the *Dutch* tax law had proved to be in conflict.

In the wake of the *Van Gend & Loos* judgment (which can properly be regarded as the *Marbury v. Madison* of European Community constitutional law), the case-law of the Court of Justice concentrated on the need to guarantee the effectiveness (*effect utile*) of Community law[14] and its uniform application in favor of those private parties - in all the Member States - holding rights under it. As we have seen, the Court had supplemented the scheme of judicial supervision of Member State compliance with Community law with one which essentially rested on the initiative of private parties to bring actions in the national courts and defend their Community law rights. The ensuing decentralization of the judicial enforcement of these rights over the national courts made it necessary for the Court of Justice to ensure that the national courts would effectively enforce the Community law rights of private parties.[15]

The Court recognized that national rules of procedure apply as long as the Community does not enact uniform rules of procedure to be observed by national courts in deciding on claims arising under Community law.[16]   But this may threaten the uniform judicial enforcement of Community law, because rules of procedure differ from one Member State to another. The Court therefore imposed obligations on national legal orders to secure the effective enforcement of Community law rights by their courts (so as to guarantee what is known as the "useful effect" of the "direct effect" of provisions of Community law). At first, the Court moved cautiously and simply required that the same rules of procedure apply to actions for the enforcement of rights arising under national law and of similar rights under Community law,[17] a more or less straightforward application of the no-discrimination principle, which is essential to the Community legal order.[18]   The Court later added that even when that no-discrimination requirement is satisfied, national rules of procedure "may not be so framed as to render virtually impossible the exercise of rights conferred by Community law."[19]   This latter condition is known as the requirement of effectiveness.[20]   Since then the Court even recognized the fundamental right of private parties to receive in the national courts an effective remedy for protecting the rights (such as the rights relating to the free movement of goods, persons, services and capital) which they draw from

Community law.[21] The Member States are obliged to create effective remedies whenever they do not exist and to eliminate obstacles to the effectiveness of existing remedies. Since the Court views this obligation as flowing from Community law (in essence from Article 5 of the EC Treaty), it will answer requests for a preliminary ruling under Article 177 of the EC Treaty with a view to filling in the precise contours of that obligation in the context of a Member State's established legal tradition. It goes without saying that these decisions of the Court are bound to be extremely sensitive, for they involve the surrender of sovereignty which the Member States had agreed to in far less explicit terms in the treaties.

Thus, the Court of Justice ruled that a national court which is called upon, within the limits of its jurisdiction, to apply provisions of Community law is under a duty to give full effect to those provisions, if necessary refusing of its own motion to apply any conflicting provision of national legislation, even if adopted subsequently, and it is not necessary for the court to request or await the prior setting aside of such provisions by legislative or other constitutional means.[22] In the grounds of the Court's judgment the requirement of effectiveness is called "of the very essence of Community law," so that any "impediment to the full effectiveness of Community law" had to be rejected even if it were only temporary.[23] As a consequence of this ruling, Italy was forced to abandon its procedural requirement that in case of conflict between a provision of Community law and subsequent national legislation, the courts refer the matter to the constitutional court first in order to have it quash the legislation on the grounds of its inconsistency with Article 11 of the Italian Constitution (which is the legal basis in the Italian legal order for the supremacy of Community law).[24]

The strong rejection of even temporary impediments to the operation of Community law indicates that the Court would not engage in a kind of balancing test, weighing the effectiveness of Community law against the possible cost in terms of national resentment against the Court's ruling. Indeed, since "the very essence of Community law" is at stake, only "full effectiveness" will do. This also underlies the Court's ruling which in effect compelled the House of Lords to abandon the age-old English rule of procedure precluding interim relief against Government decisions, when such interim relief was sought on the ground that a Government decision conflicted with Community law.[25] This ruling too led to a dramatic change in national procedural law insofar as that law provided the framework for the judicial enforcement of Community law. Outside the field of application of Community law, the law of the Member State remains, of course, unaffected by the Court's ruling, but inside that field the national courts have become the decentralized enforcers of Community law, whose full effectiveness they must protect, even at the expense of part of their own procedural autonomy. The justification for that ancillary loss of Member State judicial sovereignty is, here also, the system of Community law, as evidenced in particular by the obligations flowing for national judges from Articles 5 and 177 of the EC Treaty.[26]

The Court's most far-reaching ruling in this area is the *Francovich* judgment of November 19, 1991.[27] In that judgment, the Court stated that the Member States - again principally on the basis of Article 5 of the EEC Treaty (now EC Treaty), this time read in combination with the definition in Article 189 of the same Treaty of the "directive" as a legislative instrument of Community law[28] - must create an action for damages which could be brought against the State, if it does not fulfill its obligations to implement correctly a directive, thereby causing harm to the interests of private parties which would draw rights from such directive if it had been correctly implemented.[29] This ruling marked the first time the Court required Member States to institute a new judicial action, which might have been fully unknown in their national legal traditions, in order to provide an effective judicial remedy for the infringement of Community law on the part of the national political process.

The preceding analysis should have made it clear that the dynamics of the interaction between "federalism" and "rights" are at the core of what distinguishes the European Community from other international organizations. It is - in the words of the Court of Justice - "a Community based on the rule of law, inasmuch as neither its Member States nor its institutions can avoid a review of the question whether the measures adopted by them are in conformity with the basic constitutional charter, the Treaty."[30] This "constitutionalization"[31] of the Treaty, mainly through the recognition of enforceable rights held by private parties under the Treaty and subsequent Community legislation, served to emphasize the federal features inherent in the European Community, such as a division of powers umpired by the central Government's highest court under the provisions of that Government's constitution and the guarantee of a central set of rights which are enforceable against any public authority in the Community and in most instances against other private parties. Thus, a dual structure of sovereignty acting *vis-à-vis* the same citizens (every person holding the nationality of a Member State is indeed a citizen of the European Community[32]) came into existence, a structure in which the Community and the national Governments must respect the basic rights contained in the Treaties.[33]

It can be argued that the relationship between "federalism" and "rights" has something circular to it: the Court of Justice felt legitimized to develop step-by-step the case-law about the direct effect and the supremacy of Community law rights because the EC Treaty seemed to reveal an intention to create something more than just another international organization addressing itself only to the contracting States themselves. As we have seen, the indices were the wording of the preamble of the EC Treaty, its Articles 5, 177, and 189, as well as the creation of Community lawmaking institutions in which the people of the Member States play an important role. And yet, all of these elements would have remained of little significance if the Court of Justice had not inferred from them the structural principles of the direct effect and the supremacy of Community law rights, whose functional equivalent is taken for granted in any mature federal system. The inference of these structural principles, however, greatly increased the degree of "federalism" present in the legal order of the European Community, as well as its visibility.

JUDICIAL INTERPRETATION OF RIGHTS

We turn now to the main Community law rights and to the definition of those rights in light of the "federal" principles in the Community legal order. One must observe initially that the EC Treaty's principal focus is to lay down the ground rules for the establishment and the operation of a "common market." The basically identical concept of the "internal market" rests on "the abolition, as between Member States, of obstacles to the free movement of goods, persons, services and capital" (Article 3, c), of the EC Treaty). The Member States are therefore prohibited from discriminating against goods, persons, services, and capital on grounds of "nationality" or national origin, insofar as the nationality of another Member State is involved.[34]

"Persons" within the Meaning of the EC Treaty

The perspective of market integration (a "common market") becomes even clearer when one considers that "persons" in the EC Treaty refers to wage workers,[35] established self-employed persons,[36] or providers of services not established in the Member State where such services are provided.[37] In other words, it is the participant in the labor market (*sensu lato*), not the national of a Member State, who has the right to move freely across State lines as well as the right not to be discriminated against. But here again, the Court of Justice played a decisive role by extending the concept of "persons" beyond the mere participants in the labor market. It has applied the principle of no-discrimination on grounds of nationality to recipients of services (the Treaty text was silent on this matter). It has also, quite apart of the Treaty provisions on the free movement of goods, persons, services, and capital, offered a dynamic interpretation of the general no-discrimination clause of the Treaty (Article 6 of the EC Treaty, previously Article 7 of the EEC Treaty) which states: "Within the scope of application of this Treaty, any discrimination on grounds of nationality shall be prohibited."

In its *Cowan* judgment of February 2, 1989, the Court ruled that a tourist from a Member State must enjoy as a (potential) recipient of services the same rights in another Member State as that State grants to its own nationals in similar circumstances.[38] In *Cowan*, a British tourist in France had been attacked after leaving a subway station. The French law provides for compensation for the harm suffered only if the victim is French or holds a residence permit or is a national of a country which has entered into a reciprocal agreement on the matter with France. Despite the absence of such an agreement between Britain and France, the Court held that the prohibition of discrimination in Article 7 of the EEC Treaty supported the tourist's compensation claim.[39] Through this ruling, the Court relaxed the economic nexus which was generally believed to be a prerequisite for the applicability of the free movement principle to a national of a Member State wanting to take part in activities in the marketplace of another Member State. If the economic nexus no longer needs to be an "active" one (as wage worker, self-employed person, or provider of services) but can also be a "passive" one (as a potential recipient of services), it goes without saying that every citizen crossing Member State borders inside the Community is protected by the free movement principle and the right to equal protection in the Member States of his travel as a (potential) recipient of services. After all, just taking the bus is a service within the meaning of the Treaty.[40] What was even more striking than the apparent extension *ratione personae* of the free movement principle, was the Court's willingness to recognize an obligation for the Member States to disburse public funds by way of social or medical assistance to a "new" category of persons, *i.e.*, the (potential) recipients of services, under the same substantive conditions as applied to their own nationals.[41]

The judicial construction of the right to equal protection in favor of actual or potential recipients of services in another Member State - thus in reality in favor of all nationals of Member States as such - enhanced prospects for agreement within the Intergovernmental Conference of 1990-1992 (in fact the European Community's "constitutional convention"[42]) on the "citizenship of the Union."[43] The core provision in this respect is Article 8A (1) of the EC Treaty, which reads as follows: "Every citizen of the Union shall have the right to move and reside freely within the territory of the Member States, subject to the limitations and conditions laid down in this Treaty and by the measures adopted to give it effect." The "limitations and conditions" referred to are in the first place contained in the existing Community legislation,[44] which allows the Member States to require evidence from non-economically active nationals of other Member States that they have the necessary means of subsistence and enjoy the coverage of a health insurance regime.[45] But once these threshold requirements for entry in the host Member State are fulfilled, all nationals of other Member States, as "citizens of the Union," have the right to be treated equally as the nationals of the host Member State. Even as to political rights, which are traditionally linked to the possession of the nationality of the State in question, an important step towards a genuinely European citizenship has been taken. Thus, Article 8B of the EC Treaty states that every citizen of the Union residing in a Member State of which he is not a national shall have the right to vote and to stand as a candidate at municipal elections and elections to the European Parliament in the Member State in which he resides, under the same conditions as nationals of that State. As to the elections to the European Parliament, this principle has been implemented by a Council directive of December 6, 1993.[46]

Much of the popular resistance to the creeping "federalism" inherent in the further development of European integration stems from the fear that political rights granted irrespective of nationality will inevitably lead to a European "polity" towards which a certain allegiance will grow over time. This is seen as threatening national sovereignty or even national identity in an integrating Europe. At the same time it illustrates our thesis that the expansion of "rights" held by the person in Europe is perceived as an increase of the degree of "federalism" which characterizes the European Community, or, in other words, that rights generate federalism and only federalism is seen as fully effective in guaranteeing the rights involved. But fears remain that the balance between unity (integration) and diversity (national identity) might in due course drift completely towards the first pole rather than remain in equilibrium between the two poles. This concern contributed to the 50.7 percent of Danish *nej* (June 1992) and to the 49 percent of French *non* (September 1992) to the Treaty on European Union. In both countries the rights attached to the citizenship of the Union were at the heart of the opposition to the new Treaty. The Treaty opponents are not necessarily anti-Europeans, but they advocate intergovernmental cooperation by consensus (a kind of confederalism) which should not promote the creation of rights which citizens of the Member States could claim against Member States other than their own. However, historically the European Community has moved in the direction of properly supranational decisionmaking - with majority voting in the Council producing decisions which are binding in *all* the Member States, including those opposed to the decisions, and which most often have "direct effect." Moreover, the decisionmaking in the Council takes place on a proposal from the Commission, the guarantor of the Community interest as such, and after some interaction with the European Parliament.[47] All of this reflects a kind of federalism.

The challenge ahead is to reconcile the protection of important rights, derived from European Community law and enforceable against all Member States, with the concerns of many of those States that their national "polities" not suffer a loss of dignity or identity as a result of this development.

The other route to enhancing the status of the "person" as a bearer of Community law rights - irrespective of his/her status as a wage worker, a self-employed person, or a provider of services - was first followed in the Court's *Gravier* judgment of February 13, 1985.[48] The Court held that "the imposition on students who are nationals of other Member States, of a charge, a registration fee or the so-called 'minerval' [*i.e.*, additional tuition for foreigners] as a condition of access to vocational training, where the same fee is not imposed on students who are nationals of the host Member State, constitutes discrimination on grounds of nationality contrary to Article 7 of the Treaty."[49] The Court in *Gravier* defined "vocational training" as any course of study which "prepares students for a qualification for a particular profession, trade or employment or provides them with the skills necessary for such a profession, trade or employment."[50] This definition was later applied to almost all disciplines of higher education taught at universities.[51] The right to equal access was further extended to include not only tuition, but also fellowships covering expenses related to obtaining access to education (but not general living costs or even just costs of study[52]) and the public funding systems of universities and institutions of higher learning in general, insofar as they operated to give those institutions an incentive to favor domestic students over those from other Member States.[53]

The landmark character of these cases has to be understood against the background of the unquestioned absence of legislative competencies for the Community in the field of education. The Court, however, found the existence of enforceable Community law rights in favor of students, nationals of other Member States, by skillfully combining Article 7 of the EEC Treaty with

Article 128 of the same Treaty, which grants to the Community the power to "lay down the general principles for implementing a common vocational training policy capable of contributing to the harmonious development both of the national economies and of the common market." It was irrelevant for the Court that the Community had hardly made any use of this power, since the mere existence of the power was enough to conclude that "vocational training" came "within the scope of application of [the EEC] Treaty" (Article 7) so as to make the general prohibition of "any discrimination on grounds of nationality" apply.

Under the Court's approach, when new legislative competencies are conferred upon the Community (see, *e.g.*, in the EC Treaty, the new titles on culture, education, or consumer protection), this increases dramatically the scope of application of the no-discrimination rule, even before the Community legislature first employs such new competencies. In this instance also, the grant of further competencies to the Community produces a sort of multiplier effect in the sense that the mere existence of these competencies strengthens the protection of the rights which the citizens of the Member States enjoy under Community law. Thus, the increase of "federalism" (understood as integration) results in a better shielding of citizens' rights.

Market Integration and Conflicting "Rights"

The Court has repeatedly addressed the tension between market integration (an aspect of federalism) and "rights" held under the national law of Member States, in cases dealing with the free movement of goods, workers, self-employed persons (freedom of establishment), and services. The Treaty provisions relating to these several aspects of the free movement principle all produce "direct effect,"[54] a feature which allows interested private parties to claim rights under them. This leads in turn to requests for a preliminary ruling addressed to the Court of Justice by the national courts. In answering those requests, the Court must devise a judicially workable interpretation of the directly effective Community law provision, since being able to give such an interpretation precisely amounts to the core of what "direct effect" is all about. While the Court endeavors to safeguard the free movement principle, it must also be sensitive to the need for protection of "rights" held by private parties under national law and recognized as possible exceptions to the free movement principle either by some Treaty provisions[55] or else by the Court's case-law.[56] These latter rights cover a wide range of local values protected through the Member States' legislation, such as the protection of the health of people, the environment, consumers, the fairness of commercial transactions, etc. As the national laws involved differ from one Member State to another, they may constitute an obstacle to interstate commerce in the Community and therefore infringe the free movement principle.[57] The Court has refused to accept that the absence of full harmonization by the Community legislature of the national laws required it to permit all obstacles to the free movement principle flowing from these laws. Instead, it tried to itself arbitrate the conflict between the Community law right to free movement and the national laws protecting various rights, but impeding at the same time the right to free movement. The Court therefore introduced the concept of mutual recognition due by the Member States to each other's laws, even in cases where they are different in their actual content.[58] Under this concept, Member States are to authorize on their territory the marketing of goods and services lawfully introduced into the market of another Member State, except insofar as their own national law contains specific marketing conditions for such goods and services (conditions equally applicable to domestic and out-of-state goods and services), which are "recognized as being necessary in order to satisfy mandatory requirements relating in particular to the effectiveness of fiscal supervision, the protection of public health, the fairness of commercial transactions and the defence of the consumer."[59] The list of "mandatory requirements" is by no means comprehensive. The Court may expand the list whenever it judges that the policy goal pursued by a Member State in derogation of the free movement principle significantly advances an aspect of the general interest which is worthy of public protection by the Member State. The Court's approach thus requires a judicial policy choice identifying exceptions to the principle.[60] Using that prerogative, the Court has added the protection of the environment to the list of "mandatory requirements."[61] The Court also exercises a second policy choice in determining whether the national legislation which burdens free movement is actually "necessary" to satisfy the mandatory requirement at hand. If there were less restrictive alternatives, less burdensome for the operation of the free movement principle, yet equally - or only marginally less - effective in satisfying the mandatory requirement, the national legislation would be considered incompatible with Community law.[62] This "means-goals" test draws the Court into the balancing of conflicting "rights,"[63] and the outcome of this balancing depends entirely upon the sort of scrutiny which is to be applied. Basically, the Court has adhered to the general rule of interpretation that the principle (free movement) should be understood extensively in case of doubt, whereas the exception to the principle (the "mandatory requirement" taken care of by a Member State) receives the opposite treatment. In practice, the Member State defending its legislation will succeed only as to the proportionality test when it argues convincingly that its national situation is so specific, and hence different from that prevailing in the other Member States, that the laws of those States must be regarded as insufficient in order to satisfy its needs.[64] If accepted by the Court, this argument clears the way - as a matter of sheer logic - for the Member State to refuse the mutual recognition normally due by Member States to each other's laws, since the Court then, in effect, agrees with the proposition that, in the concrete case, there is no equivalence between the national laws.

The limited protection granted by the Member States to a certain number of rights, as a consequence of the Court's reading of the free movement principle, has resulted in a call for the protection of such rights at the Community level. The Community legislature, as it was structured in the original Treaty of 1957, appears badly equipped to harmonize the national laws protecting all sorts of rights, since decisions require a unanimous vote by the Council on a proposal from the Commission and after consulting the European Parliament.[65] The requirement of unanimity in effect gives every Member State a veto power.[66]

After the adoption of the Single European Act on July 1, 1987, the procedure for decisionmaking was changed. Article 100A of the EC Treaty permits the Council to harmonize national laws pertaining to the internal market, by a qualified majority on a proposal from the Commission in co-decision with the European Parliament. That means that Member States can be outvoted in the Council and yet bound by the Community legislation which is enacted. To cushion that "risk," Article 100A(4) provides for a mechanism whereby a Member State may continue to apply its conflicting national legislation "on grounds of major needs" if neither the Commission nor another Member State objects. If an objection is raised, however, that the Member State in question is just protecting its own market by excluding competing goods or services originating in other Member States, then the matter will be referred to the Court of Justice, which will have the final say.[67]

That the Community should take the protection of rights seriously when it exercises its competence flowing from Article 100A becomes clear through the third paragraph of this provision. It reads as follows: "The Commission, in its proposals...concerning health, safety, environmental protection and consumer protection, will take as a base a high level of protection." It should be clear that the content of the Commission's proposal is essential to guarantee an effective protection to the rights involved. A qualified majority vote in the Council is indeed sufficient to adopt the Commission's proposal,

while it takes a unanimous vote to alter it.[68]   This means that if the
Commission were to take as a base a low level of protection (*i.e.*, clearly below
the present state of the art concerning the protection of health, safety, or the
environment), it would not only infringe Article 100A (3) of the EC Treaty but
also open the way for a single Member State to veto any increase of the level
of protection (which would indeed require the unanimous approval of the
members of the Council, since it constitutes an alteration of the Commission's
proposal).[69]   It remains an open question whether the legislative act adopted
by the Council in conformity with a proposal from the Commission which
infringes Article 100A (3) could be quashed by the Court of Justice when the
validity (constitutionality) of the act is challenged in appropriate
proceedings.[70]

Social Rights

In the field of social rights, the European Community is active in
guaranteeing to women and men the right to equal treatment in labor relations
and social security schemes.[71]   Treaty provisions, legislative acts, and an
important number of judgments of the Court of Justice combine to prohibit all
forms of discrimination, whether direct or indirect.[72]   This prohibition can be
enforced against the public authorities of the Member States (both national
and local) irrespective of whether they are acting as lawmakers or as
employers.[73]   The enforcement of the no-discrimination rule against private
employers may in some cases cause more problems, because - except for the
rule of equal pay for equal work which is contained in a Treaty provision and
hence enforceable *vis-à-vis* public authorities and private parties alike - the
other aspects of the no-discrimination rule are regulated by directives. A
directive is a legislative instrument of the Community which, according to
Article 189 of the EC Treaty "shall be binding, as to the result to be achieved,
upon each Member State to which it is addressed, but shall leave to the
national authorities the choice of form and methods." Under the Court's case-
law, Member States are obliged to incorporate into their national laws all
Community directives within the time-limits set in the directives.[74]   This
obligation flows from the very nature of the directive, which requires the
adoption of national legislation before it reaches its full normative status in the
legal orders of the Member States. If a Member State does not comply with
this obligation within the stated time-limit, it runs the risk that the directive
will nevertheless be relied upon against the public authorities in that State to

judgment to receive "direct effect," *i.e.*, that they are clear, precise and unconditional so as not to leave any political discretion to the Community or the national government.[75] The idea behind this judicial construction is that it would be utterly unacceptable for a Member State to avoid its obligation to incorporate the directive into the national laws and then refuse rights which private parties would have drawn from it if it had been so incorporated. The public authorities of the Member State in question are therefore estopped from defending on the basis of the non-incorporation of the directive into national laws.[76] However, when the non-incorporated directive is invoked against another private party (in the situation here under consideration, normally an employer), that party can successfully base its defense on the non-applicability of the directive in the national legal order, a circumstance for which it obviously bears no responsibility. The enforceability of the right to equal treatment guaranteed by the Community directives might thus be endangered in the labor relations between private employers and their employees, the vast majority of labor relations in the market economies of Europe. The Court has developed some escape routes out of this situation, such as the obligation for national judges to interpret their own laws dynamically so as to make them conform to the content of the non-incorporated directive,[77] and the possibility that a private party harmed by the non-incorporation of the directive into the national laws might obtain damages from the Member State.[78] Although these "solutions" certainly promote equal treatment of women and men between private parties on the basis of the applicable Community legislation, they do not completely ensure a general enforcement of this right against public and private parties alike.

A second area of Community protection of social rights concerns the "vested rights" to social security benefits of wage workers and later also self-employed persons who make use of their fundamental right to free movement throughout the several Member States.[79] The creation of an integrated labor market is impossible if workers moving across State borders forfeited benefits accumulated in the Member State where they previously worked. The relevant Community legislation and case-law of the Court of Justice do not establish any new right to social security benefits but coordinate the applicable national laws to ensure that the effectiveness of the free movement principle is not undermined.[80] The Community law principle is that the right to social security benefits, acquired on the basis of employment in a Member State under the national legislation of that State, remains vested when wage workers or self-employed persons move to another Member State in which they may acquire further rights under the national legislation of that State. The result is a rather complicated "patchwork" of social security benefits, prorated to the time of work in each Member State, but guaranteeing that no social security benefits are lost by workers who make use of the right to free movement.

Finally, the European Community endeavors to prevent labor market integration from leading to "social dumping," the displacement of labor-intensive industries to Member States which offer less protection for the social rights of workers. The Community's legislative competence in this field is, however, limited to "improvements, especially in the working environment, as regards the health and safety of workers" and to "the harmonization of conditions in this area, while maintaining the improvements made" (see Article 118A of the EC Treaty). In addition, the Commission has "the task of promoting close cooperation between Member States in the social field" in a wide variety of matters relating to labor law and social security law.[81] Some critics, however, feared that the establishment of the internal market as of January 1, 1993 - with its entirely open inter-Member State borders - would put pressure on national legislatures to reduce social rights. To counter the critics (especially the trade unions), eleven of the twelve heads of state or government adopted during the Strasbourg meeting of the European Council of December 8-9, 1989, the "Community Charter of Fundamental Social Rights of Workers." The Charter sets ambitious policy objectives to be pursued in the years ahead, but it is not legally binding and the Community currently lacks the legislative competence to adopt the necessary implementing measures. The recent Intergovernmental conference which led to the signing of the Treaty on European Union, concluded without a consensus on the extension of the legislative competence of the Community in this respect. The twelve Member States only agreed that eleven Member States (all except the United Kingdom, as with the adoption of the Charter in 1989) could "have recourse to the institutions, procedures and mechanisms of the Treaty" to take the necessary implementing measures.[82] Although the legal status of such measures is not yet entirely clear, there can be little doubt about the political significance of the Charter as the starting point for a "federal" basic (Community) protection of the social rights of workers to be respected by the Member States.

In conclusion, the protection of social rights by the Community emerged as a by-product of the establishment of the internal market. It has been recognized that in order to make the latter project acceptable without undermining the conceptions prevailing in most Member States about the social rights of workers, a harmonization of the level of those rights through the enactment of Community legislation was essential. Here again, federalism (integration) should assure the continued protection of rights in a situation which is otherwise characterized by fierce competition between the economies of the Member States operating in a single "internal market."

Fundamental Rights

The treaties do not contain a catalogue of fundamental rights,[83] although some discrete expressions of such rights are to be found in a number of Treaty provisions.[84] In that sense, the present text of the treaties could be compared to that of the United States Constitution that came out of the Philadelphia Convention, before the addition of the first ten amendments.[85] This has not, however, prevented the Court from ensuring that in the field of protection of fundamental rights "the law is observed" (Article 164 of the EC Treaty). As it said in the *Nold* case:

> Fundamental rights form an integral part of the general principles of law, the observance of which [the Court] ensures. In safeguarding these rights the Court is bound to draw inspiration from constitutional traditions common to the Member States, and it cannot therefore uphold measures which are incompatible with fundamental rights recognized and protected by the Constitutions of those States. Similarly, international treaties for the protection of human rights on which the Member States have collaborated or of which they are signatories, can supply guidelines which should be followed within the framework of Community law.[86]

Among those treaties, the European Convention for the Protection of Human Rights and Fundamental Freedoms of November 4, 1950, is particularly important.[87] For acts of the Community institutions to be constitutional, they must be compatible "with the requirements of the protection of fundamental rights in the Community legal order."[88] And the Court added: "Since those requirements are also binding on the Member States when they implement Community rules, the Member States must, as far as possible, apply those rules in accordance with those requirements."[89] The constitutionalization of fundamental rights protection in the Community legal order did not, however, lead to a kind of EC version of the Fourteenth Amendment to the U. S. Constitution, which would have enabled the Court to incorporate selectively the several fundamental rights recognized at the level of the Community into a Community fundamental rights standard which the Court could enforce against the Member States (proceeding on the basis of the principle of supremacy of Community law).[90] The case-law has consistently held that "although it is the duty of the Court to ensure observance of

Federalism and Rights

fundamental rights in the field of Community law, it has no power to examine the compatibility with the European Convention on Human Rights of national legislation lying outside the scope of Community law."[91]   The issue then becomes, of course, whether a national act, said to be incompatible with the European Convention on Human Rights, lies or not "outside the scope of Community law."[92]   And as it appears, the solution of that issue may depend in part on the compatibility of national legislation with the Community fundamental rights standard upheld by the Court, which makes the reasoning look rather circular.   The Court indeed ruled in its *Elliniki* judgment of June 18, 1991,[93] that when Member States defend their legislation in the face of the free movement principle by reference to one of the exception clauses provided for in the EC Treaty or allowed under the Court's case-law, the legislation to be justified under such clause must be compatible with the Community fundamental rights standard.   If it is not, the reference to the exception clause will fail and the measure will by the same token be prohibited as an infringement of the free movement principle and thus come under the scope of Community law.   If it is compatible with the fundamental rights standard,[94] the reference to the exception clause can succeed, so that the national legislation will no longer come under the scope of the Community's prohibition of infringements on the free movement principle.   Thus, the Court avoids pronouncing on the compatibility of national laws or acts with the Community fundamental rights standard whenever these laws or acts are foreign to Community law,[95] but the slightest nexus between such laws or acts and Community law, such as the need of their authorization under an exception clause provided for in the Treaty or in the Court's own case-law, is sufficient to justify an inquiry regarding their consistency with the Court's fundamental rights standard.

The reluctance of the Court of Justice to examine whether actions of the Member States which fall outside the substantive scope of Community law comply with the Community fundamental rights standard does not, however, lead to a gap in the judicial protection of fundamental rights.   In such cases the other supranational legal order in Europe, the legal order established by the European Convention for the Protection of Human Rights and Fundamental Freedoms (hereinafter the "ECHR") within the Council of Europe, may intervene.[96]   All Member States of the European Community, along with fifteen other European States, are contracting parties to the ECHR.   The control machinery of this convention serves to enforce the fundamental rights of the people against the EC Member States, when they act under their residual - *i.e.*, non-Community related - powers.   All Member States of the European

Community have accepted that individual complaints can be lodged against them before the European Commission of Human Rights in accordance with Article 25 of the ECHR. They have also accepted the compulsory jurisdiction of the European Court of Human Rights.[97] This means that outside the scope of application of Community law, the EC Member States are not only bound by the ECHR, but are, in addition, equally subject to judicial review of their actions (or inaction) as to their consistency with the fundamental rights protected in the ECHR (a list which is in most respects similar to the U.S. Bill of Rights).[98]

Just like its Luxembourg counterpart did within the framework of the European Community, the Strasbourg Court of Human Rights interpreted the ECHR in a most dynamic way "having regard to the object and purpose of the Convention"[99] and stating that "unlike international treaties of the classic kind, the Convention comprises more than mere reciprocal engagements between contracting States. It creates over and above a network of mutual, bilateral undertakings, objective obligations which in the words of the preamble, benefit from a collective enforcement."[100] The reference to the supranational character of the ECHR legal order (which in this sense can be labelled as a kind of supervisory federalism) only served to strengthen the legitimacy of a far-reaching judicial protection of fundamental rights.

CONCLUSION

The European Community has long been perceived as an intergovernmental construction of a somewhat novel kind, with the Council deciding all important matters by a unanimous vote while the truly supernational organs, the Commission and the European Parliament, intervene in the decisionmaking in a lateral fashion.

After the entry into force of the Single European Act, this perception had to be corrected because qualified majority voting in the Council became the usual practice, and this for a whole range of quite essential policy choices.[101] The input of the Commission increased also because the power brokering role which it can play in the Council is definitely more effective when only a majority (albeit a qualified one) has to be obtained rather than a general consensus.[102] The European Parliament saw its role equally increased through the "cooperation" procedure.

Now that the Treaty on European Union has entered into force, the perception of the original thirty years will have to be nuanced further. With a single currency, a citizenship of the Union triggering its own set of rights, a common foreign and security policy, an internal market and "economic and social cohesion" (a catchword for financial solidarity at Community level between the richer and the poorer Member States), even the most reluctant observer will have to recognize that important features of "federalism" have found their way in the political landscape of the Community, both in the process of decisionmaking and in the constitutional rules to be observed by that process. In spite of this, the drafters of the Treaty on European Union decided not to mention the "federal vocation" of the Union in this Treaty, apparently in order not to scare away the eurosceptics. And, of course, the presence or absence of the term "federal vocation" does not really add anything to the substance of the Treaty.

What matters here, as a conclusion to our analysis, is that whether one characterizes the political process of the Community since 1957 as confederal or federal, Community law has throughout been properly federal, with the Court of Justice enforcing the "rights" conferred by Community law to private parties in their relationship to the Community institutions themselves, the Member States, and other private parties. The principles of supremacy of Community law over conflicting national law and of "direct effect" of a wide variety of provisions of Community law stand out as the most visible beacons of this kind of normative federalism, which structures the interaction between Community and Member State law. The pivotal role of the concept of "rights" held by private parties under Community law therefore belongs to the essence of what "federalism" in the European Community was all about from the beginning, and this irrespective of the further development of the federal features of the political decisionmaking at the Community level.

Has the protection of "rights" been strengthened by the establishment of the European Community? On the whole, yes. The rights to free movement and equal protection of the nationals of one Member State, in all other Member States, the several kinds of social rights and the umbrella of fundamental rights (through the interaction of the legal orders of the Community and the ECHR) all contribute in significant ways to the improvement of the "rights" status of private parties against the public authorities of their own and the other Member States as well as against other private parties (except in the latter case for some lack of efficiency as to the enforceability of such rights when they are stated in Community directives).

However, a closer look into the balance of powers inherent in Community "federalism" may lead to a more critical assessment. When the Community harmonizes - with a view to the smooth operation of the internal market - a range of national laws protecting health, the environment, consumers, or the national cultural heritage or local traditions in the field of education, the "rights" enjoyed by private parties for some matters in some Member States under the previously applicable national laws may be curtailed after their regulation at Community level. In some cases the Court of Justice expressly limited the reach of the free movement principle in order to pay heed to values of "regional" diversity, thus protecting the "rights" held by the local people under their laws,[103] but in other cases it just as clearly failed to do so.[104] The Court's case-by-case approach does not leave an overall impression of steadiness.

The political process of the Community is equally under pressure not to pursue any longer the centralized regulatory drive which has at times characterized it. Thus, the new Article 3b of the EC Treaty states that

> in areas which do not fall within its exclusive competence, the Community shall take action, in accordance with the principle of subsidiarity, only if and in so far as the objectives of the proposed action cannot be sufficiently achieved by the Member States and can therefore, by reason of the scale or effects of the proposed action, be better achieved by the Community.[105]

As a guideline for the functioning of a system of divided powers, the principle of subsidiarity aims at maximizing the protection of the people's rights by vesting the responsibility for such protection with the level of government which is best able to take care of it. If successful, the institution of the principle of subsidiarity should strike a balance of "federalism" which is acceptable to public authorities and private parties alike as a common denominator between what appears to be desirable and feasible in the protection of "rights."

NOTES

1.   See our earlier reflections on this matter in Koen Lenaerts, "Constitutionalism and the Many Faces of Federalism," *American Journal of Comparative Law*, 38 (1990): 205-263. Compare Joseph H.H. Weiler, "The Community System: The Dual Character of Supranationalism," *Yearbook of European Law*, 1 (1981): 267-306.

2.   Attempts to include in the Treaty on European Union a reference to the "federal vocation" of the Union, a new name for the integration project taking place within the broader context of the European Community, failed at the end of 1991 as a consequence of fierce opposition voiced by a minority of Member States.

3.   Article C, first paragraph, of the Treaty on European Union.   The *acquis communautaire* is the term used in all nine official languages of the Community to designate the state of Community law considered at any given moment (in this case, on the day of signing of the Treaty on European Union).

4.   Article A, second paragraph, of the Treaty on European Union.
5.   Judgment of February 5, 1963, *Van Gend & Loos v. Netherlands Inland Revenue Administration*, Case 26/62, (1963) ECR 1, at 11.
6.   Article 169 of the EEC Treaty (now EC Treaty) reads as follows:

If the Commission considers that a Member State has failed to fulfill an obligation under this Treaty, it shall deliver a reasoned opinion on the matter after giving the State concerned the opportunity to submit its observations. If the State concerned does not comply with the opinion within the period laid down by the Commission, the latter may bring the matter before the Court of Justice.

Article 170 of the EEC Treaty (now EC Treaty) reads as follows:

A Member State which considers that another Member State has failed to fulfill an obligation under this Treaty may bring the matter before the Court of Justice. Before a Member State brings an action against another Member State for an alleged infringement of an obligation under this Treaty, it shall bring the matter before the Commission. The Commission shall deliver a reasoned opinion after each of the States concerned has been given the opportunity to submit its own case and its observations on the other party's case both orally and in writing. If the Commission has not delivered an opinion within three months of the date on which the matter was brought before it, the absence of such opinion shall not prevent the matter from being brought before the Court of Justice.

For a comment on these provisions, see Ulrich Everling, "The Member States of the European Community before Their Court of Justice," *European Law Review*, 9 (1984): 215-241.
7.   For the quotations contained in this paragraph, see (1963) ECR 1, at 12.
8.   (1963) ECR 1, at 12, fourth paragraph.
9.   The Court's approach to the interpretation of the Treaty text may have appeared innovative in 1963, when it handed down its *Van Gend & Loos* judgment, but it was later confirmed in the international-law field by Article 31 of the Vienna Convention on the Law of Treaties (1969) which has entered into force for the huge majority of countries, members of the United Nations.
10.   See John Temple Lang, "Community Constitutional Law: Article 5 EEC Treaty," *Common Market Law Review*, 27 (1990): 645-681.
11.   See, *e.g.*, the *Rewe/Comet* (1976), *Simmenthal* (1978), *Factortame* (1990) and *Francovich* (1991) judgments, discussed hereinafter. The underlying philosophy of the system is exemplified by the following quote from the opinion of Advocate-General G.F. Mancini in *Jongeneel Kaas*, Case 237/82, (1984) ECR 483, at 520:

The general principles elicited by the Court from the primary and secondary provisions of Community law, and in particular from those fundamental values which are common to the legal systems of the Member States, form part of the Community legal order and may therefore be relied upon by individuals before *the national court* which, as is well known, is also *a Community court* (emphasis added).

12. (1963) ECR 1, at 13, fifth paragraph.

13. (1963) ECR 1, at 13, sixth paragraph.

14. Compare Pierre Pescatore, "The Doctrine of Direct Effect, an Infant Disease of Community Law," *European Law Review*, 8 (1983): 155-177.

15. See "Editorial Comments," *Common Market Law Review*, 28 (1991): 711-716.

16. See the judgments of December 16, 1976, *Rewe*, Case 33/76, (1976) ECR 1989, at 1997, paragraph 5 (3); and *Comet*, Case 45/76, (1976) ECR 2043, at 2053, paragraph 13:

> [In] the absence of any relevant Community rules, it is for the national legal order of each Member State to designate the competent courts and to lay down the procedural rules for proceedings designed to ensure the protection of the rights which individuals acquire through the direct effect of Community law.

17. See the end of paragraph 13 of the *Comet* judgment which immediately follows the passage of that paragraph quoted above, note 16: "... provided that such rules are not less favourable than those governing the same right of action on an internal matter." Compare the *Rewe* judgment of the same day, (1976) ECR 1989, 1997-1998, paragraph 5 (3) *in fine*: "... it being understood that such conditions cannot be less favourable than those relating to similar actions of a domestic nature."

18. Henry G. Schermers and Denis F. Waelbroeck, *Judicial Protection in the European Communities*, 4th ed. (Deventer: Kluwer, 1987), pp. 62-67, §§116-124; Koen Lenaerts, "L'égalité de traitement en droit communautaire: un principe unique aux apparences multiples," *Cahiers de droit européen*, 27 (1991): 3-41.

19. Judgment of November 9, 1983, *San Giorgio*, Case 199/82, (1983) ECR 3595, at 3612, paragraph 12.

20. This requirement was first stated in the *Comet* judgment, (1976) ECR 2043, at 2053, paragraph 16:

> The position [*i.e.*, the applicability of the rules of procedure laid down by national law] would be different only if those rules and time-limits made it impossible in practice to exercise rights which the national courts have a duty to protect.

See also the judgment of July 10, 1980, *Ariete*, Case 811/79, (1980) ECR 2545, at 2554-2555, paragraph 12, last sentence.

21. See the judgment of October 15, 1987, *Heylens*, Case 222/86, (1987) ECR 4097, at 4117, paragraph 14:

> Since free access to employment is a fundamental right which the Treaty confers individually on each worker in the Community, the existence of a remedy of a judicial nature is essential in order to secure for the individual effective protection for his right. ...[That] requirement reflects a general principle of Community law which underlies the constitutional traditions common to the Member States and has been enshrined in Articles 6 and 13 of the European Convention for the Protection of Human Rights and Fundamental Freedoms.

22. Judgment of March 9, 1978, *Simmenthal*, Case 106/77, (1978) ECR 629, at 645-646.

23. *Ibidem*, at 644, paragraphs 22 and 23.

24. "Italian Corte Costituzionale, judgment of June 8, 1984, *S.P.A. Granital v. Amministrazione delle Finanze dello Stato*," *Common Market Law Review*, 21 (1984): 764-772, with comments by Giorgio Gaja.

25. Judgment of the Court of Justice of June 19, 1990, *Factortame*, Case C-213/89, (1990) ECR I-2433, at I-2475, *dictum*; British House of Lords, judgment of October 11, 1990, *Factortame*, 1 All E R 70 (1991).

26. *Ibidem*, paragraph 19 (as to the reference to Article 5) and paragraphs 21 and 22:

> [The] full effectiveness of Community law would be...impaired if a rule of national law could prevent a court seised of a dispute governed by Community law from granting interim relief in order to ensure the full effectiveness of the judgment to be given on the existence of the rights claimed under Community law. It follows that a court which in those circumstances would grant interim relief, if it were not for a rule of national law, is obliged to set aside that rule. That interpretation is reinforced by the system established by Article 177 of the EEC Treaty whose effectiveness would be impaired if a national court, having stayed proceedings pending the reply by the Court of Justice to the question referred to it for a preliminary ruling, were not able to grant interim relief until it delivered its judgment following the reply given by the Court of Justice.

27. Joined Cases C-6/90 and C-9/90, (1991) ECR I-5357.

28. Article 189, third paragraph, of the EC Treaty: "A directive shall be binding, as to the result to be achieved, upon each Member State to which it is addressed, but shall leave to the national authorities the choice of form and methods." On the obligation for Member States to adopt the necessary implementing measures, see the judgment of the Court of Justice of May 6, 1980, *Commission v. Belgium*, Case 102/79, (1980) ECR 1473, at 1487, paragraph 12.

29. This was so in the facts of the case underlying the Court's *Francovich* judgment. The Community directive at issue had obliged the Member States to establish a national guarantee fund which should, under some circumstances, take over the financial obligations of insolvent employers *vis-à-vis* their workers. Italy had not established any such fund and now faced claims brought against it by workers who could not obtain payment of what was still due to them by their - in the meantime insolvent - employer. Another situation in which the Member State's failure to implement a directive into national law might cause harm to a private party, is that in which the directive's content is clear, precise, and unconditional and therefore capable of producing "direct effect," but should be invoked by one private party against another private party, which is not possible when the directive has not been first implemented in a provision of national law. See the judgments of the Court of Justice of February 26, 1986, *Marshall I*, Case 152/84, (1986) ECR 723, at 749, paragraph 48; of August 2, 1993, *Marshall II*, Case C-271/91, (1993) ECR I-4367; and of July 14, 1994, *Faccini Dori*, Case C-91/92, (1994) ECR not yet reported.

30. Judgment of April 23, 1986, *Parti écologiste "Les Verts" v. European Parliament*, Case 294/83, (1986) ECR 1339, at 1365, paragraph 23.

31. Compare Trevor C. Hartley, "Federalism, Courts, and Legal Systems: The Emerging Constitution of the European Community," *American Journal of Comparative Law*, 34 (1986): 229-247.

32. See Article 8 (1) of the EC Treaty. Thus, Member States are bound to grant full recognition to the operation of the other Member States' nationality laws, without having the right to subject such recognition to any further conditions. See the judgment of the Court of Justice of July 7, 1992, *Micheletti*, Case C-369/90, (1992) ECR not yet reported.

33. The European Community rests not only on the treaties which have established the three European Communities (Treaty establishing the European Coal and Steel Community, signed in Paris on April 18, 1951; Treaty establishing the European [Economic] Community, signed in Rome on March 25, 1957; and Treaty establishing the European Atomic Energy Community, signed in Rome on March 25, 1957), but also on the annexes and protocols to these Treaties (which have the same normative force as the treaties themselves - see Articles 84 of the ECSC Treaty, 239 of the EEC Treaty and 207 of the EAEC Treaty). These treaties have been amended on several occasions, *inter alia*, through the Convention on certain institutions common to the European Communities (signed in Rome on March 25, 1957), the so-called "Merger Treaty," establishing a Single Council and a Single Commission of the European Communities (*Official Journal of the European Communities*, hereinafter *O.J.E.C.*, 1967, 152), the Treaty amending Certain Budgetary Provisions (*O.J.E.C.*, 1971, L 2), the Treaty amending Certain Financial Provisions (*O.J.E.C.*, 1977, L 359), the Act concerning the election of the representatives of the European Parliament by direct universal suffrage (*O.J.E.C.*, 1976, L 278), the Single European Act (*O.J.E.C.*, 1987, L 169), and the Treaty on European Union (*O.J.E.C.*, 1992, C 224). In addition, there are three Acts of Accession, adjusting the original Treaties, the Act of 1972 on the accession of Denmark, Ireland, and the United Kingdom (*O.J.E.C.*, 1972, L 73), the Act of 1979 on the accession of Greece (*O.J.E.C.*, 1979, L 291), and the Act of 1985 on the accession of Portugal and Spain (*O.J.E.C.*, 1985, L 302). For a case in which an act of the Council was censured by the Court on the grounds that it infringed the basic rights to free movement and to equal treatment of migrant workers, see the judgment of January 15, 1986, *Pinna*, Case 41/84, (1986) ECR 1.

34. Nationals of third States can, of course, also obtain rights on the basis of Community law, but then mainly through special legal instruments, such as international agreements concluded between the Community and third States, or else as a consequence of their special situation, *e.g.*, as a member of the family of a Community national. For a recent example in the case-law, see the judgment of the Court of Justice of July 7, 1992, *The Queen v. Immigration Appeal Tribunal and Surinder Singh*, Case C-370/90, (1992) ECR not yet reported.

35. Articles 48-51 of the EC Treaty.

36. Articles 52-58 of the EC Treaty.

37. Articles 59-66 of the EC Treaty.

38. (1989) ECR 195.

39. (1989) ECR 195, at 223.

40. See Article 60, first paragraph, of the EC Treaty: "Services shall be considered to be 'services' within the meaning of this Treaty where they are normally provided for remuneration." Cf. G. Federico Mancini, "The Making of a Constitution for Europe," *Common Market Law Review*, 25 (1989): 595, at 606-608.

41. Compare Article 15 (3) of the European Parliament's Declaration of fundamental rights and freedoms (*O.J.E.C.*, 1989, C 120/51-52), providing that "anyone lacking sufficient resources shall have the right to social and medical assistance." The Declaration has no binding

legal status, but the quoted provision can be seen as the expression of the *acquis communautaire* inasmuch as it restates the right to equal treatment for the nationals of Member States who exercise their freedom of movement and of residence guaranteed by Community law in any other Member State.

42. See Article 236 of the EEC Treaty, now Article N of the Treaty on European Union. The texts adopted by such a "conference of representatives of the Governments of the Member States...shall enter into force after being ratified by all the Member States in accordance with their respective constitutional requirements." The latter may be a referendum (*e.g.*, Denmark and Ireland), a referendum at the initiative of the President of the Republic (France), or a parliamentary vote (all other Member States).

43. The "citizenship of the Union" is regulated by Articles 8 to 8E of the EC Treaty, which are justiciable provisions of the Community constitution (see Article L of the Treaty on European Union).

44. Compare David O'Keeffe, "The Free Movement of Persons and the Single Market," *European Law Review*, 17 (1992): 3, at 4-6.

45. Such requirements may not be imposed on migrant workers, self-employed persons and providers of services who all enjoy protection under the relevant Treaty Articles granting them the right to free movement in the common market. See, *e.g.*, the judgment of the Court of Justice of February 5, 1991, Case C-363/89, (1991) ECR I-273.

46. Directive 93/109/EC, *O.J.E.C.*, 1993, L 329/34.

47. See Articles 189B and 189C EC Treaty.

48. (1985) ECR 593.

49. (1985) ECR 593, at 615, *dictum* (1).

50. (1985) ECR 593, at 615, *dictum* (2).

51. See the judgment of the Court of Justice of February 2, 1988, *Blaizot*, Case 24/86, (1988) ECR 379.

52. See the judgment of the Court of Justice of June 21, 1988, *Lair*, Case 39/86, (1988) ECR 3161, at 3195, paragraph 16, and *Brown*, Case 197/86, (1988) ECR 3205, at 3243, paragraph 19.

53. See the judgment of the Court of Justice of September 27, 1988, *Commission v. Belgium*, Case 42/87, (1988) ECR 5445.

54. See the Articles 30 (goods), 48 (workers), 52 (self-employed persons/freedom of establishment), and 59 and 60 (services) of the EC Treaty, all of which were granted "direct effect" throughout the Court's case-law: see the judgments of March 22, 1977, *Iannelli*, Case 74/76, (1977) ECR 557, at 575, paragraph 13 (about Article 30); December 4, 1974, *Van Duyn*, Case 41/74, (1974) ECR 1337, at 1346-1347, paragraphs 4-8 (about Article 48); June 21, 1974, *Reyners*, Case 2/74, (1974) ECR 631, at 651-652, paragraphs 26-30 (about Article 52); and December 3, 1974, *Van Binsbergen*, Case 33/74, (1974) ECR 1299, at 1312, paragraph 27 (about Articles 59 and 60).

55. See Articles 36, 48 (3), 56, and 66 of the EC Treaty providing for exceptions to the free movement principle on grounds of public policy, public security, or public health (and some other grounds as to goods - see Article 36), which have been interpreted restrictively by the Court; see, as representative examples, the judgments of October 28, 1975, *Rutili*, Case 36/75, (1975) ECR 1219 (about Article 48 (3)), and May 20, 1976, *De Peijper*, Case 104/75, (1976) ECR 613.

56. In the field of the free movement of goods, see the "Cassis de Dijon" principle, established by the Court's judgment of February 20, 1979, *Rewe-Zentral v. Bundesmonopolverwltung für Branntwein*, (1979) ECR 649 (national legislation which is indistinctly applicable to domestic and imported goods, yet hinders inter-Member State trade, may escape from the prohibition laid down in Article 30 of the EEC Treaty if it is "necessary" to satisfy a "mandatory requirement" of general interest to the Member State in question). In the field of the free movement of services, the Court allows for "specific requirements" being imposed on the providers of the services (*e.g.*, "where they have as their purpose the application of professional rules, justified by the general good or by the need to ensure the protection of the [consumer]") even if they somewhat hinder the cross-border providing of services. But, as for goods, the Court will be extremely restrictive as to recognizing that the measures adopted to meet such requirements are really necessary and that no less restrictive alternatives are available. See the judgment of January 18, 1979, *Van Wesemael*, Case 111/78, (1979) ECR 35, at 52-53, paragraphs 28-30.

57. The Court of Justice has indeed held that "all trading rules enacted by Member States which are capable of hindering, directly or indirectly, actually or potentially, intra-Community trade are to be considered as measures having an effect equivalent to quantitative restrictions" (judgment of July 11, 1974, *Dassonville*, Case 8/74, (1974) ECR 837, at 852, paragraph 5), which are prohibited by Article 30 of the EC Treaty. Thus, national laws which are indistinctly applicable to domestic and imported goods may nevertheless be "capable of hindering" intra-Community trade, solely because the burden for manufacturers of imported goods to conform to such national laws is heavier (they will have to conform in fact to their domestic laws as well as to the laws of all the Member States to which they intend to export) than for manufacturers of domestic goods. If one looks more closely to this line of reasoning, the true cause of the hindrance of intra-Community trade simply is the divergence between the applicable national laws.

58. Mutual recognition in the field of the free movement of services means that the Member State in which the services are provided "must take into account the evidence and guarantees already furnished by the provider of the services for the pursuit of his activities in the Member State of his establishment"; see the judgment of December 17, 1981, *Webb*, Case 279/80, (1981) ECR 3305, at 3326, paragraph 20, last sentence. For a more recent application of the same line of reasoning relating to the issue of the mutual recognition of diplomas and professional qualifications, see the judgment of the Court of Justice of May 7, 1991, *Vlassopoulou*, Case C-340/89, (1991) ECR I-2357 (rather than being allowed to refuse recognition to the Greek diploma in law and the subsequent legal experience of Ms. Vlassopoulou in Germany, this Member State was put under an obligation to analyze with great care the precise extent of professional knowledge that had thus been acquired by Ms. Vlassopoulou who wanted to become "Rechtsanwalt" in Germany. Therefore, the German authorities could only impose the additional training requirements which would still seem to be necessary after having duly taken into account the legal training received, *inter alia*, in the Member State of origin).

59. See the "Cassis de Dijon" judgment, cited above, note 56, (1979) ECR 649, at 662, paragraph 8 (2).

60. See the wording of the Court's assessment that the elimination of possible abuse in the provision of manpower "amounts for [Member States] to a legitimate choice of policy pursued in the public interest":

[The] provision of manpower is a particularly sensitive matter from the occupational and social point of view. Owing to the special nature of the employment relationships inherent in that kind of activity, pursuit of such a business directly affects both relations on the labour market and the lawful interests of the workforce concerned.

(See the *Webb* judgment, cited above, note 59, (1981) ECR 3305, at 3325, quotations from paragraphs 19 and 18.) It is hard to imagine a more open kind of discussion of the judicial policy choice which has guided the Court's reasoning.

61.   See the judgment of the Court of Justice of September 20, 1988, *Commission v. Denmark*, Case 302/86, (1988) ECR 4607, at 4630, paragraph 9.

62.   For an application of the "less restrictive alternatives" test, see the so-called German beer case, in which the centuries-old law (of Bavarian origin) mandating the purity for beer brought onto the German market (which means that only beer manufactured on the basis of natural ingredients may be marketed) was considered to be inconsistent with the free movement principle, because the objectives stated for the law (health and consumer protection) could have been reached, according to the Court, through alternative means which would have been less burdensome for the cross-border trade in beer, such as an appropriate warning on the label of the bottle.   See the judgment of the Court of Justice of March 12, 1987, *Commission v. Germany*, Case 178/84, (1987) ECR 1227.

63.   See, *e.g.*, in the just cited German beer case, the Court's approach in explaining why a ban on additives is not really necessary to protect public health: "Mere reference to the potential risks of the ingestion of additives in general and to the fact that beer is a foodstuff consumed in large quantities does not suffice to justify the imposition of stricter rules in the case of beer," (1987) ECR 1227, at 1275, paragraph 49, last sentence.   The Court then in essence referred to "the findings of international scientific research and in particular the work of the Community's Scientific Committee for Food, the Codex Alimentarius Committee of the FAO and the World Health Organization," *ibidem*, at 1276, paragraph 52, to conclude that the application of the German requirement of purity to beers imported from other Member States was contrary to the free movement principle of Community law.

64.   For a case in which the defending Member State was successful at its argument, see the judgment of the Court of Justice of January 28, 1986, *Commission v. France*, Case 188/84, (1986) ECR 419 (relating to technical and safety standards for woodworking machines).

65.   See Article 100 of the EC Treaty.

66.   But see Article 148 (3) of the EC Treaty: "Abstentions by members present in person or represented shall not prevent the adoption by the Council of acts which require unanimity."

67.   See James Flynn, "How Will Article 100A (4) Work? A Comparison with Article 93," *Common Market Law Review*, 24 (1987): 689-707.

68.   See Article 189A of the EC Treaty.

69.   This would be a case of application of the just quoted Treaty provision, note 68.

70.   The applicant in an annulment action (Article 173 of the EC Treaty) could be a Member State that should have obtained the unanimous approval of all the other Member States in order to raise the level of protection proposed by the Commission, but did not succeed in this respect.   A challenge to the Council's act could also be raised through the preliminary rulings procedure (Article 177, b, of the EC Treaty).

71.   See generally A. Th. S. Leenen, "Equal Treatment of Male and Female Employees under European Community Law," *Legal Issues of European Integration*, (1986): 91-114.

72. See Thijmen Koopmans, "Equal Protection - The Social Dimension of European Community Law," *Michigan Journal of International Law*, 11 (1989): 1-10. As an illustration of the Court's approach, the judgment of May 13, 1986, can be mentioned, *Bilka v. Weber von Hartz*, Case 170/84, (1986) ECR 1607. There, the Court held that the rule of equal pay for equal work, contained in Article 119 of the EC Treaty, was infringed by an undertaking which excludes part-time employees from its occupational pension scheme, where that exclusion affects a far greater number of women than men, unless the undertaking shows that the exclusion is based on objectively justified factors unrelated to any discrimination on grounds of sex.

73. See the judgment of the Court of Justice of February 26, 1986, cited above, (1986) ECR 723, at 749, paragraph 49.

74. See above, note 73.

75. See, *e.g.*, the judgment of the Court of Justice of July 12, 1990, *Foster v. British Gas*, Case C-188/89, (1990) ECR I-3313, at I-3348, paragraph 18.

76. See, *e.g.*, the judgments of the Court of Justice of April 5, 1979, *Ratti*, Case 148/78, (1979) ECR 1629; and of January 19, 1982, *Becker*, Case 8/81, (1982) ECR 53.

77. Vested case-law since the judgments of April 10, 1984, *Von Colson & Camann v. Land Nordrhein-Westfalen*, Case 14/83, (1984) ECR 1891; and *Harz v. Deutsche Tradax GmbH*, Case 79/83, (1984) ECR 1921. For a comment, see Deirdre Curtin, "Effective Sanctions and the Equal Treatment Directive: The Von Colson and Harz Cases," *Common Market Law Review*, 22 (1985): 505-532.

78. See the judgment of the Court of Justice of November 19, 1991, *Francovich*, cited above.

79. See Article 51 of the EC Treaty and Council Regulation (EEC) No. 1408/71, as codified by Council Regulation (EEC) No. 2001/83 of June 2, 1983, *O.J.E.C.*, 1983, L 230.

80. See, *e.g.*, the judgment of the Court of Justice of July 12, 1984, *Patteri*, Case 242/83, (1984) ECR 3171.

81. See Article 118 of the EC Treaty and the extensive interpretation made of this provision in the judgment of the Court of Justice of July 9, 1987, *Germany, France, Netherlands, Denmark, and United Kingdom v. Commission*, Joined Cases 281, 283 to 285 and 287/85, (1987) ECR 3203.

82. See Article 1 of the Protocol on Social Policy, attached to the EC Treaty by the Treaty on European Union. The Protocol has the same normative status as the Treaty itself (Cf. Article 239 of the EC Treaty).

83. For an analysis of the possibility of insertion of a "Bill of Rights" in the Community Treaties, see Koen Lenaerts, "Fundamental Rights to Be Included in a Community Catalogue," *European Law Review*, 16 (1991): 367-390.

84. See, *e.g.*, Article 6 of the EC Treaty (no-discrimination on grounds of nationality) or Article 119 of the EC Treaty (equal pay for equal work performed by women and men).

85. Cf. Laurence H. Tribe, *American Constitutional Law* 2d ed. (Mineola: Foundation Press, 1988), p. 4, note 7: "The Constitutional Convention decided against including a Bill of Rights largely in the belief that Congress was in any event delegated none of the powers such a bill would seek to deny." In the European Community, the idea would rather have been that it was unthinkable that in a supranational structure of economic powers, the fundamental rights of the people, thought of during the 1950s as being solely civil and political rights, could be at risk. See Pierre Pescatore, "Referat, Der Schutz der Grundrechte in den Europäischen Gemeinschaften und seine Lücken," *Grundrechtsschutz in Europa, Europäische*

Menschenrechts-Konvention und Europäische Gemeinschaften, Hermann Mosler, Rudolf Bernhardt, and Meinhard Hilf eds. (Berlin: Springer, 1977), pp. 64-75.

86. See the judgment of the Court of Justice of May 14, 1974, *Nold*, Case 4/73, (1974) ECR 491, at 507, paragraph 13.

87. See the judgment of the Court of Justice of May 15, 1986, *Johnston*, Case 222/84, (1986) ECR 1651, at 1682, paragraph 18.

88. See the judgment of the Court of Justice of July 13, 1989, *Wachauf*, Case 5/88, (1989) ECR 2609, at 2639, paragraph 19, first sentence.

89. See (1989) ECR 2609, at 2639-2640, paragraph 19, second sentence; see also the judgment of the Court of Justice of November 25, 1986, *Klensch*, Joined Cases 201-202/85, (1986) ECR 3477, at 3507, paragraph 8.

90. For an argument in favor of a generalized applicability of the Community fundamental rights standard *vis-à-vis* the Member States, see Michel Waelbroeck, "La protection des droits fondamentaux à l'égard des Etats membres dans le cadre communautaire," *Mélanges Fernand Dehousse* (Paris-Brussels: Fernand Nathan-Editions Labor, 1979), vol 2, pp. 333-335; but see the opinion of Advocate-General F. Capotorti in Case 149/77, *Defrenne*, (1978) ECR 1365, at 1385-1386.

91. See the judgment of the Court of Justice of September 30, 1987, *Demirel*, Case 12/86, (1987) ECR 3719, at 3754, paragraph 28; see also the judgment of July 11, 1985, *Cinéthèque*, Joined Cases 60-61/84, (1985) ECR 2605, at 2627, paragraphs 25 and 26.

92. See Joseph H.H. Weiler, "The European Court at a Crossroads: Community Human Rights and Member State Action," *Liber amicorum Pierre Pescatore* (Baden-Baden: Nomos, 1987), pp. 821-842.

93. Case C-260/89, (1991) ECR I-2925.

94. See (1991) ECR I-2925, at I-2964, paragraph 42, second part, to paragraph 45.

95. The European Parliament appears to share this concern. In its Resolution of April 12, 1989, adopting the Declaration of fundamental rights and freedoms, it certainly considered that "the identity of the Community makes it essential to give expression to the shared values of the citizens of Europe," but stated in the Declaration itself that "this Declaration shall afford protection for every citizen in the field of application of Community law" [Article 25 (1)], *O.J.E.C.*, 1989, C 120/51-52,56.

96. The Convention was signed in Rome on November 4, 1950. The Council of Europe was established on May 5, 1949. Its thirty-two members are, besides the fifteen Member States of the European Union (Austria, Belgium, Denmark, Finland, France, Germany, Greece, Ireland, Italy, Luxembourg, Netherlands, Portugal, Spain, Sweden, United Kingdom), Bulgaria, Cyprus, the Czech Republic, Estonia, Hungary, Iceland, Liechtenstein, Lithuania, Malta, Norway, Poland, Romania, San Marino, Slovakia, Slovenia, Switzerland, and Turkey. Andorra is scheduled to join soon.

97. See Article 46 of the ECHR.

98. The European Court of Human Rights engages in a similar kind of fine-tuning of the fundamental rights protected in the ECHR as does the U.S. Supreme Court in relation to the Bill of Rights. The European Court appears to be at times more exigent than its American counterpart. Thus, in the judgment of February 25, 1982, *Campbell and Cosans*, 48 *Publications of the European Court of Human Rights* (Series A), Britain was found to have infringed the ECHR for making pupils liable to corporal punishment as a disciplinary measure in public schools (in the later judgment of March 22, 1983, Britain was even convicted to pay just compensation to the victims involved in the case, 60 *Publications of the European Court*

of Human Rights (Series A); whereas the United States Supreme Court accepted in *Ingraham v. Wright*, 430 U.S. 651 (1977) that corporal punishment of a schoolchild could take place without the guarantee of prior procedural due process of law within the meaning of the Fourteenth Amendment to the U.S. Constitution. For a critical assessment of this latter judgment, see Tribe, *American Constitutional Law*, p. 1333, § 15-9.

99. Judgment of the European Court of Human Rights of February 21, 1975, *Golder*, 18 *Publications of the European Court of Human Rights* (Series A), at 18, § 36.

100. Judgment of the European Court of Human Rights of January 18, 1978, *Ireland v. United Kingdom*, 25 *Publications of the European Court of Human Rights* (Series A), at 90-91.

101. See, *e.g.*, the legislation on the mutual recognition of diplomas (Article 57 of the EC Treaty) and the internal market legislation (Article 100A of the EC Treaty).

102. It must be known that the Commission is represented in all meetings of the Council and of the working parties operating inside the Council, and this on the basis of the rules of procedure of the Council itself. As a consequence, the Commission can actively mediate between opposing views presented by the several members of the Council and, if need be, adapt its proposal to the extent needed to forge the necessary majority of votes. If successful in this respect, the Commission can ask that the vote be taken (Article 5 of the rules of procedure of the Council, as amended on July 20, 1987, *O.J.E.C.*, 1987, L 291/27).

103. See, *e.g.*, the judgment of November 28, 1989, *Groener*, Case C-379/87, (1989) ECR 3967, in which the Court accepted that a Dutch national who acted as a part-time teacher of painting at the College of Marketing and Design in Dublin could be obliged by Irish legislation to show, through an examination, her knowledge of the Irish language, in order to be appointed on a permanent basis. This requirement constituted a serious obstacle to the right of the Dutch teacher to free movement as a worker in Ireland (Article 48 of the EC Treaty), because she did not know Irish. In addition, she taught in English. But the Court was sensible to the Irish Government's argument of principle that the "identity" of the country within the European Community was at stake. It therefore approved "the linguistic requirement in question...as part of a policy for the promotion of the national language which is, at the same time, the first official language" (*ibidem*, at 3995).

104. See the judgment of June 18, 1991, *Piageme v. Peeters*, Case C-369/89, (1991) ECR I-2971, in which the Court held the Belgian law imposing the use of the official language (Dutch in Flanders, French in Wallonia, both Dutch and French in Brussels) for the labelling of products marketed in the several Belgian regions, to be incompatible with the EEC Food Labelling Directive 79/112, which would only require that consumers be sufficiently informed in a language that is easily understandable to them or by any other circumstance. The reaction to this judgment, especially in Flanders, has been particularly negative. It was argued that the Court had been insensitive to the fact that the official language of Flanders is Dutch and that Flemish people have - as much as English, French, or German people - the right to receive information in their own languages about the products which they buy. There should not, in other words, be a presumption that the peoples of Europe speaking a "small" language necessarily understand some other "big" language, whereas the same presumption is not made for the native speakers of the "big" languages. Apparently, in this case, the Court was not ready to tolerate the additional cost of multilingual labelling of products caused by the Belgian law to those manufacturers who commercialize their products throughout the common market, probably because it feared that this additional cost would constitute a real obstacle to the free movement principle. It based its reasoning on a reading of the Directive, which - if the Court

had wanted to favor the opposite value, *i.e.*, the recognition of linguistic diversity in the European Community - could have been different.

105. See further Koen Lenaerts, "The Principle of Subsidiarity and the Environment in the European Union: Keeping the Balance of Federalism," *Fordham International Law Journal*, 17 (1994): 846-895.

CHAPTER 9

CAN THE CENTER HOLD? FEDERALISM AND RIGHTS IN CANADA

Irwin Cotler

The defining moment in the dialectics of federalism and human rights in Canada came with the enactment of the *Constitutional Act* of 1982,[1] which involved three elements: first, the "patriation"[2] of the Canadian *Constitution* and the final severance of the constitutional umbilical cord with the United Kingdom; second, a domestic amending formula[3] for a "made in Canada" constitution; and third, the centerpiece of constitutional reform, the *Canadian Charter of Rights and Freedoms*.[4] All this was accomplished with but a passing wink at "federalism" or the distribution of powers between the federal government and the provinces which had been the dominant constitutional motif for the first 115 years of Canadian constitutional history, 1867-1982.

Indeed, notions of "renewed federalism" were preempted by the Proclamation on April 17, 1982, of this *Charter of Rights* which the then Minister of Justice, Mark MacGuigan, now a Justice of the Federal Court of Appeal, characterized at the time as the "most significant legal development in Canada in this century." Five years later, Madam Justice Claire l'Heureux-Dube, of the Supreme Court of Canada, spoke of the attempt "to stretch the constitutional blanket as far in five years in Canada as it has taken the United States 200 years to do." While on the occasion of the tenth anniversary of the

Charter on April 17, 1992, the Chief Justice of the Supreme Court of Canada, Antonio Lamer, referred to this "epoch-making" event as a "revolution" comparable to the "discoveries of Pasteur in science."

This is not to say that there were no discordant voices at the time, and these reasserted themselves on the tenth anniversary of the *Charter*. Law enforcement authorities argued, not unlike their counterparts in the United States, that the *Charter of Rights* was inhibiting police and prosecutorial work, some even suggesting that it has resulted in the "coddling of criminals." There was, as well, a "federalism" subset to this "crime control" argument; for, since the authority and legitimacy of federalism were arguably dependent on its ability to maintain public order and security in Canada, and since, it was argued, the "rights explosion" would undermine public order and security, *ergo*, the argument continued, the rights explosion would erode the authority and legitimacy of federalism itself.

Some legislators, and commentators, lamented the transfer of power from parliament to the courts, invoking Alexander Bickel's "anti-majoritarian paradox" - the specter of unelected, unaccountable judges vitiating the will of Parliament; or the "government of judges," as it has been called, frustrating the will of the people. Still others, including civil libertarians among them, wondered whether the courts were even up to the task of judicial watchdogs. Their concern was not simply the "anti-majoritarian paradox," but the *mediocrity* of those who would exercise it.

Some, particularly in Quebec, even saw this transfer of power from Parliament to the courts as an enhancement of federal power at the expense of the provinces. The thesis here was that giving more judicial power to the Supreme Court - a group of federally appointed judges - meant not only the transfer of power from Parliament to the courts, but the transfer of provincial to federal power. For them, the Supreme Court, as former Quebec Premier Rene Levesque put it, was the "Leaning Tower of Pisa" - always leaning in the federalist direction - so that an enhancement of judicial authority was necessarily an enhancement of federal authority. It did not seem to matter to the adherents of this position that the empirical data suggested otherwise, that while the *British North American Act 1867*[5] was admittedly one of the most centralist documents of any federal state, the "centrifugal" judicial review of both the Privy Council and the Supreme Court of Canada had effectively rewritten the federalist equilibrium; the metaphor then of the "Leaning Tower of Pisa" continued to permeate the consciousness of Quebecers.

Some "critical legal theorists" also wondered whether the *Charter* was the "people's package" as its supporters claimed, or the instrument of "corporate

Canada," as these critics decried. They argued that the *Charter* leaned in favor of those who could afford to invoke it, while prejudicing the "doubly disadvantaged," *i.e.*, prejudicing those against whom it was invoked because of their situation of disadvantage, who could not themselves afford to invoke it.

Still others were concerned that the *Charter*, with its multiplicity of "rights claimants," would erode the "communitarian character" of Canada, and undermine the "rights-duties" equilibrium of the Canadian legal culture - in a word, a nation of "grievers" would undermine the fragile mosaic.

Finally, and not unrelated to the Charlottetown Constitutional Referendum[6] of 1992, many in Quebec in 1992 - the philosophical legatees of the then Quebec *Pequiste* (separatist) government that had rejected the *Charter* in 1982 - were concerned that the *Charter* would erode Quebec as a "distinct society";[7] while still others - including former Canadian Prime Minister Pierre Elliot Trudeau, the architect of the *Charter* - argued that the inclusion of a "distinct society" clause in the Charlottetown Accords would erode both Canadian federalism and the *Charter*.

Whatever the merits of these allegations, one thing is clear: the notion of *"plus ca change, plus c'est la meme chose"* (the more things change, the more things are the same) has been turned on its head. Everything has changed, and nothing will be the same again. The *Charter* has wrought a revolution not only in how we teach law, but in how we practice it; not only in how we litigate, but in how we live.

We are witnessing today in Canada the phenomenon of the "constitutionalization of everyday life." Wherever we go, we bump into a constitutional process in one form or another; wherever we go as governments, as groups, as individuals, we bump into - or bump up against - the *Constitution* and the *Charter*. There is a constitutional process associated with every executive or legislative act; every major policy initiative is now subjected to a dual constitutional filter: first, the "federalism" or "jurisdictional" filter, *i.e.*, is the challenged act within the legislative competence of the enacting authority? - the continuing legacy of the classical "powers" process of Canadian constitutionalism; and, second, does the challenged act violate any provisions of the *Charter*?- the "rights process."

Thus the question arises: if everything is so good, why is everything so bad? Why did the former Chief Justice of the Supreme Court of Canada say that Canada "was facing the greatest peacetime crisis in its history"? Why did Herman Melville's metaphor of a "tempest bursting" not characterize the Canadian political landscape? Is it a case that Canada, as someone once put it, is a "solution looking for a problem"? What is this "rights revolution," and what is the relationship between federalism and human rights in Canada? Why was the Charlottetown process of constitutional reform considered "counter-revolutionary" by some (Trudeau and some other federalists) and "not revolutionary enough" by others (the Quebec nationalists and independence movements)?

The balance of this essay will attempt to answer these questions and will be organized around four basic themes: (1) the legal status of civil rights in pre-*Charter* Canada; (2) the revolution wrought by the *Charter* - the movement from a "powers" process to a "rights" process; (3) the dramatic jurisprudence under the *Charter* where rights issues that were formerly filtered through the rubric of federalism were now addressed through the prism of rights, and (4) the implications of the widely supported constitutional amendments.

THE LEGAL STATUS OF CIVIL LIBERTIES
IN PRE-CHARTER LAW

Any inquiry into the Canadian constitutional process in the first 115 years of Canadian constitutional history - 1867 to 1982 - would reveal a continuing preoccupation with the power of government at the expense of the rights of the people. More particularly, traditional constitutional analysis and reform has revolved around the division of powers between the federal government and the provinces - otherwise known as "legal federalism" - as distinct from limitations on the exercise of power, whether federal or provincial - otherwise known as "civil liberties." The result was that the powers of government tended to precede, if not obscure, the rights of people, when it is the rights of the people that should precede the powers of government. The outcome was a political or legal theory in which the constitutional discourse was about federalism or "power," and not about "rights" or people.

In a word, constitutional law developed in Canada as a "powers process" - a battle of "sovereign jurisdictional rivalry" between the federal government and the provinces - with the courts as the arbiters of that process, rather than as a "rights process" with the courts as the guardians of those rights. It is not surprising, therefore, that while in the United States the popular metaphor of the American *Constitution*, "life, liberty and the pursuit of happiness," is a rights-based, people-oriented metaphor, the popular metaphor of the Canadian *Constitution*, "peace, order and good government," is a power-based, government-oriented metaphor, with a clear federalist, if not centralist, orientation.

Professor Bora Laskin (who went on to become Chief Justice of Canada) summed up his constitutional experience in one pithy sentence: "The basic constitutional question," he wrote, "was which jurisdiction should have the power to work the injustice, not whether the injustice itself should be prohibited." Or, as he commented in another context: "The constitutional issue is simply whether the particular suppression is competent to the Dominion or the Province, as the case may be."

This obsession with the division of powers not only obscured the claims to protection of civil liberties, but very often determined the disposition of the claims themselves. In a word, legal federalism became the "looking glass" for the determination and disposition of civil liberties issues. Accordingly, whenever a federal or provincial statute appeared to offend against civil liberties, the central question for judges became, "Is the alleged denial of civil liberties within the legislative competence of the denying legislature?" If it was, that was the end of the matter, however much this analysis may have obscured, let alone denied, the civil liberties issue.

Sometimes this "jurisdictional" technique worked to uphold civil liberties, although more often it did not. Even when it worked, however, it left the disturbing inference that if the same offensive legislation had been passed by the competing legislature, that legislation under this "jurisdictional logic" would have been valid.

For example, in the early case of *Union Colliery Company Ltd. v. Bryden*[8] a provincial statute prohibiting the employment of "Chinamen" in any coal mine below ground was held to be unconstitutional by the Judicial Committee of the Privy Council, not on the grounds that it discriminated against the Chinese as a race, but on the grounds that the provincial legislation involving Chinamen who had not been naturalized encroached on the authority of the federal government. Presumably, therefore, if the federal legislature had passed identical (discriminatory) legislation, it would have been valid. Several years later, in *Cunningham and A. G. B. C. v. Tomey Homma and A. G. Can,*[9] the result was not as sanguine. The Privy Council upheld discriminatory provincial legislation which provided that no Japanese or Chinaman, whether naturalized or not, was entitled to vote in provincial elections, holding that the act did not encroach on federal authority. Once again, as in *Bryden*, there was virtually no reference in the case to discrimination because of race or color. In this case, however, the jurisdictional technique failed to protect rights.

Lest the *Bryden* example and others like it be dismissed as anachronistic judicial review by an unenlightened Judicial Committee of the Privy Council, at least this much might be said for it: it did the right thing for the wrong reason. In 1978, in the Supreme Court cases of *McNeil*[10] and *Dupond*,[11] on the very eve of the *Charter*, one almost looks back nostalgically to *Bryden*. In the *McNeil* case, the Supreme Court upheld provincial censorship legislation used to ban the showing of the film *Last Tango in Paris* on the grounds that it was legislation "in relation to property," a provincial power, while summarily dismissing the argument that the legislation involved a violation of fundamental freedoms. Even the powerful dissent of Chief Justice Bora Laskin, while acknowledging that the province sought "an unqualified power...to determine the fitness of films for public viewing on considerations that may extend beyond the moral and may include the political, the social and the religious," and that this determination was not limited to films but to "what is indecent...in a publication, what is morally fit for public viewing, whether in films, in art, or in a live performance," would have invalidated the legislation on the grounds that it is "within the exclusive power of the Parliament of Canada under its enumerated authority to legislate in relation to the criminal law." Such reasoning, while comporting well with the niceties of legal federalism, might once again leave the disturbing inference that if the federal Parliament had passed such legislation, it would be valid regardless of its effect on civil liberties.

Nor is the *Dupond* judgment, handed down by the Court on the same day, any more inspiring. Faced with a constitutional challenge to the validity of a City of Montreal anti-demonstration ordinance, the Supreme Court upheld the validity of the legislation on the grounds that it was legislation in relation to provincial power over "matters of a local and private nature within the Province," while refusing to even characterize the subject matter of the ordinance as legislation involving "fundamental freedoms" of speech or assembly.

Thus, the preoccupation with the division of powers analysis was as preeminent on the eve of the *Charter* as it was when the judiciary first embarked upon a disquisition of legal federalism some 100 years ago. The result in the ensuing period was to relegate civil liberties, however compelling, to a secondary status in Canadian constitutional law - a kind of "constitutional afterthought."

Moreover, the division of powers analysis has not only obscured the civil liberties issues, leaving the disturbing inference that the impugned legislation would be valid if enacted by the competent authority, but has even led -

perhaps inadvertently - to a "double standard" in the judicial invalidation of legislation offending civil liberties. For while the Court was striking down offensive provincial legislation for trespassing on federal authority, it was upholding offensive federal legislation as being within the competence of federal powers. The federal law-making power may not have been regarded as being as offensive to a "rights sensibility" as its provincial counterparts. Nevertheless, the upholding of federal legislation (such as that which discriminated against Japanese-Canadians) implied, in its double standard, a differential status of federal and provincial legislatures.

Interesting enough then, in the matter of human rights, the *Charter* might be seen as redressing a certain imbalance in legal federalism where discriminatory federal legislation would be upheld while its provincial parallel would be invalidated. In this sense, the *Charter* can be seen as accommodating both a rights theory and a renewed federalism.

None of this is intended to suggest that civil liberties were unprotected in Canada before the *Charter*. There were, as befits a "constitution similar in principle to that of the United Kingdom,"[12] certain civil liberties protections available, although admittedly, they were vulnerable without an entrenched *Charter of Rights*. There were, for example, the principles of the common law to the effect that "a person is free to do anything except that which is expressly prohibited by law, and governments can do nothing except that which is expressly authorized by law." But from the point of view of constitutional theory - *i.e.*, the theory of Parliamentary Sovereignty encased in legal federalism - the power of abridge any civil liberty was "exhausted" somewhere between the combined "sovereignties" of federal and provincial power. Thus, in the absence of a *Charter of Rights*, the essential question remained, "which jurisdiction should have the power to work the injustice?" The result was that the common law protection could often be turned on its head; individuals could seemingly do nothing except that which was authorized by law and governments could do anything except that which was prohibited by law. Civil liberties were the residue after the determination was made of what a person may not do.

Nor was the Canadian *Bill of Rights*, enacted in 1960, of much help. It was an unentrenched federal statute, limited to federal acts of Parliament, without a remedial provision, and judicially treated as a canon of construction rather than overriding federal legislation. The result was that only one case, the *Drybones* case, ever held a federal provision of law inoperative by reason of the fact that it offended against the *Bill of Rights*.

There were some judges who questioned whether civil liberties should be seen purely as adjuncts to legal federalism. In other words, while the Preamble of the *B.N.A. Act* imported for some a theory of parliamentary sovereignty and the accompanying notion that Parliament could undo any civil liberty, the notion of a "constitution similar in principle to that of the United Kingdom" imported for others an implied bill of rights protective of civil liberties. More particularly, if parliamentary sovereignty meant "which power could work the injustice," there were those jurists and judges who "wanted to confront directly the question whether any legislative body in Canada should have the power to impair fundamental civil liberties."[13]

In other words, the countervailing theory that there are some "injustices" that should be prohibited completely became the inspiration for an "implied bill of rights" doctrine. Regrettably, however, this judicial doctrine was as limited as it was short-lived. It was never the *ratio* in any case; was applied to provincial statutes only; was limited to political rights alone; was ultimately grounded in the jurisdictional niceties of legal federalism; and experienced a veritable death-blow in the *McNeil* and *Dupond* cases on the eve of the *Charter*.

In summary then, while there were certain protections affirmed by the common law and related principles, there was no real constitutional protection for civil liberties on the eve of the *Charter*. The best protection, ironically enough, came from the dialectics of legal federalism, so that whenever a statute (usually a provincial law) violated civil liberties such that it particularly offended judicial sensibilities, the court would find a jurisdiction trespass. But there were no entrenched rights, no constitutional role for the courts to protect rights, and no constitutional anchorage for a process of judicial review to invalidate legislation on rights grounds as distinct from jurisdictional grounds.

THE REVOLUTION WROUGHT BY THE CHARTER

The very enactment of the *Charter* brought about a revolution in Canada even before the *Charter* was itself the subject of litigation. For the first time in the history of Canadian constitutional law, civil liberties now had an independent constitutional status distinct from a derivative jurisdictional status as an adjunct to federalism. In other words, the *Charter* was now part of the Constitution, part of the "supreme law of the land."[14] Any act, federal or provincial, that violated the *Canadian Charter of Rights and Freedoms* was of no force or effect. For the first time, therefore, the courts now had the power (indeed, the responsibility) to strike down legislation on "rights" grounds rather than on "jurisdictional" grounds. For the first time - and this became particularly important as it formed the "consciousness" backdrop to what went on in the Referendum - persons had standing to seek relief from any legislative act, or executive decision, that breached any of the rights guaranteed by the *Charter*.

People now regarded themselves, and were so regarded by the *Charter*, as "rights bearers" or "rights claimants." For the first time, anyone whose rights had been violated could seek an appropriate and just remedy from a court of competent jurisdiction. At the same time, the international rights revolution, involving the internationalization of human rights and the humanization of international law, provided an international support system dovetailing with the Canadian rights revolution.

Moreover, the *Charter* was important not only because of the constitutionalization and judicialization of rights, but also because of the range of rights involved. While an elaboration of these rights is beyond the scope of this essay, an enumeration of the ten categories of rights that have been constitutionalized is necessary so as to appreciate the scope of this revolutionary event. The categories of rights include: political rights, democratic rights, mobility rights, legal rights, equality rights, minority language rights, aboriginal rights, rights of visible minorities, and the like.

As well, the *Charter* has features unique among rights charters generally and rights charters in federal systems more specifically. One example is Section 1 of the *Charter*, which is not only a basic principle of the *Charter*, but whose meaning dovetails with comments made in other chapters in this book respecting individual rights and communitarian obligations. Section 1 provides that

> the *Canadian Charter of Rights and Freedoms* guarantees the rights and freedoms set out in it subject only to such reasonable limits, prescribed by law, as can be demonstrably justified in a free and democratic society.

In other words, the *Charter* acknowledges that rights are not absolute, that they can be limited, and that there is an important communitarian dimension that can be invoked to limit rights if it can pass a four-pronged test: first, it must be reasonable; second, it must be prescribed by law; third, it must be demonstrably justifiable; and fourth, it must be compatible with the norms of a free and democratic society.

A second feature which distinguishes the Canadian *Charter* from rights charters in other countries is the "notwithstanding" clause, or "override" provision of Section 33, a necessary concession to the provinces to get the *Charter* approved in the first place.   Section 33 authorizes the federal Parliament or any provincial legislature to "override" parts of the *Charter of Rights and Freedoms* - particularly Section 2 and Sections 7-15, or the categories dealing with fundamental freedoms, legal rights, and equality rights - by including in any legislative enactment the phrase that "the law shall apply notwithstanding the [enumerated] sections of the *Charter*." This capacity to blunt the efficacy of the *Charter* through the use of this override is clearly present. The hope was that this provision would only rarely be used; in fact, it has been only rarely used. But when it has been invoked - as when Quebec effectively overrode a Supreme Court decision which had struck down Quebec legislation violative of free expression and minority language rights - the whole issue of individual rights versus collective powers came into play, and became part of the existential backdrop to the Referendum, as discussed below.

A third unique provision is one which revolves around the concept of "multiculturalism." For Section 27 of the *Charter* provides that "this *Charter* shall be interpreted in a manner consistent with the preservation and enhancement of the multicultural heritage of Canadians." Multiculturalism, then, became a basic principle of constitutional interpretation in Canada. But, for many in Quebec, this principle of multiculturalism suggested that Quebec was but one of many cultures, and diminished for many Quebecers the notion of Quebec as a "distinct society" - the notion that Quebec *"n'est pas une province commes les autres."*   For many in Quebec, therefore, multiculturalism was not so much a "rights principle" as it was a principle contracting Quebec "powers." This view also became part of the existential backdrop to the Referendum.

A fourth unique feature was Section 28 of the *Charter* - the gender equality principle - and the only provision in the *Charter* which begins with the words "notwithstanding anything in this *Charter*...," and goes on to proclaim that the "rights or freedoms referred to in it are guaranteed equally to male and female persons." This principle was effectively "smuggled" into the *Charter* since many Canadians did not fully appreciate what was happening at the time. But to the credit of Canadian women, they knew what they needed and got it. Thus, the Canadian *Charter*, unlike the *Constitution* of the United States, has an *Equal Rights Amendment*.

Protection for women's rights had already been anchored in the general Equality Rights provision of Section 15 which guaranteed that every individual is equal before and under the law and has the right to the equal protection and equal benefit of the law without discrimination and, in particular, without discrimination based on race, national or ethnic origin, colour, religion, sex, age, or mental or physical disability.

This equality rights principle was enlarged further in Section 15(2) which constitutionalized affirmative action programs and provides:

Subsection (1) does not prelude any law, program or activity that has as its object the amelioration of conditions of disadvantaged individuals or groups including those that are disadvantaged because of race, national or ethnic origin, colour, religion, sex, age, or mental or physical disability.

But Canadian women, mindful of the pre-*Charter* intellectual and judicial legacy that had been insensitive to, and unprotective of gender equality, were not satisfied. They sought and obtained, therefore, a specific gender equality provision in Section 28 that would obtain "notwithstanding" anything else in the *Charter*.

Fifth, there are unique provisions respecting aboriginal rights, guaranteeing in Section 25 that the *Charter* "shall not be construed as to abrogate or denigrate any aboriginal treaty, or other rights or freedoms that pertain to the aboriginal peoples of Canada"; and, in Section 35, "recognizing and affirming the existing aboriginal and treaty rights of the aboriginal peoples." Both provisions have been interpreted by the courts to entrench and expand aboriginal rights.

Sixth, continuing in the vein of constitutionalizing group rights, the *Charter* incorporates and expands upon minority language rights protections which were first constitutionalized in Section 133 of the *B. N. A. Act*; and continues through Section 29 of the *Charter*, the protection accorded to denominational rights under Section 93 of the *B.N.A. Act* - although the latter is a double-edged sword because the "denominational rights" have a certain privileged character to them.

These unique and compelling provisions respecting minority language rights and aboriginal rights reflect a concern with group rights distinguishable from the ethos of the United States *Constitution,* but which are consistent with the notions of diversity and pluralism that resonate throughout this book.

Finally, there is an express reference to international law in Section 11(G) of the *Charter* which provides that retroactivity shall not avail as a defense to prosecution "where the crimes are criminal according to international law or according to the general principles of law recognized by the community of nations." This provision was included in order to authorize criminal prosecutions of Nazi War Criminals, and to allow for the enactment of domestic criminal law for that purpose - and which now finds expression in the 1987 amendments to the Canadian *Criminal Code*. In the United States, no such prosecutions are undertaken, as the United States regards such prosecutions as constitutionally suspect; in Canada, however, Section 11(G) of the *Charter* has effectively constitutionalized such initiatives, while effecting an important "nexus" between domestic and international law.

LITIGATING THE VALUES OF A NATION: THE REVOLUTIONARY RIGHTS JURISPRUDENCE

There have been a number of landmark decisions constituting a critical mass of litigation that has literally revolutionized constitutionalism in Canada. For reasons of economy, I shall refer to only two of these decisions here, particularly as each has an American counterpart. The first was a case launched in 1983 by a coalition of peace, environmental, women's, labor, and aboriginal groups - known effectively as the *Operation Dismantle* case after the peace group of the same name. The suit sought to prevent Canada from testing the cruise missile. The case has its American parallel in the *Greenham Women* case in which women from the United Kingdom came to American courts to challenge the legality of the testing and the deployment of the cruise missiles on the grounds that they were a threat to the rights of life and security of the person. They were supported by some American congressmen who also argued that the deployment of the missiles was a usurpation of congressional authority. In this American case, the courts held that the issue was non-justiciable, that it was a political question, and that it was not ripe for decision.

In Canada, *Operation Dismantle* was one of the first cases to come before the courts under the *Charter*. May I make full disclosure at the outset: I acted as counsel to the petitioners in this case - much to the surprise of many of my colleagues who regarded the proceeding as frivolous. Accordingly, when the federal government argued that our action was frivolous, vexatious, and an abuse of process, these same colleagues concurred and wondered what I was doing in this case. But the case - apart from the merits of the action itself - had several crucial constitutional and *Charter* considerations at issue, for the federal government argued (after its motion to dismiss our action as frivolous was denied), that its action was not subject to review by the courts. It organized its submission around three major propositions, each of which was germane to the efficacy of the *Charter* generally.

First, the government argued that the *Charter* did not apply to acts of the executive, only to acts of Parliament. Second, it argued that even if it applied to acts of the executive, it did not apply to the executive's exercise of the Royal Prerogative - that residue of executive authority that reposed in the Crown. Finally, the government argued that even if the *Charter* applied to acts of the Royal Prerogative, it did not apply to the Royal Prerogative in matters of defense and foreign policy. Clearly, if these propositions were to be accepted, it would not only have defeated our action on the merits, but it basically would have immunized executive action from judicial review. The *Charter* then would apply only to acts of Parliament, not to acts of the executive.

The danger, of course, was that this rather unusual case might indeed be characterized only as a "frivolous" proceeding, thereby making and deflecting the larger constitutional questions at issue. Accordingly, I was delighted when we were told that the presiding judge in the court of the first instance was regarded as somewhat "eccentric," for I thought that only a somewhat eccentric judge might be responsive to our arguments. Fortunately, that was the case and we won in the court of the first instance - the last victory we were to have on the merits of the case, for we were unanimously reversed on every other level thereafter. Indeed, when we won at the first level, it was characterized in newspaper headlines as "the shock heard around the world - even in the Kremlin," causing some to regard us as naive and unsuspecting agents of the Kremlin.

Nevertheless, while the Supreme Court ultimately dismissed our claim as "having no reasonable cause of action," it did hold with us on three points of crucial importance for the efficacy of the *Charter* generally. First, it held that the *Charter* did apply to decisions of the executive. Second, it held that the *Charter* did apply even to the exercise by the executive of the Royal Prerogative. And third, it held, albeit in *obiter*, that decisions in matters of defense and foreign policy may be judicially cognizable by the courts. From a rights litigation point of view, this opened an important window of opportunity should such issues ever arise again.

In addition, there have been a series of historic cases which reversed 75 years of jurisprudence in Canada that had upheld the Lord's Day Act, or an establishment of religion; or had upheld compulsory prayers in the schools; or had sanctioned compulsory religious education. These practices respecting "church in state" were still valid in Canada, even into the 1980s. But these practices were invalidated by the Supreme Court under the *Charter* with ringing declarations respecting freedom on conscience and religion in a free and democratic society. Indeed, if the critical mass of rights jurisprudence of the last ten years could be cited in this essay, one could understand Madame Justice Claire L'Heureux-Dube's dictum that Canada "has stretched the cords of liberty more in five years than the United States has in 200 years;" for some of the most progressive jurisprudence in the world can be found in the *Charter* case-law of the Canadian Supreme Court in matters of women's rights, the rights of minorities, the rights of the accused, and the rights of immigrants and refugees.

And now to repeat the earlier question: "If things are so good, why are they also so bad?" If there is a veritable revolution, why did the former Chief Justice of Canada, the Right Honourable Brian Dickson, warn on the eve of the Referendum that "Canada was facing the gravest peace-time crisis in its history"? Why was Canada characterized - in Herman Melville's words - as a "tempest bursting," by both federalist and anti-federalist forces in the recent Referendum? Why did the Referendum have to take place at all? And why was there a *Charlottetown Accord?*

BACK TO THE FUTURE - CAN THE CENTER HOLD?

The *Charlottetown Accords*, like the predecessor *Meech Lake Accords*, were designed, as Prime Minister Mulroney then remarked, "to bring Quebec back into the constitutional process with honour and enthusiasm." But, as Quebec sociologist Maurice Pinard put it, this ignored the fact that before Mulroney began this process, there were few in Quebec who were concerned with the constitutional process, or who thought they had been excluded from it. In fact, 86 percent of Quebecers had supported the adoption of the constitutional package in 1982, and only one percent had even heard of the *Meech Lake Accords* when that process was first launched in the late 1980s.

But by 1992, Canada was clearly a country with "tempest bursting" of which it may well have been said that "things fall apart; the center cannot hold." The economy appeared to be in a free fall, with 500,000 jobs lost - 300,000 in manufacturing in the three years before the Referendum alone. The *Free Trade Agreement* with the United States was regarded as an agreement which only one side could win - and it was not the Canadian side. Unemployment was at a record high, - some 75,000 bankruptcies had been recorded in 1991 alone, - and food banks were proliferating across the country. The western provinces appeared more alienated than ever before, while Quebec now felt, in retrospect, that it had been betrayed in 1982, and that nothing less than its recognition as a "distinct society" could bring it back into the constitutional process. The aboriginal peoples had developed a similar sense of grievance and exclusion. Indeed, the facts regards the aboriginal peoples were appalling: 80 percent of aboriginal people on reserves were unemployed; aboriginal persons were seven times more likely to commit suicide that any other person in Canada; eight of ten women on reserves reported that they were victims of sexual abuse. It is no wonder that aboriginal people were spoken of as a form of "third world apartheid" in Canada.

Accordingly, a set of proposals was designed "to give something to everyone" - except perhaps to the federal government. For example, Quebec was to be guaranteed 25 percent of the representatives in the federal Parliament in perpetuity, regardless of how the demographics might change - a proposal that did not endear itself to British Columbia. Quebec was also guaranteed four seats on the Canadian Supreme Court, which seats were to be filled from a list of candidates drawn up by the Premier of Quebec, who could be an *independaniste* committed to separation. Quebec was not only to be recognized as a distinct society, but it was to have the executive and legislative power to promote this status; six major areas of jurisdiction were to be transferred to Quebec, including jurisdiction over culture.

However, in order to sell the transfer of these powers to Quebec, they were also offered to all the other provinces. This was a prescription for the further devolution and decentralization of federal power. In addition, the western provinces were to be mollified by reform of the Senate and the aboriginal peoples were not only to secure the right of self-government, but also by constitutional recognition as a third order of government. Accordingly, Canada would now have three orders of government - a federal government, provincial governments and a set of aboriginal governments. But, since aboriginal people in Canada were organized around some 600 self-governing bands, one had the prospect of multiple sovereignties representing this third order of government.

These proposals were supported by the federal government, the opposition parties in the federal Parliament, every provincial parliament, the territorial governments, the aboriginal leaders, and every elite group in Canada; yet, incredibly, the *Charlottetown Accords* were defeated at the polls. One newspaper observed that it was a typically Canadian populist revolt - one in favor of the *status quo*. Clearly, however, there were other dynamics at work, dynamics which may have relevance to whether the center will, or will not hold. These dynamics may not only say something about Canada at this juncture in our history, but about other societies as well, for they represent socio-cultural dynamics that inhere in many "free and democratic" countries.

First, there is what may be called "the politics of anti-incumbency." One has heard a great deal about this dynamic in the United States, but it is doubtful whether the American center ever experienced an indictment such as that which took place in Canada. For this was not just an indictment of the substance of the Referendum, but an indictment of all the political leaders and elite groups across the nation, thereby challenging the traditional elite accommodation theory. Admittedly, the politics of anti-incumbency has also found expression in U. S. presidential politics, but in the recent congressional elections most of the incumbents were still returned. In Canada, however, the Referendum rejected every messenger, as well as the message itself. It raised a serious question of whether the center can hold - for there was a massive indictment of all those who purported to speak on behalf of the center, as they defined themselves, although those representatives often spoke in very equivocal terms about the center, which is part of the problem and not of the solution.

The second dynamic - more like Europe than the United States - is that of the "politics of independence." Some 25 percent of Quebecers (allowing for certain variations at different times), would oppose any agreement that pre-supposes the continuation of a federal system with Quebec as part of Canada. For these 25 percent, any federalist package - whatever it may be - would be unacceptable. For them, from an existential point of view, the political center is not Canada, but an independent Quebec. For them, the metaphor is Havel's "Velvet Revolution" as distinct from the Balkan metaphor. Canadians generally, it may be assumed, would also follow the metaphor of the Velvet Revolution; they would not oppose any independence for Quebec that would arise out of a referendum on this issue, however difficult negotiating the break-up would be. The question is whether the center can hold when a hard-core minority of some 25 percent regards it as illegitimate.

A third dynamic is what may be called the "politics of nationalism," with particular reference to the ethnocentric politics of Quebec. In a word, in addition to the 25 percent for whom independence is the threshold, there is another 30-35 percent for whom the nationalistic threshold must be satisfied. Here the question becomes: can the center accommodate the nationalistic, ethnocentric politics for whom the matters may be, "not necessarily independence, but independence if necessary?" Can it respond to the wellspring of sometimes primordial, sometimes communitarian, but always nationalistic impulses of this 30-35 percent without eroding the center threshold necessary for a viable federalism?

Fourth, and again a dynamic distinguishable from the United States, is that of the case and cause of the aboriginal peoples in Canada. Since the aboriginal communities are composed of some 35-50 distinct peoples, involving some 600 bands with eleven languages and multiple dialects, can the center accommodate a right of self-government involving a third order of aboriginal governments. More specifically, can the center accommodate multiple aboriginal "sovereignties" with multiple claims? Moreover, there are any number of hidden agendas in the support for, or opposition to, any one or more of the claims. For example, support for the aboriginal peoples' claims may mask opposition to the claims of Quebecers, which, it is felt, would be undermined by the securing of the aboriginal peoples' claims. Conversely, support for Quebec as a distinct society may be a coded way of diminishing the claims of aboriginal peoples.

A fifth dynamic, one that is characteristic of Europe but exists in America, is the growing "tribalization of consciousness" - the proliferation of interest groups and single-issue lobbies that is increasingly fragmenting the mainstream political culture. Thus the question arises: can the center cope with a fragmenting confrontational civil society, particularly when that tribalization-fragmentation is accompanied by a certain "culture of meanness" - a zero-sum culture of complaint and grievance whose every benefit conferred or right secured is seen as the deprivation or denial of another?

A sixth dynamic is the seeming irreconcilable "politics of polarization" between Quebec and the rest of Canada. The nationalistic threshold position - let alone the *independantiste* position - is one which the rest of Canada seems unwilling or unable to meet. Conversely, the federalist threshold position of the rest of Canada is one which the distinct society of Quebec (and it is a distinct society) seems equally unwilling or unable to accommodate.

Moreover, the implications of the defeat of the *Charlottetown Accords* are interpreted differently in Quebec than in the rest of Canada. For the *independantistes (Pequistes)* of Quebec, the defeat of the *Charlottetown Accords* is being read as support for the independence option. As *Pequiste* leader Jacques Parizeau has put it, since Quebec resisted the "fear-mongering" of federalist elites, it demonstrates that Quebec has now developed the political maturity needed to secure independence.

Conversely, however, it can equally be argued that the defeat of the Referendum signaled not so much a victory for independence-minded Quebecers over the federalist fear-mongering, but that the center saw in the defeat of the Referendum a vindication of the rights theory. It is equally arguable that just as the *Charter of Rights* ushered in a rights revolution (a new center organizing idiom), the *Charlottetown Accords*, with its emphasis on provincial powers - and not just for Quebec - was seen as subordinating rights to powers, and was thus heralding a reversal back to the powers process of Canadian federalism, rather than the rights revolution occasioned by the *Charter of Rights and Freedoms*.

I would submit that the answer to my original question - "Federalism and Rights: Can the Center Hold?" - will depend on whether the federalism/rights configuration can be regarded as complementary rather than contradictory; whether the entitlement/communitarian configuration can be seen as mutually reinforcing rather than a zero-sum game; and whether the federalist/Quebec configuration can result in the *epanouissment* of each rather than the diminution of both.

It may well depend on a restatement - and assertion - of federalism itself as a rights theory rather than just as a powers process; of the emergence of a credible federal leadership that espouses the legitimacy of federalism rather than equivocates about it; of federalism as an accounting theory - a *federalisme rentable* or bookkeeping entry - but as a constitutive political and legal theory that is more than just the sum of its constituent parts; that, in a word, of federalism as a statement of principle, organized around notions of political and gender equity, democratic pluralism, cultural diversity, individual and collective rights, multicultural and district societies, and aboriginal peoples.

I say this because there could be a federal election wherein the *independantiste* party - the *Bloc Quebecois* - would contest in all federal ridings, and a populist, protest right-wing movement known as the Reform Party would field candidates in all ridings except Quebec, thus providing the seeds for a rump Parliament and a rump center. Parizeau could then argue that not only is Quebec a nation, entitled to independence, but that Canada is ungovernable and Parliament unmanageable and so a peaceful exit for Quebec - a Velvet Revolution - would benefit both Quebec and the rest of Canada. In other words, as Parizeau might argue - with the Bloc Quebecois as evidence - the center would hold better with Quebec out than in; that there will either be two centers - Quebec and the rest of Canada - or none.

In an article on Canada entitled "Nice Country, Nice Mess," the *Economist* wrote that the Canadian model - whether of disintegration or of holding together in some new, post-modern version of the nation-state - is going to be an example to avoid or follow for all but a few federations, for all multicultural societies, especially immigrant ones, for countries whose borders reflect conquest more than geography, and for all states riven or driven by nationalism. In this sense Canada has something for almost everyone.[15]

It is sometimes said that a constitution is the "autobiography of a nation"; Canada may perhaps be said to be a nation - with a Constitution - in search of its autobiography. The "constitutional tempest" of federalism and rights may yet determine not only what kind of nation it will be, but whether it will ever be a nation at all.

NOTES

1. *The Constitutional Act of 1982* is schedule B of the *Canada Act of 1982*, c. 11 (U.K.).
2. See P. Hogg, "Patriation of the Canadian Constitution," *Queen's Law Journal*, 8 (1983): 123.
3. *Constitution Act 1982*, Part V - "Procedure for Amending Constitution of Canada."
4. Part I of the *Constitution Act of 1982*. For commentary on the Charter of Rights, see Tarnopolsky and Beaudoin, eds., *The Canadian Charter of Rights and Freedoms: Commentary* (1982), and 2nd Revised Edition, Beaudoin and Ratushny, eds. (1989).
5. Renamed the *Constitution Act of 1867* in 1982.
6. This was a nationwide referendum on the *Charlottetown Accords*, the constitutional package that had something in it for everyone, and was supported by the federal government, all ten provincial governments, the two territorial governments, the Assembly of Free Nations - all of the political and power elites - yet was defeated in the Referendum itself. As one commentator put it, while it purported to have something in it for everyone, everyone seemed to find something in it to hate.
7. The socio-legal characterization of Quebec that asserted itself as a "bottom-line" claim by the Quebec government in the constitutional negotiations surrounding both the *Meech Lake* and *Charlottetown Accords*.
8. [1899] A. C. 580 (P. C.).
9. [1903] A. C. 151 (P. C.).
10. *McNeil v. N.S. Board of Censors* (1978), 84 D. L. R. (3rd) 1 (S. C. C.).
11. *A. G. Canada v. Dupond* (1978), 2 S. C. R. 770.
12. In the words of the Preamble of the *B.N.A. Act.*
13. P. W. Hogg, *Constitutional Law of Canada* (Toronto: Carswell Co., 1977), p. 429.
14. Section 52 of the *Constitution Act 1982*.
15. The *Economist* (June 29, 1991).

INDEX

on censorship, 178
constitutional experience of, 177
Last Tango in Paris, banning of, 178
Law's Empire (Dworkin), 22, 33
Lee, Richard Henry, 60
on Constitution, 59
Lenaerts, Koen: on EC federalism, xix
"Less restrictive alternatives" test, 168n62
Levesque, Rene, 174
Lewis, Anthony: on *New York v. Sullivan*, 127
L'Heureux-Dube, Claire, 186
on Canadian Charter of Rights and Freedoms, 173
Libel, tort law of, 127, 128
Liberty, 30, 58, 64
Anti-Federalists and, 60, 61
division of power and, 66
federalism and, xv, 8-9, 31, 118
Federalists and, 61
large republics and, 61
local majorities and, 61
maintaining, 12, 59, 67, 68, 70
majoritarian, 43
personal, 52n40
public, 49
threats to, 69
See also Civil liberties
Limited government, 5, 58
Lincoln, Abraham: federalism and, 77
Linde, Hans A., 119n32
Lipset, Seymour Martin, 55n69
Local governments, 14
educational function of, 13
Localism, 11, 16, 20, 85
federalism and, 15, 19
freedom and, 54n48
Lord's Day Act, 185

McConnell, Grant, 76
on Madisonian principles, 75
MacGuigan, Mark: on Canadian Charter of Rights and Freedoms, 173
McNeil case (1978), 178, 180
Madison, James, 32, 58, 61
on amendment process, 63-64
Anti-Federalists and, 73n18

Bill of Rights and, 35-36, 102
Constitution and, 62, 65
corrective federalism and, 82-86, 92, 93, 99
double security and, xii
on federalism, x, xvii, 12, 18, 31, 67-68, 76, 85, 94
on group differences, 47
on House of Representatives, 62-63
on liberty, 60, 65
on limited monarchy, 83
nationalism and, 70
on ratification process, 62
republicanism and, 69, 83-84, 96
on rights, 49n3, 84
on union, 85
Virginia Resolutions and, 68
Madison Federalism, 81, 94
Hamilton Federalism and, 98
Magna Carta, 21
Majority rule, ix, xv, 96
Make No Law (Lewis), 127
Maltz, Earl M. on
nationalization/Fourteenth Amendment and, 42
on reapportionment, 52n37
Mandatory requirements, 152-53, 167n56
Mapp v. Ohio (1961), 121n66
Marbury v. Madison (1803), 73n26, 144
Market integration, conflicting rights and, 151-54
Marketplace
competition of, 52n30
federalism and, 38
Marshall, John
Barron v. Baltimore and, 31, 92
judicial review and, 12
Masaryk, Thomas, 25
Mason, George, 14, 26n11
Massachusetts Declaration of Rights, privacy issue and, 116
Massachusetts Supreme Judicial Court, *Upton* case and, 107, 109
Massachusetts v. Upton, 106-7, 109, 116
Massey, Calvin, 37

Massive Resistance, era of, 21
Mayer, David N.: on Anti-Federalists, 60
Medical malpractice law, federal, 127-28
Meech Lake Accords, 186, 191n7
Member States (EC), 146, 164n28, 170n96
  Community law and, 141, 142, 143-44, 145, 150-51
  customs duties and, 140
  ECHR and, 158
  European Court of Justice and, 158
  federalism and, 143-44, 160
  free movement principle and, 148, 152
  fundamental rights standard and, 157-58
  nationality laws of, 165n32
  rights and, 149, 153, 154, 156-57, 161, 163n16
  services and, 167n58
  veto power for, 153
Michigan v. Long (1983), 105-6, 113
Minimum wage laws, 17, 124
Minorities, rights of, 183-84, 186
Missouri Plan, 136-37
Montesquieu
  on federalism, 77
  on small republics, 59
Moral philosophy, 52n33
  constitutional law and, 33
Mulroney, Brian: Charlottetown Accords and, 186
Multiculturalism, 182, 190

Nagel, Robert F.: on federalism/rights, 50n7
National Association of Manufacturing, 126
National government, expansion of, 67
Nationalism, politics of, 188-89
National League of Cities v. Usery (1976), 41
  minimum wage laws and, 124
National Treasury Employees Union v. Von Raab (1990), privacy and, 116-17
National values, litigating, 184-86
Nationhood, sense of, 23-24

Natural rights, ix, 3, 34-35, 44, 76, 79, 87, 88, 91, 93, 100n9
  abortion and, 51n23
  commitment to, 35-36
  delegitimation of, 45
  triad of, 89-90
Netherlands Inland Revenue Administration, 140
Neutrality, federalism and, 38
New Deal, 40
  civil society and, 4
  federalism and, 75
New State Ice Co. v. Liebmann (1932), 109
New York v. Sullivan (1964), 127
Nineteenth Amendment, 17
Ninth Amendment, 112
Nixon, Richard: new federalism and, 70
NLRB v. Jones and Laughlin (1937), 98
No-discrimination principle, 144, 148, 151, 154
Nold case (1974), fundamental rights and, 157
Non-incorporated directive, 155
"Not in my backyard" sentiment, 15
Nozick, Robert: on rights, 87

Obligation, rights and, 8
"Obsolescence of Federalism, The" (Laski), 134
O'Connor, Sandra Day
  Cruzan v. Missouri and, 109-10
  Garcia v. San Antonio and, 18
Operation Dismantle case, 184
Operation Greylord, 135
Oregon Court of Appeals
  double jeopardy and, 108
  Kennedy case and, 108
Oregon Supreme Court
  Kennedy case and, 107
  Sterling v. Cupp and, 107-8
Oregon v. Hass (1975), 105
Oregon v. Kennedy (1980), 107
  double jeopardy and, 108

Pangle, Thomas: on Anti-Federalists/Bill of Rights, 41
Parental consent, privacy rights and, 113

CONTRIBUTORS

ELLIS KATZ is Professor of Political Science and Fellow of the Center for the Study of Federalism, Temple University. He is the author or editor of *Ethnic Group Politics, American Models of Revolutionary Leadership, The Pennsylvania State Constitution,* and *The Government and Politics of Pennsylvania.*

G. ALAN TARR is Professor of Political Science, Rutgers University (Camden) and a Fellow of the Center for the Study of Federalism. He is the author of *Judicial Process and Judicial Policymaking,* coauthor of *American Constitutional Law* (4th edition) and of *State Supreme Courts in State and Nation,* and editor of a 52-volume series on state constitutions.

DOROTHY TOTH BEASLEY is Presiding Judge, Court of Appeals of Georgia. She is the author of several articles on state constitutional law, including "The Georgia Bill of Rights: Dead or Alive?" *Emory Law Journal* (1985).

IRWIN COTLER is Professor of Law, McGill University. He is an international human rights lawyer and frequent litigator of issues under the *Canadian Charter of Rights and Freedoms.*

TALBOT D'ALEMBERTE is President of Florida State University. He is a former President of the American Bar Association and author of *The Florida State Constitution.*

DANIEL J. ELAZAR is Professor of Political Science and Director of the Center for the Study of Federalism, Temple University; Professor of Political Science, Bar Ilan University and President of the Jerusalem Institute for Federal Studies. He is the founding editor of *Publius: The Journal of Federalism*, and author of numerous books, including *American Federalism: A View from the States*, *The American Constitutional Tradition* and *Exploring Federalism*.

A. E. DICK HOWARD is White Burkett Miller Professor of Law and Public Affairs, University of Virginia. He is the author of numerous books and articles on American federalism and constitutional law, including *Commentaries on the Constitution of Virginia* and *The Road to Runnymede: Magna Carta and Constitutionalism in America*.

GARY JEFFREY JACOBSOHN is Woodrow Wilson Professor of Political Science, Williams College. Among his books are *Apple of Gold: Constitutionalism in Israel and the United States*, *The Supreme Court and the Decline of Constitutional Aspiration*, and *Pragmatism, Statesmanship and the Supreme Court*.

KOEN LENAERTS is Judge of the Court of First Instance of the European Communities (Luxembourg) and Professor of European Community Law, University of Leuvan (Belgium). He is the author of several books and articles on comparative constitutional law, including "Constitutionalism and the Many Faces of Federalism," *American Journal of Comparative Law* (1990), and "Some Reflections on the Separation of Powers in the European Community," *Common Market Law Review* (1991).

JEAN YARBROUGH is Professor of Political Science, Bowdoin College. She is the author of numerous studies in American Political Theory, including "Rethinking the *Federalist*'s View of Federalism," *Publius: The Journal of Federalism* (1985).

MICHAEL P. ZUCKERT is Dorothy and Edward Congdon Professor of Political Science, Carleton College. His books and articles include *Natural Rights and the New Republicanism* and "Completing the Constitution: The Fourteenth Amendment and Constitutional Rights," *Publius: The Journal of Federalism* (1992).